T0245307

Complex Systems and Clouds

Complex Systems and Clouds

A Self-Organization and Self-Management Perspective

Dan C. Marinescu
Computer Science Department
University of Central Florida
Orlando, FL, USA

AMSTERDAM • BOSTON • HEIDELBERG • LONDON
NEW YORK • OXFORD • PARIS • SAN DIEGO
SAN FRANCISCO • SINGAPORE • SYDNEY • TOKYO

Morgan Kaufmann is an imprint of Elsevier

Morgan Kaufmann is an imprint of Elsevier
50 Hampshire Street, 5th Floor, Cambridge, MA 02139, United States

Library of Congress Cataloging-in-Publication Data
A catalog record for this book is available from the Library of Congress

British Library Cataloguing-in-Publication Data
A catalogue record for this book is available from the British Library

ISBN: 978-0-12-804041-6

For information on all Elsevier publications
visit our website at https://www.elsevier.com/

Working together
to grow libraries in
developing countries

www.elsevier.com • www.bookaid.org

Publisher: Todd Green
Acquisition Editor: Brian Romer
Editorial Project Manager: Lindsay Lawrence
Production Project Manager: Priya Kumaraguruparan
Cover Designer: Matthew Limbert

Typeset by SPi Global, India

To Vera Rae and Luke Bell.

CONTENTS

PREFACE

In 2003, IBM researchers formulated the autonomic computing challenge. A decade and more than 8,000 papers, 200 conferences, and 200 patents later, a few small- or medium-scale systems were the signs of success of the autonomic computing movement [137]. In the mean time we kept building systems with increasingly larger numbers of components interacting with each other in intricate ways.

The first cloud computing services were introduced a decade ago. In 2006, Amazon Web Services (AWS) started offering storage and computing services, S3 and EC2. The number of Cloud Service Providers (CSPs) has increased year after year, as larger numbers of individuals and large organizations have enthusiastically joined the cloud computing user community. A decade later, the most powerful processors with large cache and memory and attached GPU co-processors, storage arrays, interconnected by a hierarchy of networks populate the cloud computing infrastructure of many CSPs.

The complexity of computer clouds is undeniable and yet, their design is based on traditional, mostly deterministic hierarchical management. The time has come to ask if the elusive goal of self-organization and self-management can be achieved for large-scale systems such as computer clouds. The best place to start looking for an answer is to understand what are the defining attributes of a complex system.

The first chapter of the book covers complex systems. After a brief review of the evolution of thinking about systems consisting of an ensemble of components, we analyze nondeterminism, nonlinearity, and phase transitions in complex systems. A range of topics pertinent to complexity, such as self-organization, self-organized criticality, power law distributions, computational irreducibility, and quantitative characterization of complexity are then covered. Cybernetics and the interdisciplinary nature of complexity are the last topics of the chapter.

Nature is a good place to look for ideas regarding complex systems and the second chapter is dedicated to nature-inspired algorithms and systems. Disciplines such as evolutionary computation, neural computation, artificial immune systems, swarm intelligence, and Ant Colony Optimization (ACO) draw from nature their inspiration for new problem-solving techniques. Cellular automata, epidemic algorithms, genetic algorithms, ACO algorithms, swarm intelligence, DNA computing, quantum information processing, and membrane computing are then presented. A discussion of the scope and the limitations of nature-inspired algorithms and of realistic expectations from DNA computing and quantum information processing concludes the chapter.

The third chapter is dedicated to managing the complexity of cyber-physical systems. Most large-scale systems are cyber-physical systems integrating computation, communication, sensing, and physical processes. Cyber-physical systems are now ubiquitous and their undeniable complexity is caused by a set of factors reviewed in the first sections of the chapter, which also discusses how software has pushed the limits of system composability. Challenges specific to large-scale cyber-physical systems, autonomic computing, and scalable system organizations are the topics of the next sections. The discussion of virtualization by aggregation and coalition formation is followed by a survey of cooperative games for coalition formation. An in-depth analysis of a self-organization protocol for very large sensor networks concludes the chapter.

The fourth chapter covers computer clouds. Computer clouds have altered our thinking about computing and we first provide a down-to-earth view of the new paradigm and present the cloud delivery models. The hierarchical organization of the cloud infrastructure, consisting of multiple warehouse-scale computers is discussed next. Cloud elasticity, the effects of over-provisioning on costs and energy consumption, and existing Cloud Resource Management (CRM) policies and mechanisms for implementing these policies are analyzed. Alternative CRMs based on market mechanisms, such as auctions and server coalitions are then introduced. Combinatorial auctions allow access to packages of resources for applications with a complex workflow.

The last chapter analyzes cloud self-organization and Big Data applications in science and engineering. Computational science and engineering applications exacerbate the shortcomings of existing CRM for Big Data applications. Significant enhancements of cloud infrastructure have been noticeable since 2010, when a comparison between the performance of HPCC applications on supercomputers and AWS instances was reported.

Nevertheless, the 2016 AWS does not provide the best environment for data-intensive applications exhibiting fine grain parallelism. The relatively high latency and low bandwidth of a cloud interconnect are partially responsible for this state of affairs. The analysis of the tensor network contraction, an application in the area of condensed matter physics, reveals that a better CRM could alleviate some of performance problems due to the architectural limitations. Simulation results show that the solution proposed, a reservation system based on coalition formation and combinatorial auctions, can guarantee spatial and temporal locality thus, reduce the communication overhead. The system is application-centric, resources allocated match exactly the needs of an application, rather than providing a limited menu of instances.

Time is the critical ingredient for self-organization and adaptation in nature. It took millions of years for biological species to adapt to natural conditions. It seems thus, hopeless to believe that a man-made system can self-organize, manage, and repair itself. But time can be compressed, as the rate of events that change the state in computer clouds and other large-scale systems is extremely high. This means that sophisticated learning algorithms could identify in days, weeks, or months patterns of interactions with the environment and use this knowledge to adapt and optimize the performance of the system. The research of Dan Marinescu is partially supported by the NSF CCR grant 1525943 "Is the Simulation of Quantum Many-Body Systems Feasible on the Cloud?".

CHAPTER *1*

Complex Systems

Informally, we say that a system or a phenomenon is complex if its behavior cannot be easily described and understood [121]. Biological systems shaped by evolution, physical phenomena such as turbulence, the mixture of biology and social components involved in spreading of infectious diseases, and man-made systems such as the Large Hadron Collider (LHC) exhibit elements of complexity.

Complex systems are difficult to model, thus it is difficult to study them and understand the laws governing their evolution. A complex system is characterized by intricate interactions among its components and the emergence of novel properties that cannot be inferred from the study of the individual system components. The behavior of a complex system is subject to statistical laws which affect the individual system components, as well as the interactions among them.

We review philosophical concepts related to the nature and scope of knowledge and the defining attributes of complexity, including nondeterminism, self-similarity, emergence, nonlinearity, and phase transitions. We analyze the interactions of a complex system with the environment. In this chapter, we discuss fractal geometry, Power Law distributions, self-organized criticality, and quantitative characterization of complexity. We conclude with a discussion of the interdisciplinary nature of complexity studies.

1.1 THE THINKING ON COMPLEX SYSTEMS THROUGH THE CENTURIES

Abstract questions about systems consisting of an ensemble of components have preoccupied the minds of humans since antiquity. Plato, a student of Socrates, and Aristotle's mentor, laid the very foundations of Western philosophy and science. He founded one of the earliest known schools in Athens, the Academy. In *The Republic,* Plato introduces the concept of "level of knowledge," ranging from total ignorance to total knowledge. Plato was influenced by Pythagoras in believing that abstract thinking represents

Complex Systems and Clouds. http://dx.doi.org/10.1016/B978-0-12-804041-6.00001-3

the basis for philosophical thinking and sound theses in science, as well as morals. In *A History of Western Philosophy*, Bertrand Russel argues that Pythagoras should be considered the most influential Western philosopher.

Aristotle, in *Metaphysics, Book H* states "... the totality is not, as it were, a mere heap, but the whole is something besides the parts ...," i.e., the whole is other than the sum of the parts. Zino of Eleea, a Greek philosopher living in the 5th century BC, is famous for his paradoxes. One of his paradoxes was that a distance of any length could be divided into an infinite number of shorter segments, therefore covering the distance required traversing an infinite number of shorter segments taking an infinite amount of time; we obviously do cross distances in finite time! Aristotle's answer was that a length was first and foremost a whole.

The philosophy of science has always been that the world can be understood by discovering the properties of its simple building blocks. The traditional scientific method, based on analysis, isolation, and the gathering of complete information about a phenomenon, is a reflection of the reductionist principle. The Greek philosopher Leucippus of Miletus thought the material world is composed of tiny indivisible particles called atoms.[1] Democritus (c.460–371 BC), a disciple of Leucippus, was inspired by his mentor's book, *The Greater World System* and he refined and extended the concept.

The atomic theory of Democritus states that matter is composed of atoms separated by empty space through which the atoms move and that atoms are solid, homogeneous, indivisible, and unchangeable. Some 2500 years later, we are still struggling to better understand the properties of the visible physical matter which accounts for only 4% of the universe. We know even less about the dark matter and the dark energy, which represent 23% and 73%, respectively, of the universe.

Classical mechanics, formulated by Newton and further developed by Laplace and others, was accepted as the foundation for all scientific disciplines until the beginning of the 20th century. *Epistemology* is a branch of philosophy concerned with the nature and scope of knowledge. Newtonian epistemology is based on the principle of *analysis* formulated by the French mathematician and philosopher Descartes, who laid the

---

[1] In Greek the prefix "a" means "not" and the word "tomos" means cut.

foundation of 17th century *rationalism*. According to this principle, also called *reductionism*, to understand a complex phenomenon one has to identify its components and understand their properties and if these components are also complex, the reduction process should be applied recursively until reaching the simplest, or atomic, components with well understood properties.

Newtonian epistemology is based on a reflection-correspondence view of knowledge and on sound philosophical monisms including materialism, reductionism, and determinism. Newtonian epistemology had a pervasive influence on scientific thinking for several centuries, not only because its basic paradigm is compelling by its simplicity, coherence, and apparent completeness, but also due to the fact that it is largely in agreement with intuition and common sense.

More precise reflections of the reality of newer theories, such as special and general relativity and quantum mechanics lack this simplicity and intuitive appeal and are sometimes questioned. For example, the EPR paradox is a thought experiment in quantum mechanics proposed by Einstein, Podolsky, and Rosen in 1935. This thought experiment claims to show that the wave function does not provide a complete description of physical reality, thus, the Copenhagen interpretation[2] is unsatisfactory. John Stewart Bell contributed important ideas to the philosophy of science, showing that local hidden variables cannot reproduce the quantum measurement correlations that quantum mechanics predicts, and that carrying forward EPR's analysis leads to the famous Bell's theorem and Bell's inequality [24].

Newtonian epistemology cannot accept creation and novelty. During the first decades of the 20th century, philosophers such as Bergson and Whitehead realized that the whole has properties that cannot be inferred from the properties of the parts. The term "holism" is defined by Jan Smuts as "the tendency in nature to form wholes that are greater than the sum of the parts through creative evolution" [213].

Causality is a fundamental principle embraced by scientists and philosophers alike in their quest to understand the world. The belief that every event has a cause, the *determinism*, is also critical to the process of thought and gathering knowledge. *Downward causation* is the belief that even if

---

[2]Copenhagen interpretation is an explanation of quantum mechanics principles formulated in the mid-1920s by Niels Bohr and Werner Heisenberg.

we have complete information about the parts of a system, as well as about the environment, the "ensemble" can enforce constraints on the parts and have an unpredictable evolution. Downward causation is related to emergence and self-organization.

1.2 THE MANY FACETS OF COMPLEXITY

There is no universally accepted definition of complexity; typically, the concept is conveyed by particular examples. Systems with a very large number of components, such as the human brain with more than 100 billion neurons, are examples of complex systems. The space shuttle,[3] a modern fighter jet, a multicore processor with several billion transistors,[4] or the Internet with more than 1 billion hosts as of January 2014, are examples of complex man-made systems. Arguably, one of the most complex system, to date is LHC, the particle accelerator, together with its seven particle detectors at CERN in Geneva. Data recorded by the LHC detectors fill around 100,000 dual-layer DVDs each year and led to the discovery of the Higgs boson, and provided new insights into the structure of the matter. Computer clouds are also complex systems consisting of millions of servers. Clouds deliver the computing cycles and the storage, allowing analysis of large data sets such as those produced by LHC.

Percolation, the movement and filtering of fluids through porous materials, and turbulence, the violent flow of a fluid, are examples of complex phenomena occurring in nature. Some of these phenomena, such as turbulence, are not fully understood in spite of significant progress in the field of fluid dynamics and their importance in the design of systems critical for modern society. It is reported that on his deathbed, Werner Heisenberg, one of the pioneers of quantum mechanics and the author of the *Uncertainty Principle*, declared that he had two questions for God: "Why relativity and why turbulence?" Heisenberg said "I really think that He may have an answer to the first question" [92].

---

[3]"The main elements of the space shuttle ... are assembled from more than 2.5 million parts, 230 miles of wire, 1040 valves and 1440 circuit breakers." (Columbia Accident Investigation Board, Report, vol. I, pp. 14, August 2003, at www.nasa.gov/columbia/caib/html/report.html.
[4]As of 2014 Intel's 15-core Xeon Ivy Bridge had the highest transistor count in a commercially available CPU, more than 4.3×10^9 transistors. A 5.4×10^9 transistor chip built with 28 nm technology has one of the highest transistor counts of any chip ever produced.

A side-by-side comparison of generic attributes of simple and complex systems shows that complex systems *are nonlinear, operate far from equilibrium, are intractable at the component level, exhibit different patterns of behavior at different scales, require a long history to draw conclusion about their properties, exhibit complex forms of emergence, are affected by phase transitions, and scale well.* In contrast, simple systems are linear, operate close to equilibrium, are tractable at a component level, exhibit similar patterns of behavior at different levels, relevant properties can be inferred based on a short history, exhibit simple forms of emergence, are not affected by phase transitions, and do not scale well.

Natural sciences, including chemistry, molecular biology, neuroscience, and physics, study different aspects of complexity and complex phenomena. For example, *self-organized criticality* discussed in Section 1.8 was an important discovery in statistical physics in the second half of the 20th century [22]. Bak et al. analyzed mechanisms supporting natural complexity, and the spontaneous emergence of complexity from simple local interactions. They concluded that [21] "the complexity observed in nature does not depend on fine details of the system, several model parameters could have ample variations without affecting the emergence of critical behavior."

Complexity plays a role whenever we model intricate processes in fields such as economics, meteorology, psychology, earthquake prediction, or sociology. Friedrick Hayek, a philosopher and Nobel prize economist, and Karl Popper, both associated with the Austrian school of economics, made significant contributions to the understanding of complexity in economics. More recently, Paul Krugman, the 2008 winner of the Nobel Prize in Economic Sciences for his contributions to New Trade Theory and New Economic Geography, analyzed the application of self-organization in economy [142].

Ludwig von Bertalanffy, who initiated the study of open systems, stresses that: "It is necessary to study not only parts and processes in isolation, but also to solve the decisive problems found in organization and order unifying them, resulting from dynamic interaction of parts, and making the behavior of the parts different when studied in isolation or within the whole" [36]. The patterns of the interactions between the components of a complex system can be stable over longer periods of time or short-lived [49].

The concept of *emergence* describes phenomena characteristic of complex systems and is related to self-organization [104]. *Emergence* is the formation of larger entities, patterns, and regularities through interactions among smaller and/or simpler entities that themselves do not exhibit such properties. Emergence has been discussed since the time of Aristotle. Aldous Huxley observed [123]: "now and again there is a sudden rapid passage to a totally new and more comprehensive type of order or organization, with quite new emergent properties, and involving quite new methods of further evolution."

Emergent behavior is increasingly harder to predict as the number of system components and the complexity of interactions among them increase. Emergence is often associated with positive feedback. Positive feedback amplifies changes in the behavior of individual components and favors the formation of new patterns of behavior. On the other hand, negative feedback tends to stabilize the system behavior and makes emergence less likely.

In 1948, Warren Weaver observed that there is a conceptual distinction between organized and disorganized complexity [246]. Correlated relations between the parts and *emergence,* the fact that the entire system can manifest properties that cannot be inferred from the study of the individual parts, are at the core of *organized complexity*. On the other hand, *disorganized complexity* is characteristic of systems and phenomena when the number of variables is very large and the variables have an erratic or unknown behavior. In spite of the behavior of the individual variables, the system as a whole possesses certain orderly and analyzable average properties.

The properties of an entire system characterized by disorganized complexity can be understood by using probability and statistical methods. The study of disorganized complexity was triggered at the beginning of the 20th century by life sciences, including biology, and now has applications in many fields. For example, although a life insurance company does not have any knowledge of how long a particular individual will live, it has dependable knowledge of the average lifetime of individuals.

Complexity can be measured by the total number of properties of an object or phenomenon detected by an observer. Complexity can also be associated with the probability of a state vector of a physical system. In network theory, complexity reflects the connectivity among the nodes. In software engineering, complexity measures the interactions between system components. Several measures of system complexity are discussed in [173].

In theoretical computer science, computational problems are classified according to their inherent difficulty reflected by the resources necessary to solve them. The *time complexity* of a problem equals the number of steps used by the most efficient algorithm to solve an instance of the problem, as a function of the size of the input, and the *space complexity* measures the amount of the memory used by the algorithm. The study of complexity is not limited to computer science and fields such as artificial intelligence, artificial life, or evolutionary computing.[5]

Conceptually, there is no limit to the number of cores, processors, clusters, and collections of clusters linked together by a hierarchy of networks that can be operating in concert under the control of sophisticated software. Such complex systems are now an integral part of the critical infrastructure of the society and require a different thinking about system design and implementation.

1.3 LAWS OF NATURE, NONDETERMINISM, AND COMPLEX SYSTEMS

The basic laws of physics are expressed by simple mathematical formulas. For example, Newton's Second Law states that $a = \frac{f}{m}$, the acceleration a of an object as produced by a net force f is directly proportional to the magnitude of the force, and inversely proportional to the mass m of the object. The ideal gas law, the equation of state of a hypothetical ideal gas is expressed as $pV = nRT$ where p is the pressure, V is the volume, n is the amount (in moles), R is the ideal gas constant, and T is the temperature of the gas; this law is a good approximation of the behavior of many gases under many conditions. The thermodynamic entropy, S is given by the equation $S = k_B \Omega$ with k_B the Boltzman's constant and Ω the number of micro-states of the system.

Some of the systems described by the laws of physics can be considered "ordered" assemblies of large number of atoms and molecules, while others are random collections of atoms; crystals are an example of ordered assemblies, while gasses form random, disorganized systems. The ideal gas law relates macroscopic quantities, such as temperature and

---

[5]Evolutionary computing is a subfield of computational intelligence using algorithms inspired by Darwin's theory of evolution to solve global optimization problems.

pressure. The temperature reflects the kinetic energy of the ensemble of gas molecules but gives no indication of the kinetic energy, or the movement of individual molecules. Explaining in detail natural phenomena based on the fundamental laws of physics is a hopeless endeavor due to the large variability of the systems and the phenomena in nature.

Complex systems are characterized by a large variability and this makes it impossible to condense the detailed observations of individual components into crisply formulated laws. *The theory explaining the behavior of complex systems must be statistical, ergo, unable to describe the behavior of individual system components.*

Abstraction is a technique for managing system complexity; it establishes the level of detail we want to represent in a model of the system. It is very hard to construct a model of a complex system, making the study of such systems even more challenging. It is even harder to construct a tractable model of a complex system, the state space is so large that traditional methods of investigation, whether analytical or numerical simulation, are impractical.

It has been observed that the existence of stable intermediate forms in chemistry and biology has a powerful effect on the evolution of complex forms. Herbert Simon made an interesting observation relating problem-solving by humans to intermediary forms in biological evolution: "cues signaling progress play the same role in the problem-solving process that stable intermediate forms play in the biological evolutionary process" [210]. As a practical example on how cues reduce the complexity of problem-solving, consider the problem of opening a safe with 10 dials, each one with 100 settings. A trial-and-error strategy has to examine 10^{100} possible combinations. If, on the other hand, a click is heard once a dial is set and the corresponding setting is identified, the number of trials is dramatically reduced to an average of $10 \times 50 = 500$.

It has long been accepted that a legitimate way to relate empirical observations with theory is by predicting the statistics of the phenomena, rather than determining the specific outcome of an experiment. As Democritus observed more than 2000 years ago, "Everything existing in the universe is the fruit of chance and necessity."

Nondeterminism is critical for understanding the behavior of complex systems. Nondeterminism is at the heart of physical reality models. In quantum mechanics the Heisenberg inequality states that we cannot possibly simultaneously determine the momentum, as well as the position of a quantum particle with arbitrarily high precision. In computer science, a nondeterministic algorithm is an algorithm that, as opposed to a deterministic algorithm, even for the same input, can exhibit different behaviors on different runs.

Complexity science is an interdisciplinary discipline devoted to the study of complex systems. The variability of complex organization precludes the possibility that any large number of detailed observations of nature can be condensed into simple laws similar to the laws of physics. It is thus understandable that complexity science cannot explain any detailed fact in nature, but the study of complex systems has stimulated the development of new scientific theories. The study of complex biological, chemical, or physical phenomena led to the development of new disciplines, such as the theory of evolution, bifurcation, and catastrophe theory,[6] the theory of cellular automata, and fractal geometry.

Important ideas regarding evolution and the selection of biological systems were formulated in the middle of the 19th century by Charles Darwin [67]. More recently, Dawkins [68] and Gould made important contributions to the theory of evolution. Gould and Eldredge [97] formulated the thesis that evolution is a chaotic process with long periods of equilibrium, followed by bursts of dramatic changes. The study of chemical systems by Prigogine and his group led to the concept of *dissipative structures* encountered in systems far from thermodynamical equilibrium. Such systems tend to self-organize by exporting entropy to the environment [177, 189].

Modern studies of complex systems are based on nonlinear dynamics, statistical physics, and network theory. There are countless applications of nonlinear dynamics in science and engineering of deterministic systems: in physics, celestial mechanics, geophysics, physiology, neurophysiology, and many other areas. Many systems in nature are nonlinear and *chaos theory* studies nonlinear systems highly sensitive to initial conditions. In a chaotic system, even a minute change in the initial conditions can have dramatic effects over time [63, 65]. Chaos theory has applications in meteorology, but also in sociology, physics, engineering, economics, biology, and philosophy.

---

[6]The French mathematician René Thom in the 1960s, and Christopher Zeeman in the 1970s, developed the catastrophe theory [221, 241].

For example, the weather exhibits chaotic behavior. Catastrophe theory considers cases where an extended stable equilibrium can be identified with the minimum of a smooth, well-defined potential function. It analyzes points where the first, as well as one or more higher derivatives of the potential function, are zero.

Statistical physics introduced new ideas about prediction, formulated solutions to multibody problems in terms of ensembles, and promoted the study of discrete models, such as cellular automata. The study of critical phenomena is based on the scaling hypothesis and scaling laws relating the critical-points exponents.[7] The universality of critical behavior expresses the fact that exponents and scaling functions are the same in the vicinity of the critical point for systems in the same universality class. It follows that one may choose to study the most tractable system in a universality class and expect the results to hold for the other systems in the same class [12].

Network theory plays an important role in understanding complex systems. The study of networks was initiated by the famous mathematician Leonhard Euler. His famous Königsberg bridge puzzle [79] was formulated as: "In the town of Königsberg in Prussia there is an island, called Kneiphoff, with the two branches of the river Pregel flowing around it. There are seven bridges, a, b, c, d, e, f, and g, crossing the two branches. The question is whether a person can plan a walk in such a way that he will cross each of these bridges once, but not more than once. [...] On the basis of the above I formulated the following very general problem for myself: Given any configuration of the river and the branches into which it may divide, as well as any number of bridges, to determine whether or not it is possible to cross each bridge exactly once."

Euler distinguished odd from even nodes based on the number of links directly connected to the node and showed that: (a) the sum of degrees of the nodes of a graph is even; (b) every graph must have an even number of odd nodes; (c) if the number of odd nodes is greater than 2, no Euler walk exists; (d) if there are no odd nodes, Euler walks can start at an arbitrary node. He concluded that all four nodes in the Königsberg bridge are odd, thus there was no solution to his puzzle. The contributions to graph theory by Paul Erdös [78], as well as scale-free networks [29, 30] and Small World networks [244], are discussed in Section 3.7.

---

[7]Critical exponents describe the behavior of physical systems near continuous phase transitions. It is generally believed that critical exponents do not depend on the details of the physical system, and therefore are universal.

1.4 SELF-SIMILARITY: FRACTAL GEOMETRY

The laws of physics describing ordered systems such as solids, where atoms are organized in a lattice, are based on *translational symmetry.* Translational symmetry is the invariance of the equations describing the system under either continuous or discrete translations. The distance between the atoms in an atomic lattice or the mean free path for gases represent a *characteristic length scale.* The assumption of *a characteristic length scale is a basic concept in physics, chemistry, biology, and other disciplines.*

By contrast, complex systems are characterized by a new type of invariance, the *self-invariance,* also called *self-similarity* [106]. Self-similarity means that an object is either exactly, or approximately similar to a part of itself; *the object looks about the same at any scale.* Fractals are infinitely complex patterns that are self-similar across different scales. Fractals are recursive, the process leading to their construction gets repeated indefinitely.

The idea of fractals can be traced to the study of continuous, but not differentiable functions, and the seminal work of famous 19th century mathematicians Bernard Bolzano, Bernhard Riemann, and Karl Weierstrass. Fractal geometry was developed by Benoit Mandelbrot [154] who coined the term "fractal" from the Latin word "fractus" meaning "broken" or "fractured." According to Mandelbrot, "Clouds are not spheres, mountains are not cones, coastlines are not circles, and bark is not smooth, nor does lightning travel in a straight line." Fractals describe the objects in nature, such as clouds, mountains, coastlines, or trees, better than the Euclidian geometry (see Fig. 1.1).

Fig. 1.1 Fractals describe, better than Euclidian geometry shapes, encountered in nature such as clouds, mountains, and coastlines.

The *dimension of a fractal*, $M(bL)$, is a real number b showing how detail in a fractal pattern changes with the scale at which it is measured. For example, given a line segment of size L when we divide it in two $M(\frac{1}{2}L) = \frac{1}{2}M(L)$; for an $L \times L$ square $M(\frac{1}{2}L) = \frac{1}{2^2}M(L)$; for an $L \times L \times L$ cube $M(\frac{1}{2}L) = \frac{1}{2^3}M(L)$. The fractal dimension d is given by Eq. (1.1)

$$M(b \times L) = b^d M(L). \tag{1.1}$$

An example of fractals, the Sierpinski gasket, is generated using the following rules: (1) start with an equilateral triangle and divide it in four equal triangles; (2) leave the center triangle in place; (3) repeatedly apply rules (1) and (2) to every other triangle. Self-similarity is an isotropic property, the change of scale is the same in every direction in space as we can see in Fig. 1.2. The dimension of the Sierpinski gasket is given by Eq. (1.2)

$$M\left(\frac{1}{2}L\right) = \frac{1}{3}M(L) \quad \text{and} \quad M\left(\frac{1}{2}L\right) = \frac{1}{2}^d M(L) \Rightarrow d = \frac{\log 3}{\log 2} = 1.585. \tag{1.2}$$

An *attractor* is a set of numerical values toward which a dynamic system tends to evolve, for a wide variety of initial system conditions. Attractors are critical elements in the theory of self-organization of Ashby [17]. There is a close relationship between fractals and chaotic systems which exhibit fractal attractors.

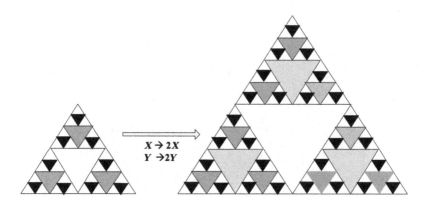

Fig. 1.2 Siorpinski gasket. Self-similarity is an isotropic property, the change of scale is the same in every direction in space.

Fractals have applications in medicine to model heartbeat dynamics or Alzheimer's plaque, in economics to model stock market dynamics, in biology to model DNA molecules, in technology to model the Internet, and for image compression. The recursive formalism for fractal description facilitates numerical simulation.

1.5 POWER LAW DISTRIBUTIONS: ZIPF'S LAW

There are many instances of phenomena where large events are rare, but small ones are quite common and *there is no typical size of the events.* For example, according to the Gutenberg-Richter Law, there are few large earthquakes, but many small ones. For 10 earthquakes of magnitude 6 on the Richter scale there are 100 of magnitude 5, and some 1000 of magnitude 4. *We cannot talk about a typical earthquake magnitude!* The population rankings of cities in various countries follow the same rules, there are a few with a large population and many small ones. Talking about a typical population size of a city makes no sense, either.

Mandelbrot counted the number of months with a given cotton price variation and observed that the price variations are *scale-free,* meaning there is no typical size of the variations. When looking at the coastal map of Norway, one ponders "how long is a typical fjord?" There is no answer to this question; the map shows a hierarchical structure of fjords, with fjords within fjords, and fjords within fjords within fjords. The phenomena of fjord creation are scale-free.

In 1949, George Kingsley Zipf, a professor of statistics at Harvard University, observed that *the log-log plot of rank versus frequency of many phenomena is a straight line with slope near unity* and formulated the so-called Zipf's Law [242]. Zipf counted the frequency of words in James Joyce's *Ulysses* and in a collection of newspapers. He plotted the frequency of the English words versus their rank and noticed that the frequency of occurrence of the words "the," "I," and "say" ranked $1, 10$, and 100 was 9%, 1%, and 0.1%, respectively. Zipf's Law predicts that given N elements, the frequency of elements of rank k, $f(k; \gamma, N)$, is

$$f(k; \gamma, N) = \frac{k^{-\gamma}}{\sum_{i=1}^{N} i^{-\gamma}}. \qquad (1.3)$$

Zipf's Law holds if the number of occurrences of each element are independent and identically distributed random variables with Power Law distribution $p(f) = \alpha f^{(-1-\frac{1}{\gamma})}$. The simplest case of the Zipf's Law states that the size of the kth largest occurrence of the event is inversely proportional to its rank

$$f(k) \approx k^{-\gamma}, \quad \text{with} \quad \gamma \approx 1. \tag{1.4}$$

It follows immediately that

$$\log f(k) \approx -\gamma \log k, \tag{1.5}$$

thus the exponent γ is the slope of the straight line (Fig. 1.3A).

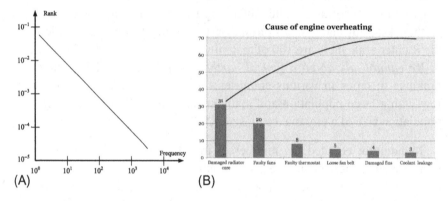

(A)   (B)

Fig. 1.3 (A) Zipf's Law: log-log plot of rank versus frequency; the size versus the number of avalanches in the sandpile model [22], discussed in Section 1.8. (B) Example of Pareto chart showing the causes of overheating in an internal combustion engine. https://upload.wikimedia.org/wikipedia/commons/6/6a/Pareto_analysis.svg.

Instead of asking what the kth largest event is, the Italian economist Vilfredo Pareto[8] asked how many events are greater than x. *Pareto's law* is formulated in terms of the cumulative distribution function (CDF), i.e., the number of events larger than x is an inverse power of x:

$$P[X > x] \approx x^{-k}. \tag{1.6}$$

For example, in terms of income distribution, Pareto's Law says that there are a few multibillionaires, but most people have a modest income.

A *Power Law* distribution gives the number of events of magnitude exactly x rather than the number of events with a magnitude greater than x.

---

[8]In 1896, Pareto published the paper "Cours d'economie politique" in connection with population and wealth. He noticed that 80% of Italy's land was owned by 20% of the population.

The Power Law distribution is the probability distribution function (PDF) associated with the CDF given by Pareto's Law

$$P[X = x] \approx x^{-(k+1)} = x^{-a}, \tag{1.7}$$

where $a = 1 + k$ and k is the Pareto distribution shape parameter. A *Pareto chart* contains both bars and a line graph; the individual values are represented in descending order by bars, and the cumulative total is represented by the line (Fig. 1.3B).

The authors of [9] report on the diameter of the World Wide Web. They used the data collected by a robot which constructed a database of URLs and determined the probabilities $P_{out}(k)$ and $P_{in}(k)$ that a document has k outgoing and incoming links, respectively. Their analysis shows that both probabilities follow a Power Law over several orders of magnitude. The link distribution is different from the Poisson distribution predicted by the classical theory of random graphs and by the bounded distribution found in random network models. This distribution shows that the probability of finding documents with a large number of links is significant. The network connectivity is dominated by highly-connected web pages.

1.6 EMERGENCE, NONLINEARITY, AND PHASE TRANSITIONS

Emergence is generally understood as *a property of a system not predictable from the properties of individual system components.* Emergent structures occur in nature, e.g., the shapes of hurricanes are emergent structures. The growth of crystals can lead to emerging structures, or the random motion of water molecules can give rise to complex orderly structures.

The number of interactions between the components of a system increases exponentially with the number of system components, and implicitly creates the conditions for subtle types of behavior, including emergence. Emergence is often a product of particular patterns of interaction, e.g., positive feedback allows local variations to grow into global patterns. Emergence may be related to dual-phase evolutions; during the first phase, patterns form or grow, and during the second, these patterns are either refined, or removed.

Goldstein defined emergence as: "the arising of novel and coherent structures, patterns, and properties during the process of self-organization in complex systems." He identified several characteristics of emergence [96]:

- Radical novelty—emergent features are not predictable from lower components.
- Coherence—emergent properties maintain a sense of identity and coherence over time.
- Global level—emergent phenomena occur at a global level.
- Dynamical evolution—emergent phenomena arise as a complex system evolves over time. Emergence is associated with new attractors in dynamical systems.
- Ostensive—the nature of complex systems implies that emergent phenomena will be different to some degree from previous ones.

There is a distinction between *weak emergence* and *strong emergence*. The former describes new properties due to interactions at an elemental level. Such properties cannot be determined by an a priori analysis, but by observing or simulating the system. The latter describes properties irreducible to the system's constituent parts, properties representing the direct causal action of the high-level system upon its components. Though the very existence of strong emergence seems to invoke some form of magic, a class of physical systems that exhibits noncomputable macroscopic properties has been reported [101].

Traditional physics has studied order and complete randomness, but emergent structures appear somewhere in the middle, and have eluded traditional physics. Crutchfield attributes this to the fact that [64] "there are not physical principles that define and dictate how to measure natural structure." Holland distinguishes between authentic emergent phenomena and "serendipitous novelty," such as the play of light on leaves in a breeze [119]. Interestingly enough, emergent behavior is used to explore the origins of novelty, creativity, and authorship in literature, art, history, and linguistics.

The argument that emergent behavior decreases the entropy of the system and violates the second law of thermodynamics, ignores the fact that open systems extract information and order out of the environment.

Linear systems satisfy the *superposition principle*. This principle states that *the response of a linear system caused by two or more stimuli is the sum of the responses caused by each stimulus acting alone*. If input i_1 produces response r_1 and input i_2 produces response r_2, then input $i_1 + i_2$ should produce response $r_1 + r_2$. Many physical systems can be modeled as linear systems. In mathematics, a linear function $f(x)$ satisfies additivity or superposition and homogeneity expressed as:

$$f(x + y) = f(x) + f(y) \quad \text{and} \quad f(\alpha x) = \alpha f(x). \tag{1.8}$$

Nonlinearity characterizes phenomena when there is a disproportionate relationship between cause and effect. A nonlinear system does not satisfy the superposition principle.

Nonlinear phenomena are harder to study and the nonlinear equations describing such phenomena are more difficult to solve. For example, the *Navier-Stokes equations* describe the motion of viscous fluid and are used to model the weather, ocean currents, water flow in a pipe, and air flow around an airplane wing. The *Boltzmann transport equation* describes the behavior of a thermodynamic system not in a thermodynamic equilibrium, e.g., when the random transport of particles of a fluid with a temperature gradient causes heat to flow from hotter regions to colder ones. More generally, the equation describes the change of a macroscopic quantity in a thermodynamic system, such as energy, charge, or particle number.

General relativity expressed by the Einstein field equations describes the curvature of spacetime directly related to the energy and the momentum of matter and radiation. General relativity presents a unified description of gravity as a geometric property of space and time, and is the simplest theory of gravitation consistent with all experimental data. The Einstein field equations are nonlinear and very difficult to solve.

There are many other types of nonlinear behavior, including *chaos* which describes systems with unpredictable behavior or systems oscillating between multiple stable states with unstable points between the stable points, or the so-called *multistability*. There are also *solitons* caused by cancellation of nonlinear and dispersive effects in the medium.

In complex systems, the relation between cause and effect is often unpredictable; small causes could have large effects, and large causes could have small effects. This phenomenon is caused by *feedback*, the results of an action or transformation are fed back and affect the system's behavior. Negative feedback negatively affects the causes that trigger the action, while positive feedback reinforces these causes.

A fair number of nested or otherwise related positive and negative feedback loops affect the state of a complex system. For example, in the case of the stock market, the number of stocks bought and sold depends upon the price and the price depends on how many stocks are bought and sold. An increase in price has a negative effect on the demand thus, the price will eventually fall, but, at the same time, it stimulates the appetite for speculation, making the stocks more attractive to the buyers. Eventually, the Nash equilibrium is reached.

Avalanche phenomena could occur in a packet-switched[9] networks without congestion control mechanisms. When the network load increases, routers with limited buffer space start dropping packets, the senders do not receive acknowledgments, time out, and resend packets, and eventually the network ceases to transport packets. Similar phenomena could occur in computer systems when processor scheduling algorithms fail to detect *thrashing* and take adequate measures. For example, two memory-intensive processes could generate a large rate of page faults and cause frequent context switching, preventing competing processes or threads from making progress.

Minor faults could trigger an unforeseen and undesirable chain of events and cause a complex system, such as the cloud infrastructure of a Cloud Service Provider (CSP) to collapse. Such a sequence of events led to the failure of Amazon Web Services (AWS) on June 30, 2012 at 11:21 PM, when a severe thunderstorm caused the North Virginia site to go down. Several companies, including Netflix, Instagram, and Pinterest, as well as a large number of individual AWS users, were affected by this outage.

Avalanche phenomena pose a serious threat to large concentrations of resources contributing to the critical infrastructure of the society. The financial crisis of 2007–2008 threatened the collapse of large financial institutions. The "too big to fail" theory asserting that the failure of large financial institutions would be catastrophic was then used to justify the intervention of the government. Mechanisms for early detection of such phenomena should be included in the initial design of such systems to ensure graceful degradation, rather than total collapse.

The concept of *phase transition* comes from the field of thermodynamics and describes the transformation, often discontinuous, of a system from one phase/state to another, as a result of an often relatively small change in the environment. Examples of phase transitions in physical systems are: *freezing*, transition from liquid to solid and its reverse, *melting*; *deposition*, transition from gas to solid and its reverse, *sublimation*; and *ionization*, transition from gas to plasma and its reverse, *recombination*.

Phase transitions often involve a symmetry breaking process. For example, cooling of a fluid into a crystalline solid breaks continuous

---

[9]A packet-switched network carries data as suitably sized blocks called packets transmitted through via a shared medium.

translation symmetry. Each point in the fluid has the same properties, but each point in a crystal does not have the same properties. In thermodynamics, a *critical state* is one in which phase boundaries vanish. For example, the liquid-vapor critical point designates conditions when a liquid and its vapor coexist.

Two types of phase transitions exist. During a *first-order phase transition*, a system either absorbs or releases a fixed amount of energy per volume, while the temperature of the system remains constant as heat is added; in this "mixed-phase regime," some parts of the system complete the transition and others do not. *Continuous phase transitions* are characterized by a divergent susceptibility, an infinite correlation length, and a Power-Law decay of correlations near criticality.

Phase transitions have been observed in ad hoc wireless networks. The authors of [141] show that there exists a critical level of radio transmission power for all nodes. Above this level, the multihop network formed by n nodes randomly located in an area, has a very high probability to be connected. Below the critical level, the probability that the network is connected is nearly zero. The most efficient operating point for the system is just to the right of this transition point.

1.7 OPEN SYSTEMS AND THE ENVIRONMENT

An *isolated* physical system does not exchange matter, energy, or information with its environment; thus, an isolated system has a limited supply of energy. A *closed* physical system exchanges energy, but not matter with the environment.

In contrast, an *open system* interacts with its environment transferring, matter, energy, and/or information through the boundary separating it from its environment. An open system is receptive to new information. The theory of open systems was formulated in the mid-1950s by the biologist Ludwig von Bertalanffy [36].

Living systems are open to exchange matter, energy, and information, while in thermodynamically closed systems the entropy only increases. Complex systems interact with their environment, therefore, they are *open* systems. For example, living systems have to exchange matter and energy with the environment in order to survive.

Open systems are analyzed in [132]. The author stresses that open systems evolve as cycles of events and have several defining properties:

- they import energy from the environment;
- they transform the resources available to them;
- they export some resources to the environment;
- they generate negative entropy;
- they have a negative feedback loop to maintain a steady-state;
- they dynamically achieve homeostasis;
- they strive to achieve differentiation and specialization;
- they include mechanisms for integration and coordination; and
- they enjoy equifinality.

Homeostasis describes the successful survival of an organism, and *equifinality* means that a given end state can be reached by many potential means [36].

Open systems are classified in several categories in the order of their complexity [40]:

1. systems comprising static structures, e.g., crystals;
2. simple dynamic systems with predetermined motions, e.g., clocks or the solar system;
3. systems capable of self-regulation with an externally prescribed target, the cybernetic systems, e.g., a thermostat;
4. systems capable of self-maintenance through exchange of resources with the environment, e.g., a cell;
5. blueprint-growth systems, e.g., systems reproducing through seeds or eggs;
6. systems with a detailed awareness of their environment, e.g., animals;
7. self-consciousness systems, e.g., humans;
8. social systems groups sharing a common order and culture; and
9. transcendental systems—"absolutes and inescapable unknowables."

The concept of open systems has many applications, not only in natural sciences, but also in social sciences and economics. In computing, an open system supports a combination of interoperability, portability, and open software standards. The idea of open computer systems, initially referred to systems based on Unix, in contrast to the proprietary systems of vendors such as IBM, HP, or Microsoft

1.8 SELF-ORGANIZATION AND SELF-ORGANIZED CRITICALITY

Self-organization is the spontaneous emergence of global coherence out of local interactions. The behavior of many systems seems chaotic and unpredictable, but a closer analysis discovers self-organization. Positive feedback sometimes amplifies random fluctuations and generates different forms of self-organization in physical, chemical, biological, robotic, social, and cognitive systems. This point of view reflects the principle of "order from noise," formulated in 1960 by Heinz von Foerster [229].

Self-organization could open a new era in the design and implementation of large-scale computing systems and networks [166, 178]. Self-organization is prevalent in nature [199], for example, molecular self-assembly, self-assembly of monolayers, and the formation of liquid and colloidal crystals and many other examples in chemistry. Spontaneous folding of proteins and other bio-macromolecules, the formation of lipid bilayer membranes, thermal convection of fluids, chemical oscillation, and crystallization are manifestations of self-organization in nature. The flocking behavior of different species, the creation of structures by social animals, and animal swarming are manifestation of self-organization of biological systems. Ecosystems are examples of systems where individuals have competing interests and conflicts are inherent, but still some form of equilibrium is reached.

An interesting question addressed by the 1977 Nobel laureate in Chemistry, Ilya Prigogine, is how self-organization can be reconciled with the second law of thermodynamics, which states that the entropy of a system can never decrease. Prigogine studied *dissipative structures* such as the Benard cells which exhibit dynamic self-organization and are examples of systems far-from-equilibrium. Benard cells are ordered hexagonal convection cells, or atomic-molecular structures that spontaneously form in viscous mediums, such as silicon oil or whale oil, when placed on a hot plate and heated past a bifurcation point into the turbulent flow regime. Such open systems continuously generate entropy and export it to the environment. *The system circumvents the second law of thermodynamics by exporting its excess entropy;* living organisms are examples of dissipative systems [177].

According to W. Ross Ashby, a deterministic dynamic system will automatically evolve towards a state of equilibrium that can be described in terms of an attractor in a cluster of surrounding states [17]. Ashby believes that at the core of the concept of *organization* lies *conditionality*: "... as soon as the relation between two entities A and B becomes conditional in C's value or state, then a necessary component of organization exists ... The presence of organization between variables is equivalent to the existence of a constraint in the product-space of probabilities."

Recently discovered, *self-organized criticality is the spontaneous emergence of complexity from simple local interactions.* A classical example of self-organized criticality is a sandpile modeled as a cellular automaton on a square lattice [22]. Call $z(x,y)$ the height of the pile at cell (x,y) of the lattice. The sand pile at cell (x,y) collapses and dispenses sand to all neighboring cells when $z \geq K$, with K a critical value. The grains of sand leave the system if the cell is at the boundary. This process is modeled by three transitions

$$z(x,y) \rightarrow z(x,y) - K,$$
$$z(x \pm 1, y) \rightarrow z(x \pm 1, y) + 1, \qquad (1.9)$$
$$z(x, y \pm 1) \rightarrow z(x, y \pm 1) + 1.$$

The order in which the transitions occur at the same cell and different cells is arbitrary. This model describes an "Abelian sandpile," as additions corresponding to successive topplings are commutative. A cascade of transitions occur at cell (x,y) until

$$z(x,y) < K. \qquad (1.10)$$

The measurement begins when this minimally stable state occurs. The height $z(x,y)$ is increased by one, the value of the random perturbation, and the resulting avalanche are evaluated. Fig. 1.4 shows the evolution of a two-dimensional sandpile [22]. When a cell collapses, the height of its four

Diagram 1

1	2	0	2	3
2	3	2	3	0
1	2	3	3	2
3	1	3	2	1
0	2	2	1	2

Diagram 2

1	2	0	2	3
2	3	2	3	0
1	2	4	3	2
3	1	3	2	1
0	2	2	1	2

Diagram 3

1	2	0	2	3
2	3	3	3	0
1	3	0	4	2
3	1	4	2	1
0	2	2	1	2

Diagram 4

1	2	0	2	3
2	3	3	4	0
1	3	2	0	3
3	2	0	4	1
0	2	3	1	2

Diagram 5

1	2	0	3	3
2	3	4	0	1
1	3	2	2	3
3	2	1	0	2
0	2	3	2	2

Diagram 6

1	2	1	3	3
2	4	0	1	1
1	3	3	2	3
3	2	1	0	2
0	2	3	2	2

Diagram 7

1	3	1	3	3
3	0	1	1	1
1	4	3	2	3
3	2	1	0	2
0	2	3	2	2

Diagram 8

1	3	1	3	3
3	1	1	1	1
2	0	4	2	3
3	3	1	0	2
0	2	3	2	2

Diagram 9

1	3	1	3	3
3	1	2	1	1
2	1	0	3	3
3	3	2	0	2
0	2	3	2	2

Diagram 10

1	3	1	3	3
3				1
2				3
3	3			2
0	2	3	2	2

Fig. 1.4 The evolution of a two-dimensional 5×5 sandpile when the critical value is $K = 4$. The initial state is shown by the diagram in the top left corner. In the next 8 diagrams of the pile, we follow a sequence of 9 cell toppling events, starting with a grain of sand falling to the center cell of the sandpile. The cells that have toppled are the 8 dark ones in the last diagram of pile in the second row.

neighboring cells at N, S, E, and W increases by one unit and the height of the cell becomes zero.

All cells affected by the avalanche are members of a cluster of size s. $D(s)$ is the cluster distribution. Simulations for two- and three-dimensional piles show that $D(s)$ fits the Power Law

$$D(s) \approx s^{-\tau} \tag{1.11}$$

with $\tau \approx 0.98$ for a two-dimensional lattice of size 50×50, and $\tau \approx 1.35$ for a three-dimensional lattice of size $20 \times 20 \times 20$. For small values of s, the distribution D is affected by the spacing of the lattice; for large values of s, D is affected by the system size.

The distribution of fluctuation lifetimes

$$s(t) \approx t^{\tau + \gamma} \tag{1.12}$$

was calculated assuming

$$D(t) = \frac{s}{t} D(s(t)) \frac{ds}{dt} \approx t^{-(\gamma+1)\tau + 2\gamma} = t^{-\alpha} \tag{1.13}$$

with γ describing how the cluster grows.

An interesting observation related to self-organized criticality is: "...evolution cannot be seen as a drive towards more and more fit species despite the fact that each of the steps that constitute evolution may improve the fitness" [22] and reflects the fact that "fitness" is not invariant, it may change as a period of stability during which little or no evolutionary change in a lineage is replaced by another stasis. This observation may explain why sometimes genetic algorithms are not as effective as expected [152].

1.9 CYBERNETICS

The word *Cybernetics* comes from the Greek word, *kybernetes*, meaning *rudder, pilot*, a device used to steer a boat, or to support human governance. This word was first used by Plato in *Alcibiades I*[10] to signify the governance of people. In the 1830s, the French physicist Ampere used it to describe

---

[10]The first Alcibiades is a dialog between Alcibiades and Socrates attributed to Plato. Alchibiades was an aristocrat and a prominent Athenian orator, politician and general involved in the Peloponnesian War.

the science of civil government. Norbert Wiener defined cybernetics as "the study of control and communication in the animal and the machine" [248].

Cybernetics is concerned with concepts at the core of understanding complex systems such as learning, cognition, adaptation, emergence, communication, and efficiency. Cybernetics has been influenced by and, in turn, has applications in fields as diverse as psychology and control theory, philosophy and mechanical engineering, architecture and evolutionary biology, or social sciences and electrical engineering.

There is little wonder that philosophers and scientists have different definition of cybernetics. Cybernetics is "the art of creating equilibrium in a world of constraints and possibilities," according to the philosopher Ernst von Glasersfeld. The famous mathematician Andrey Nikolaevich Kolmogorov defines cybernetics as the "science concerned with the study of systems of any nature which are capable of receiving, storing, and processing information so as to use it for control."

Other remarkable definitions of cybernetics are: "The art of steersmanship: deals with all forms of behavior in so far as they are regular, or determinate, or reproducible: stands to the real machine—electronic, mechanical, neural, or economic—much as geometry stands to real object in our terrestrial space; offers a method for the scientific treatment of the system in which complexity is outstanding and too important to be ignored," by the famous psychiatrist and pioneer of cybernetics, William Ross Ashby. It is also "the science and art of understanding," according to the biologist Humberto Maturana, known for creating concepts such as structural determinism and structure coupling. Several other definitions of cybernetics can be found at the site of the American Association of Cybernetics, http://www.asc-cybernetics.org/foundations/history.htm.

In recent years, scientists have shown some reluctance to use the term *cybernetics* because the discipline covers a very broad range of concepts and applications in so many areas of human endeavor. Nevertheless, core concepts of cybernetics, such as *feedback* are essential for understanding complex systems, simply because such systems have to adapt their behavior based on feedback from the environment they operate in. Two feedback loops allow the system to learn and to adapt; one, used frequently, makes small adjustments and enables learning, while the other, used less frequently, senses the need to replace obsolete information with new information, thus enabling adaptation. According to Ashby [17], *learning* implies that a system discovers patterns of successful behavior in the environment it operates in and repeats successful actions, while avoiding unsuccessful ones. *Adaptation* means that the system learns a new pattern of behavior after recognizing that the environment has changed and the old pattern is no longer successful.

Ashby defines a *machine* as a system whose internal state, together with the state of the environment, dictates the next state. The *regulator* is the element controlling the evolution of the system, and it can do so by using the feedback to assess how far the system deviates from a prescribed behavior, and by reacting to disturbances of its environment. The regulator must have information linking cause and effect in the system environment. The repertoire of actions required by the feedback should reflect the variety of the perturbations; this is the Ashby's *Law of the requisite variety* [17]. Faced with an unforeseen sequence of events, we have the option to increase the variety in the regulator, or reduce the variety in the system being regulated. Based on these principles, we expect that an isolated dynamic system obeying unchanging laws will adapt to its environment. As a corollary, it follows that only the ensemble consisting of the system and its environment can be rightfully called *self-organizing.*

Heinz von Forster, along with McCulloch, Wiener, Ashby, and von Neumann, are considered the founders of cybernetics. In an interview at Stanford University, Heinz von Forster talks about his quantum theory of memory, "I can't remember whether Caesar came before Augustus or after Augustus... So I thought I would make myself a table, a historical table... I observed that the closer to the present you came, the more densely filled the paper was with data; conversely, the further you went back the thinner the table... The best way to represent such data is to plot it logarithmically. Every decade, or every power of ten, covers the same distance and that means that, as you go further back into the past, ten years are as big as one year, and then one hundred years are as big as ten year, etcetera..." (http:http://web.stanford.edu/group/SHR/4-2/text/interviewvonf.html). This observation could be useful in compressing the past history of an adaptive system and giving a larger weight to a more recent set of events.

1.10 QUANTITATIVE CHARACTERIZATION OF COMPLEXITY: ENTROPY

Qualitative, as well as quantitative, characterization of phenomena and entities is common to all scientific disciplines, so it seems appropriate to address the question of quantitative measures of complexity. Disciplines such as computer science, systems engineering, biology, finance, or game theory, have developed their own measures of complexity. These measures reflect answers to questions such as: How difficult is it to describe the system or the organization of the system? How difficult is it to create a model of the system?

The first quantitive characterization of a system complexity, sometimes called *abstract complexity*, can be formulated only in terms of its structure. If we consider a system with n components forming S substructures, the degree of complexity could be measured as $D = S/n$. Then, the abstract complexity of the system depends on the degree of complexity and the cardinality of the set of substructures, and can be expressed as

$$C = D \times S = \frac{S^2}{n}. \tag{1.14}$$

Consider a hierarchical structure of n elements and L levels. The number of substructures at levels $0, 1, \ldots L - 1$, are respectively

$$S_0 = n, S_1 = N_1, \ldots, S_{L-1} = N_{L-1}. \tag{1.15}$$

Then the abstract complexity of the entire structure can be expressed as

$$C_L = \prod_{i=1}^{L-1} C_i = \frac{N_1^2}{n} \times \frac{N_2^2}{N_1} \times \cdots \times \frac{N_{L-2}^2}{N_{L-3}} \times \frac{N_{L-1}^2}{N_{L-2}} = \frac{N_{L-1}}{n} \prod_{i=1}^{L-1} N_i. \tag{1.16}$$

We have to accept that the quantitative characterization of a system's complexity is more challenging. It has to reflect all factors contributing to complexity, including: the number of components, the diversity of the components, the interaction patterns among the components, how far can the system be from equilibrium, how extensive should the knowledge of the system's history be to give us some understanding of its behavior, and what type of feedback, what is its intensity, and how is it applied in time?

Typically, we operate with a model of a system and quantify aspects of this model as a proxy for the complexity of the system. For example, we can measure the actual amount of information needed to describe the system [34], the number or the types of the components [169], a measure of the interactions among the system components, or a combination of these metrics.

The entropy and the Kolmogorov complexity discussed in this section, the fractal dimension mentioned in Section 1.3, and the Fisher information[11] are expressed as the number of bits. The entropy is a measure of the lack of information about the state of a system.

We briefly discuss thermodynamic entropy, Shannon entropy, and von Neumann entropy. *Thermodynamic entropy* is a measure of the number of specific ways in which the individual atoms and molecules, i.e., the micro-states, which comprise the macroscopic state of the system may be arranged. It is a measure of disorder in the system defined by Boltzman as

$$S = k_B \ln \Omega, \tag{1.17}$$

with k_B the Boltzmann's constant and Ω the number of micro-states of the system.

Shannon entropy measures the surprise caused by the occurrence of an event. Consider an event which happens with probability p; we wish to quantify the information content of a message communicating the occurrence of this event, and we impose the condition that the measure should reflect the "surprise" brought by the occurrence of this event. An initial guess for a measure of this *surprise* would be $1/p$, such that the lower the probability of the event, the larger the surprise. But this simplistic approach does not resist scrutiny; the surprise should be additive. If an event is composed of two independent events which occur with probabilities q and r, then the probability of the event should be $p = qr$, but we see that

$$\frac{1}{p} \neq \frac{1}{q} + \frac{1}{r}. \tag{1.18}$$

On the other hand, if the *surprise* is measured by the logarithm of $1/p$, then the additivity property is obeyed

$$\log \frac{1}{p} = \log \frac{1}{q} + \log \frac{1}{r}. \tag{1.19}$$

All logarithms are in base 2 unless stated otherwise. Given a discrete probability distribution with $\sum_i p_i = 1$ we see that the uncertainty is in fact equal to the average *surprise*

---

[11] The Fisher information is a way of measuring the amount of information that an observable random variable X carries about an unknown parameter θ upon which the probability of X depends. The Fisher-information matrix is used to calculate the covariance matrices associated with maximum-likelihood estimates.

$$\sum_i p_i \log \frac{1}{p_i}. \tag{1.20}$$

The entropy is a measure of the uncertainty of a single random variable X before it is observed, or the average uncertainty removed by observing it [60]. This quantity is called entropy due to its similarity to the thermodynamic entropy. The Shannon entropy of a random variable X with a probability density function $p_X(x)$ is

$$H(X) = -\sum_x p_X(x) \log p_X(x). \tag{1.21}$$

The entropy of a random variable is a positive number. Indeed, the probability $p_X(x)$ is a positive real number between 0 and 1 therefore, $\log p_X(x) \leq 0$ and $H(X) \geq 0$. Let X be a binary random variable and $p = p_X(x = 1)$ be the probability that the X takes the value 1; then the entropy of X is

$$H(p) = -p \log p - (1 - p) \log(1 - p). \tag{1.22}$$

If the logarithm is in base 2, then the binary entropy is measured in bits. The entropy has a maximum of one bit when $p = 1/2$, and goes to zero when $p = 0$ or $p = 1$; intuitively, we expect the entropy to be zero when the outcome is certain, and reach its maximum when both outcomes are equally possible.

Shannon channel source coding theorem establishes the limits to possible data compression and gives an operational meaning of the Shannon entropy.

There is a relationship between thermodynamics and Shannon entropy. When the N molecules of the system are grouped together in m micro-states depending on their energy, then the number of bits required to label the individual micro-states is

$$Q = H(p_1, p_2, \ldots, p_m), \tag{1.23}$$

with $H(p_1, p_2, \ldots, p_m)$ the Shannon entropy of a system with m states. If n_i is number of molecules in state i then $p_i = n_i/N$ is the probability of the system being in state i.

The *von Neumann entropy* of a quantum system with the density matrix ρ,

$$S(\rho) = -\text{tr}\left[\rho \log \rho\right] \tag{1.24}$$

is equal to the Shannon entropy if the system is prepared in a *maximally mixed state*, a superposition state where all pure states are equally likely.

Another measure of complexity is the *relative predictive efficiency* defined as $e = E/C$ where E is the excess entropy and C is the statistical complexity [65]. The *excess entropy* measures the complexity of the stochastic process, and can be regarded as the fraction of historical information about the process that allows us to predict the future behavior of the process. The *statistical complexity* reflects the size of the model of the system at a certain level of abstraction.

Complexity could be related to the description of a system and may consist of structural, functional, and, possibly, other important properties of the system [45]. The question of how to measure the descriptive complexity of an object was addressed by Kolmogorov [139].

The *Kolmogorov complexity* $K_V(s)$ of a string s with respect to the universal computer V, is defined as the minimal length over all programs $Prog_V$ that print s and halt

$$K_V(s) = min[Length(s)] \text{ over all Prog: } V(Prog_V) = s. \qquad (1.25)$$

The intuition behind Kolmogorov complexity is to provide the shortest possible description of any object or phenomena. Gell-Mann argues that the Kolmogorov complexity has a fundamental flaw; it is never known if a more efficient compression scheme exists or will be discovered in the future, leading to a shorter description of the object or phenomenon [89].

1.11 COMPUTATIONAL IRREDUCIBILITY

There are systems whose behavior is repetitive, or can be expressed by a straightforward interaction of a relatively small number of easy-to-describe components. In this case, there are shortcuts that allow us to reduce the computational effort to model such systems, and we say that the behavior of such systems is *computationally reducible*. So the natural question is if there are shortcuts that allow us to describe the behavior of complex systems in a simple way, and thus, to create simple models and simplify the simulation of such systems.

In his book, *A New Kind of Science*, Stephen Wolfram [250] introduced *computational irreducibility* to describe systems for which it is not possible to describe their behavior in a simple way, and thus, to find shortcuts for a program simulating the behavior of such systems. Computational irreducibility implies that there are cases where theoretical predictions are not possible and there are normally computationally irreducible phenomena. Wolfram conjectured that there is no easy theory for any behavior that seems complex.

Shortly after the introduction of the concept of computational irreducibility, it was shown in [125] that some computationally irreducible elementary cellular automata have properties that are predictable, therefore their properties are computationally reducible. These cellular automata can emulate reducible cellular automata by coarse-graining. This is the case of a universal cellular automaton described by rule 110.

A result confirming Wolfram's conjecture is discussed in [162]. The dynamic behavior of a system can be modeled as the trajectory of the system in the phase space. A phase space is an abstraction where each possible state of the system is represented by a unique point. Each dimension of the phase space represents a degree of freedom of the system. Individual trajectories have different probabilities, with some of them more likely than others.

In [162] it is shown that for a complex system, the highly probable trajectories in the phase space are dominant. The paper analyzes random walks in fully connected finite state machines, and shows that the cardinality of the set of highly probable trajectories is very large; its lower bound is exponential in the number of states traversed by the random walk, and in an expression of system entropy (see Fig. 1.5).

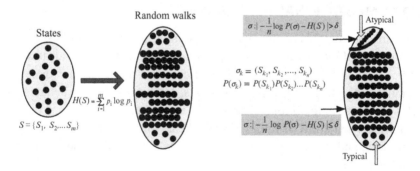

Fig. 1.5 In fully connected finite state machines the cardinality of the set of highly probable trajectories is very large, its lower bound is exponential in the number of states traversed by the random walk and in an expression of system entropy. From D.C. Marinescu, High probability trajectories in the phase space and system complexity, Complex Syst. 22 (3) (2013) 233–246.

1.12 THE INTERDISCIPLINARY NATURE OF COMPLEXITY

The interdisciplinary nature of complexity is reflected by the scientists who made major contributions to the field; papers authored by biologists, chemists, physicists, mathematicians, computer scientists, economists, and others, introduced seminal ideas for the study of complexity [112, 153, 243, 251]. The idea that physical, biological, chemical, social, economic, linguistic, and any other systems and their properties should be viewed as wholes, not as collections of parts, is the main theme of *Holism and Evolution*, a book written by the South African statesman Ian Smuts in 1926 [213].

Charles Darwin [67] is the creator of the theory of evolution. More recently, Richard Dawkins [68] made important contributions to the theory of evolution, and Stephen Gould and Niles Eldredge formulated the thesis that evolution is a chaotic process with long periods of equilibrium followed by bursts of dramatic changes [97]. Sir Julian Sorell Huxley was a British scientist proponent of natural selection, a leading figure in the mid-20th century modern evolutionary synthesis, and in ethics in science [123]. Karl Ludwig von Bertalanffy was an Austrian biologist, one of the founders of general systems theory [36].

Ilya Prigogine was a Belgian physical chemist and Nobel Laureate noted for his work on dissipative structures, complex systems, and irreversibility [177, 189]. Self-similarity was investigated by Shlomo Havlin [106] and fractal geometry was developed by Benoit Mandelbrot [154]. George Kingsley Zipf formulated the so-called Zipf's Law [242], based on the observation that the log-log plot of rank versus frequency of many phenomena is a straight line with slope near unity. The study of networks was initiated by Leonard Euler [79]. Paul Erdös made seminal contributions to graph theory [78]. More recent contributions to networks theory are due to R. Albert and A.-L. Barabási for the study of complex networks and their applications [9–11, 29, 30], and to D.J. Watts and S.H. Strogatz for the Small Worlds networks [244].

James Crutchfield worked in nonlinear dynamics, and studied critical phenomena and phase transitions, chaos, and pattern formation [63–65]. Self-organized criticality was introduced by Per Bak et al. [21]. An extensive discussion of this phenomena is presented in Bak's book *How Nature Works* [22].

Herbert Simon's research in cognitive science, computer science, philosophy of science, sociology, and political science, led to fundamental ideas regarding the decision-making process and contributed to better understanding of complex systems [209, 210]. John Holland, a computer science professor at the University of Michigan, was a pioneer in genetic algorithms and chaos theory who wrote several books on chaos theory [118, 119]. Warren Weaver coauthored with Claude Shannon the seminal paper "The Mathematical Theory of Communication," published in 1949, and developed the philosophical implications of Shannon's theory. He also noted the distinction between organized and disorganized complexity [246].

Norbert Wiener's book *Cybernetics: Or Control and Communication in the Animal and the Machine* [248], along with the seminal work of W. Ross Ashby, "Principles of Self-organizing Systems" [17], are required readings for those interested in cybernetics. Much is due to James Goldstein for his studies of emergence [96]; the distinction between strong and weak emergence is discussed in [101]. Applications of self-organization in economics are presented in [142].

The manner in which nature works has inspired algorithms for solving complex problems. A deeper understanding of the structure of matter has triggered the search for new ways of computing. These are the topics discussed in the next chapter.

CHAPTER 2

Nature-Inspired Algorithms and Systems

Richard Feynman believed that computing and physics and, particularly, quantum mechanics, are in a symbiotic relationship [82]. In 1998, Leonard Adleman expressed his conviction that "Biology and computer science— life and computation—are related. I am confident that at their interface great discoveries await those who seek them..." [7]. A significant number of research results in quantum and DNA computing have proven that the two visionary scientists were right.

The study of insect and animal behavior, immunology, molecular biology, genetics, the study of the nervous system, and of the human brain are only a few disciplines that have inspired new problem-solving techniques and principles for systems design and implementation. Evolutionary computing is inspired by Darwin's theory of evolution, and membrane computing draws its inspiration from the organization of cells where different components interact through permeable cellular walls.

Neural computation attempts to emulate the brain [120], and amorphous computing draw their ideas from morphogenesis, investigated by Alan Turing at the beginning of the 1950s [224]. The behavior of groups of insects, birds, and animals is the source of ideas for swarm intelligence, and self-replication led to the development of cellular automata. The study of the natural immune system inspired the study of artificial immune systems.

We wish to understand the laws governing complex systems in nature and, whenever feasible, apply the lessons learned in designing and building increasingly more complex man-made systems. *Bio-inspired computing* and *organic computing* are two areas driven by the desire to apply lessons learned from nature to system design. Bio-inspired computing aims to model the living phenomena using computers, and, at the same time, improve the use of computers though modeling the behavior of living organisms. Organic computing assumes that we shall soon be surrounded by networks of intelligent systems aware of their environment through arrays of sensors, and capable of acting by using sets of actuators, and that such systems will self-organize to optimize their activities.

Complex Systems and Clouds. http://dx.doi.org/10.1016/B978-0-12-804041-6.00002-5

Natural computing is a generic name for disciplines, such as evolutionary computation, neural computation, artificial immune systems, swarm intelligence, and Ant Colony Optimization, that draw their inspiration for the development of new problem-solving techniques from nature. There are also disciplines that employ natural elements, such as DNA, molecules, membranes, or quantum systems to compute, and disciplines that use computers to synthesize natural phenomena that are also part of the natural computing landscape [131]. In this chapter we review seminal ideas in these fields and their potential applications to challenging computational problems and to self-management in large-scale systems.

2.1 CELLULAR AUTOMATA

Cellular automata are spatially and temporally finite-state discrete computational systems composed of a finite set of cells evolving in parallel at discrete time steps. Cellular automata are abstract structures that can be used as general models of complexity. They can also be used for the study of nonlinear dynamics.

Cellular automata are inspired by self-reproducing/self-replicating living organisms. Under favorable circumstances, viruses and bacteriophage particles, viruses that infect and replicate within a bacteria, can reproduce themselves. The same principle applies to the multiplication of nucleic acid complexes in chromosomes. Knowing that self-reproducing properties of nucleic acid depend on its highly complex structure, we should expect that a man-made, self-replicating, system should be rather complex. Self-replication allows not only the division of a cell, but also the growth and repair of a complete organism.

Cellular automata can be specified in mathematical terms and can be implemented in physical structures. Only local interactions can be modeled with cellular automata; the state of a cell is updated by taking into account the states of the cells in its neighborhood. Cellular automata can compute functions and solve algorithmic problems and, with suitable rules, can emulate a universal Turing machine.

The idea of cellular automata is credited to Stan Ulam and John von Neumann, who collaborated during their work on Project Manhattan at Los Alamos. Ulam was studying crystal growth and von Neumann was interested in self-replicating systems. John von Neumann, one of the greatest minds of the 20th century, introduced in the early 1940s the *von Neumann cellular automata*, and its logical follow-up, the *von Neumann Universal Constructor* [236]. The deceptively simple thought-experiments using these concepts led to the idea of *self-replication*.

John von Neumann's cellular automaton deals exclusively with the flow of information. Its 2-D physical space is theoretically infinite and homogeneous. The cells are identical, they have the same internal architecture, and the same connections with their neighbors. The state, determined by the values in the cell internal memory, distinguishes a cell from its neighbors. Replication involves the creation of an exact clone and is a special case of growth.

We briefly describe the construction, the translation, the copy, and the self-replication of von Neumann's cellular automaton [155]. Initially, the system has a cluster of five 29-state cells. At time step $t = 1$, *constructor C* transforms a 1-D description of the machine M, $d(M)$, into a 2-D description generated at time step $t = 2$ using *rule #1*

$$\begin{array}{ll} t=1 & t=2 \\ \hline C \quad \mathbf{O} \;\rightarrow\; C \quad M \; \mathbf{O} \\ d(M) \qquad\quad d(M) \end{array} \qquad (2.1)$$

with $\mathbf{O}$ an empty symbol. The constructor needs $d(M)$, a tape describing the machine M. Self-replication implies the existence of a tape describing the constructor, including its own description. To remove an infinite regression $d(C[d(C[d\ldots)$ von Neumann split the construction in two steps:

1. a translation carried out by a translator $\mathcal{T}$ able to build any computing machine, M, given a tape containing its description, m;
2. a transcription mechanism carried out by a copier $\mathcal{C}$, able to realize a copy of the contents of the tape, i.e., the description of any computing machine, including the description of the constructor itself with its empty tape.

The translation is done according to *rule # 2*

$$\begin{array}{ll} t=1 & t=2 \\ \hline \mathcal{T} \quad \mathbf{O} \;\rightarrow\; \mathcal{T} \quad M \; \mathbf{O} \\ m \qquad\qquad m \end{array} \qquad (2.2)$$

Rule #3 prescribes how to build two computing machines, $M1$ and $M2$ from a concatenated description $m1m2$:

$$
\begin{array}{c|c}
t = 1 & t = 2 \\
\hline
\mathcal{T} \quad \mathbf{O} \;\rightarrow\; & \mathcal{T} \quad M1 \quad \mathbf{O} \\
m1m2 & m1m2 \quad \emptyset \\
& M2
\end{array}
\tag{2.3}
$$

Rule #4 describes the process carried out by copier C

$$
\begin{array}{c|c}
t = 1 & t = 2 \\
\hline
m \quad \mathbf{O} \;\rightarrow\; & m \quad m \quad \mathbf{O} \\
C &
\end{array}
\tag{2.4}
$$

Rule #5 describes the process carried out by copier C to apply the concatenated description $m1m2$ of two computing machines $M1$ and $M2$

$$
\begin{array}{c|c}
t = 1 & t = 2 \\
\hline
m1m2 \quad \mathbf{O} \;\rightarrow\; & m1m2 \quad m1m2 \quad \mathbf{O} \\
C &
\end{array}
\tag{2.5}
$$

Finally, *rule #6* allows self-replication by combining *rule #3* and *rule #5* and using the combined translator-copier $\mathcal{T}C$ with its description tc

$$
\begin{array}{c|c|c|c}
t = 1 & t = 2 & t = 3 & t = \ldots \\
\hline
\mathcal{T} \quad \mathbf{O} & \mathcal{T} \quad \mathcal{T} \quad \mathbf{O} & \mathcal{T} \quad \mathcal{T} \quad \mathcal{T} \quad \mathbf{O} & \\
\text{tc} \quad \mathbf{O} \;\rightarrow\; & \text{tc} \quad \text{tc} \quad \mathbf{O} \;\rightarrow\; & \text{tc} \quad \text{tc} \quad \text{tc} \quad \mathbf{O} \;\rightarrow\; & \ldots \\
C & C \quad C & C \quad C \quad C &
\end{array}
\tag{2.6}
$$

A self-replicator consistent with this description was implemented in 2004 [155].

The elegance and subtlety of von Neumann's idea is inescapable. Only several years later, in 1953, Crick and Watson published their discovery of the double-helix, the structure formed by double-stranded molecules of nucleic acids, such as DNA. The double-helix elucidated the mechanism by which genetic information is stored and copied in living organisms [62].

The *Game of Life*, invented by John H. Convey in 1970, gave a new impetus to the study of cellular automata [87]. The game models the effect of under-population, over-population, survival, and reproduction. Cells in an infinite two-dimensional orthogonal grid can be in one of two states, alive or dead. Each cell interacts with its eight adjacent cells and, at each time step, the following transitions occur:

- A live cell with fewer than two live neighbors dies—under-population.
- A live cell with more than three live neighbors dies—over-population.

- A live cell with two or three live neighbors lives—survival.
- A dead cell with exactly three live neighbors becomes a live cell—reproduction.

The classification of cellular automata is due to Stephen Wolfram [249]. Cellular automata are now used for traffic modeling, structural design, and even music composition. Analytical methods based on lattice-gas cellular automata are used in fluid dynamics studies. Stochastic cellular automata model physical processes characterized by a large set of parameters. Other applications of cellular automata are in the study of urban growth, pattern recognition, and statistical mechanics.

2.2 EPIDEMIC ALGORITHMS

Epidemic algorithms provide effective ways to spread information in large-scale systems when individual systems/nodes have only limited knowledge of the network topology and the capabilities of other nodes. Epidemic algorithms mimic the process of spreading an infectious disease in nature. Such algorithms are easy to implement and guarantee information delivery in heterogeneous environments. The *Game of Life* is one of the most popular examples of epidemic algorithms.

An epidemic algorithm requires that each member of a population of size n is to be in one of the following states at time t:

Susceptible—the individual is susceptible to some stimulus; a living organism can be infected; a node can get information from its neighbors in a distributed system;
Infective—the individual has been infected and is capable of spreading the infection; it has some information and it will spread it to its neighbors, in a distributed system;
Recovered/Removed—the individual is immune to infection and does not spread it; in a distributed system, the node knows the information and does not transmit it to its neighbors.

Several classes of epidemic algorithms are known: *Susceptible-Infective* (SI), *Susceptible-Infective-Susceptible* (SIS), and *Susceptible-Infective-Removed* (SIR). We shall now only use the language of infectious disease-spreading, the translation to information dissemination is straightforward.

In SI, almost all members of the population are infected and each individual remains infected until the entire population is infected.

The population can be represented by a randomly chosen directed graph $G = (V, E)$ where V, the set of nodes represents the population and E, the set of directed edges represents the contacts within a given round. The graph changes as each node chooses β, the set of communication partners in each round. The chance to get infected is equal to the number of incoming edges of the node. p_z, the probability of a node to have no incoming edges in one round, thus, not to get infected, is $4^{-\beta} \le p_z \le e^{-\beta}$ for $\beta \le n - 1/2$ [42].

Unlike SI, the individual members of the population in SIS are able to stop spreading the disease before the entire population is infected, but recovered members can become infective again. The number of infective individuals in a population of size n in round t is

$$n_{inf}(t) = \frac{1-p}{1 + \left(\frac{1-p \times n}{(n_{inf}(0)-1)}\right)} \times n \qquad (2.7)$$

with $p = n_{rem}/n_{inf}$, the ratio of recovered versus infective individuals per round [42].

Recovered individuals remain recovered in SIR. For instance, an individual who did not spread the disease in the last r rounds, stops spreading that specific information by assuming that the entire population is already infective. Mathematical modeling of this case is rather difficult.

2.3 GENETIC ALGORITHMS

Evolution has been an inspiration for a long time for solving optimization problems and, in particular, for genetic algorithms. Genetic algorithms, often abbreviated as GAs, are heuristics for finding exact or approximate solutions to optimization problems when an exhaustive search is unfeasible. To realize the dramatic increase of the search space, consider a scheduling problem where we have N tasks and M machines and (N, M) increase. When $(N, M) = (10, 5)$ there are 9.8×10^6 possible solutions; this number increases to 1.0×10^{20} and then to 1.92×10^{35} for problems of size $(20, 10)$ and $(30, 15)$, respectively.

The basic steps of the GA are: (1) generate a population of solutions, (2) assign a *fitness* to each solution, and (3) create a new generation by selecting the most fit solutions and then breeding them. Breeding involves crossovers and mutations with a low probability. The algorithm stops when a sufficiently good solution has been found. GAs are easily parallelizable and have application in many fields, from economics to robotics, physics, chemistry, bioinformatics, computer science, and manufacturing.

The canonical GA described by John Holland in a seminal work published in 1975 [117], starts with a population encoded as a binary string of length L. The *evaluation function f* is a measure of performance relative to a set of parameters, and the *fitness function* transforms such an evaluation into an allocation of reproductive opportunities [247]. The measure $f_i/\bar{f}$ is used for the selection process, the decision of how many copies of the string i, if any, are included in the intermediate population; in this expression, $\bar{f}$ is the average evaluation of all strings. Selection is followed by recombination when crossovers between random strings are carried out.

For example, given the strings 10110011101011001101 and aababb-baaabbaaabbabb with a and b the binary values 0 and 1, we randomly choose a recombination point after the 8 leftmost symbols and the crossover leads to the following offsprings

10110011 ∧ 101011001101

$\qquad\qquad\Rightarrow\qquad$ 10110011aabbaaabbabb & aababbba101011001101.

aababbba ∧ aabbaaabbabb

After recombination, mutations change bit values with probability p.

John Holland explained in [117] how a genetic algorithm carries out the search by sampling hyperplane partitions of a search space. Each L-bit string, a "chromosome" or a "genotype" in GA terminology, is represented by a vertex of an L-dimensional hypercube. An L-bit string containing the symbol *, which has the usual meaning, a wild card, is called a *schemata* and represents a hyperplane in the hypercube representation.

Consider, for example, a hypercube of dimension $L = 3$ and a second one of dimension $L = 4$ embedding the first, as in Fig. 2.1. We see that the inner hypercube, the one of dimension $L = 3$, corresponds to the hyperplane $1 * **$; the outer hypercube of dimension $L = 4$ corresponds to $0 * **$ and the string $*0 * *$ corresponds to the front planes of both hypercubes. The *order of a hyperplane* is the number of bits in the hyperplane description. All three hyperplanes in our example are of order 1, the hyperplane $*01*$ is of order 2, while the hyperplane $01 * 1$ is of order 3.

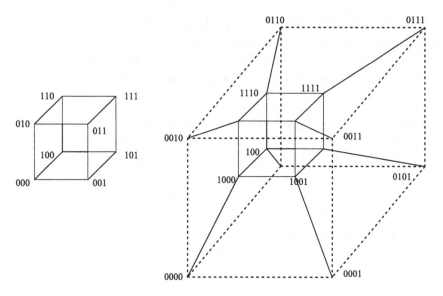

*Fig. 2.1 Hypercube interpretation of GA search. A hypercube of order L can be constructed using 2^L vertices labeled with L-bit binary numbers and connecting two vertices by an edge whenever the Hamming distance of their labels is 1. An L-bit string containing the symbol * represents a hyperplane. A genetic algorithm searches by sampling hyperplane partitions of a search space [117]. Shown are a hypercube of dimension L = 3 and its embedding into a hypercube of dimension L = 4.*

Population-based search represents the core idea of GAs. Indeed, a set of sample points provides information about many hyperplanes and low-order hyperplanes are sampled by numerous points in the population [247]. Holland argues that "many hyperplanes are evaluated in parallel each time a single string is evaluated ... the cumulative effects of evaluating a population provides statistical information about any particular subset of hyperplanes. ... the true fitness of the hyperplane partition corresponds to the average fitness of all strings that lie in that hyperplane partition. The genetic algorithm uses the population as a sample for estimating the fitness of that hyperplane partition" [247].

It can be argued that random mutations in local search heuristics mimic asexual evolution and work well in many cases. The contrast between local search and GAs which mimic sex-based evolution deserves to be investigated to understand why genetic algorithms have rarely produced better results than other approaches [183] It turns out that natural selection is not as effective for improving the fitness of a population as scientists have believed for a long time.

In a recent paper [152] with the suggestive title "A Mixability Theory of the Role of Sex in Evolution" the authors report extensive simulation results showing that natural selection under sex is not a good optimizer of fitness, instead it promotes another quality of the genotype called *mixability*. Mixability could be informally described as "genetic tolerance," as it reflects the ability of forming viable combination with other genes. The conclusion of [152] is that GAs are most suitable for problems when the objective we wish to optimize is unknown, fuzzy, or time varying.

2.4 ANT COLONY OPTIMIZATION

Ant Colony Optimization (ACO) is a metaheuristic[1] for solving hard combinatorial optimization problems introduced in [74]. The biological inspiration of ACO is that ants find the shortest path from their nest to a source of food using *pheromone trails,* chemicals left on the ground marking the path for other ants to follow.

Stigmergy[2] is a phenomenon observed in social insects; it describes a process when individuals leave in the environment a trace stimulating the actions of other members of the population. Subsequent actions reinforce and build on each other, leading to the spontaneous emergence of coherent, apparently systematic activity. Stigmergy is a form of self-organization.

A *combinatorial optimization problem, $P = (S, \Omega, f)$,* is an optimization problem where S is a search space over a set of discrete decision variables containing a finite set of possible solutions, Ω is a set of constraints among the discrete set of decision variables, and f is an objective function $f: S \mapsto R+$ that assigns a positive cost value to each solution. The goal is to find within a reasonable amount of time, either a solution of minimum cost value, or a good enough approximate solution [182].

The concise presentation of the ACO algorithm in this section uses the notations in [75, 76]. Given a set of discrete variables $X_i, i = 1, \dots, n$, with values $v_i^j \in D_i = \{v_i^1, \dots, v_i^{|D_i|}\}$ the elements of the search space S are full

---

[1] A metaheuristic is a high-level procedure to generate or select a heuristic providing a sufficiently good solution to an optimization problem. A metaheuristic sample is a search space too large to be completely sampled and it is particularly useful when we have incomplete or imperfect information and limited computation resources.

[2] The word stigmergy is derived from two Greek words, *stigma* meaning sign or maker, and *ergon* meaning builder.

assignments. In these assignments, each variable X_i has a value v_i^j assigned from its domain D_i. The set of feasible solutions S_Ω is given by the elements of S that satisfy all the constraints in the set Ω. A solution $s^* \in S_\Omega$ is called a global optimum iff $(s^*) \le f(s)$, $\forall s \in S_\Omega$. Solving a global optimization problem means finding a solution $s^* \in S_\Omega^*$ where $S_\Omega^* \subseteq S_\Omega$ is the set of all globally optimal solutions.

The critical component of the ACO is the *pheromone model*. This model is used to probabilistically generate solutions by assembling them from a finite set of components. The model consists of a vector $\mathcal{T}$ whose components are pheromone trail parameters, $\mathcal{T}_i \in \mathcal{T}$. The pheromone trail parameters are usually associated with *pheromone values* τ_i. An ACO algorithm updates the pheromone values using previously generated solutions aiming to direct the search to regions of the search space containing high quality solutions.

The metaheuristics consists of an initialization phase and two scheduled activity phases executed repeatedly

```
Set parameters; initialize pheromone trails;
BeginScheduleActivities
    ConstructAntSolutions;
    UpdatePheromone
EndScheduleActivities
```

An optional, problem-specific phase, involving centrally controlled activities which cannot be implemented by individual ants, is sometimes performed after the first phase.

Solution construction. A solution component c_{ij} is the instantiated decision variable $X_i = v_i^j$ and C is the set of all possible solution components. A pheromone trail value τ_{ij} is associated with each c_{ij}. We define the graph $G_C(V, E)$ where either the vertices V, or the edges E, are associated with the solution components C and allow the ants to move from vertex to vertex along the edges of this graph and deposit pheromones either along the edges or on the vertices. The next groups of ants use the pheromone values to incrementally construct a solution.

The solutions are constructed starting with $s^p = \emptyset$. Constructing solutions corresponds to a path selection on the graph $G_C(V, E)$. The set $\mathcal{N}(s^p)$ corresponds to the allowed paths for the partial solution s^p. The probability update rule is

$$p(c_{ij}|s^p) = \frac{\tau_{ij}^{\alpha} \cdot \eta_{ij}^{\beta}}{\sum_{c_{il} \in \mathcal{N}(s^p)} \tau_{il}^{\alpha} \eta_{il}^{\beta}}, \quad \forall c_{ij} \in \mathcal{N}(s^p). \tag{2.8}$$

In this expression, τ_{ij}^{α} represent pheromone values, η_{ij}^{β} are heuristic values associated with component c_{ij}, and α, β are positive real numbers, the weights of pheromone and heuristic values, respectively.

Pheromone updating. This process aims to amplify the pheromone values corresponding to good solutions and lower them for bad solutions. The intensity of a pheromone changes in time, pheromone values decrease due to evaporation with evaporation rate $0 \le \rho \le 1$, and are intensified for good solutions. The pheromone update rule is

$$\tau_{ij} \leftarrow (1 - \rho) \cdot \tau_{ij} + \rho \cdot \sum_{s \in S_{upd}|c_{ij} \in s} F(s) \tag{2.9}$$

with S_{upd} the set of solutions used for the update and $F : S \mapsto R+$ a fitness function, with the property

$$f(s) \le f(s') \Rightarrow F(s) \ge F(s'), \quad \forall s \ne s' \in S. \tag{2.10}$$

The AS algorithm. There are several variants of ACO algorithms with different probabilistic rules, including the *Ant System* (AS) [74] which assumes a population of m artificial ants. In this case the pheromone update is

$$\tau_{ij} \leftarrow (1 - \rho) \cdot \tau_{ij} + \rho \cdot \sum_{k=1}^{m} \Delta \tau_{ij}^{k}. \tag{2.11}$$

The quantity of the pheromone left on edge (i,j) by the kth ant is a function of L_k, the tour length of this ant

$$\Delta \tau_{ij}^{k} = \begin{cases} \frac{1}{L_k} & \text{if ant } k \text{ used edge } (i,j) \text{ in its last tour,} \\ 0 & \text{otherwise.} \end{cases} \tag{2.12}$$

Given the partial solution s_k^p for ant k, call $\mathcal{N}(s_k^p)$ the set of components that do not belong to this partial solution. The transition probability of ant k to traverse the edge (i,j) under the rule of AS is

$$p(c_{ij}|s_k^p) = \begin{cases} \frac{\tau_{ij}^{\alpha} \cdot \eta_{ij}^{\beta}}{\sum_{c_{il} \in \mathcal{N}(s_k^p)} \tau_{il}^{\alpha} \eta_{il}^{\beta}} & \text{if } j \in N(s_k^p), \\ 0 & \text{otherwise.} \end{cases} \tag{2.13}$$

In this expression τ_{ij}^{α} represent pheromone values, $\eta_{ij}^{\beta} = 1/d_{ij}$ are heuristic values with d_{ij} the length of components c_{ij}, and α, β are positive real numbers, the weights of pheromone and heuristic values, respectively.

Several adaptations of the ACO algorithms are discussed in the literature [74, 111] including the traveling salesman problem (TSP) and bin packing. TSP, discussed next, has numerous applications, ranging from computing optimal delivery routes, to machine scheduling, network optimization, and protein folding.

An n city TSP adaptation assumes that each one of the m ants builds its own tour starting from a randomly selected city and while the tour is completed, deposits the pheromone on each visited city. An ant maintains a *tabu list*, $\mathcal{B}$, the list of those already visited, and chooses the next town function of the distance and the amount of pheromone on the selected link to the town. A version of the rule in Eq. (2.8) is used

$$p(ij) = \frac{\tau_{ij} \cdot \eta_{ij}^{\beta}}{\sum_{g \notin \mathcal{B}} \tau_{ig} \eta_{ig}^{\beta}}, \tag{2.14}$$

where the heuristic, called in this case *visibility*, chooses the nearest town, $\eta_{ij} = 1/d_{ij}$. The pheromone update rule is

$$\tau_{ij} = \rho \cdot \tau_{ij} + \Delta\tau_{ij} \quad \text{with} \quad \Delta\tau_{ij} = \sum_{k=1}^{m} \Delta_{ij}^{k}. \tag{2.15}$$

The pheromone contribution of ant k is

$$\Delta\tau_{ij}^{k} = \begin{cases} \frac{Q}{L_k} & \text{if ant } k \text{ used edge } (i,j) \text{ in its last tour,} \\ 0 & \text{otherwise.} \end{cases} \tag{2.16}$$

with Q a constant. In the first step, the pheromone intensities on all links are set and each ant k initializes its tabu list $\mathcal{B}^k$ with the randomly selected starting city. Then each ant moves from city to city following the probability rule given by Eq. (2.14). After crossing n links, the tabu lists $\mathcal{B}^k$, $1 \le k \le m$ are full and L_k and Δ_{ij}^{k} are computed. The shortest path is saved, tabu lists are reset, and the next iteration is carried out. The process stops when the tour counter reaches maximum or until all ants make the same tour.

2.5 SWARM INTELLIGENCE

Swarm intelligence is a form of collective intelligence observed in some collections of organisms, such as flocks of birds, schools of fish, ant colonies, herds of bisons, or packs of wolves [39]. Swarms of organisms display abilities not shown by individuals. The collective intelligence emerges from individual experiences of the members of the organization combined with their ability to communicate with one another.

The collective intelligence is the result of simple rules easily followed by the individual members of the swarm. For example, the need for cohesion requires individual members to stay in close proximity to one another and, at the same time, to avoid conflicts or collisions with other members of the group; whenever the group moves, all the members of the group should move together.

Particle swarm optimization (PSO) algorithms [133] are applicable when the cardinality of the set of participants is limited to a few thousands and all individuals collaborate to optimally achieve a common objective. Such algorithms are robust, asynchronous, do not require a central control, and can be parallelized with relative ease. PSO algorithms are easy to implement and only a few parameters of the model are required.

A population of random solutions is generated during an initialization phase of a PSO algorithm. Then the search for optimal solutions, called *particles*, is carried out by updating generations. Unlike in genetic algorithms, there are no crossover or mutation evolution operators in this evolution. A fitness function evaluates the individual fitness values of all particles to identify the particle(s) with optimal trajectory. Then all particles flow through the problem space, tracing the trajectory of the current optimum particle(s).

The high-level description of the algorithm presented next follows the notations used in [111, 133]. We assume n particles with positions $X(i) \in \mathbb{R}^m$, and velocities $V(i) \in \mathbb{R}^m, i \in \{1, n\}$ in a space with m dimensions. The fitness function $f: \mathbb{R}^m \to \mathbb{R}$ is used to determine *XLocalOpt(i)*, the optimal position of particle $i \in \{1, n\}$, and the global optimum *XGlobalOpt*. Three parameters, w, a, and b are used in the following high-level description of the algorithm

1. Generate random vectors R and Q with $R(i), Q(i) \in U[0, 1]$ and $i \in \{1, n\}$.
2. Update velocity and position of each particle ($\circ$ is a scalar product of two vectors)

$$V(i) \leftarrow wV(i) + a \times R \circ (XLocalBest(i) - X(i)$$
$$+ \, b \times Q \circ (XGlobalOpt - X(i)) \qquad (2.17)$$
$$X(i) \leftarrow X(i) + V(i).$$

3. Find local and global optima; for a minimization problem

Local minima : $XLocalOpt \leftarrow X(i)$ if $f(X(i)) < f(XLocalOpt(i))$.
$$(2.18)$$

Global minima : $XGlobalOpt \leftarrow x_i$ if $f(X(i)) < f(XGlobalOpt)$.
$$(2.19)$$

For a maximization problem the updates are carried out if $f(X(i)) > f(XLocalOpt(i))$ and $f(X(i)) > f(XGlobalOpt)$, respectively.

Swarm intelligence has applications in robotics and modeling of social systems. Swarm intelligence is also used for routing in communication networks and in searching for the optimal organization structure in industrial engineering. Other applications of swarm intelligence are in data mining, clustering algorithms, pattern recognition, and space exploration [115].

2.6 DNA COMPUTING

Rather than drawing inspiration from biology and using biological processes as a metaphor, deoxyribonucleic acid (DNA) computing proposes to actually use biological material, rather than silicon, for the implementation of computer gates and circuits. This is particularly tempting because living organisms process information in parallel, are nondeterministic, and capable to deal with complex stimuli.

DNA is the hereditary material residing in the nucleus of every cell[3] of almost all organisms, including humans. The hereditary information is encoded using a four-letter alphabet, embodied by the four chemical bases: adenine (A), guanine (G), cytosine (C), and thymine (T). Units called *DNA base pairs* are formed by A paired with T, and C paired with G. To each base, are also attached a sugar molecule and a phosphate molecule. *Nucleotides*

---

[3]There is also a small amount of mitochondrial DNA.

consisting of a base, sugar, and phosphate are arranged in two long strands that form a *double helix*. When a cell divides, a DNA strand serves as a pattern, allowing each new cell to inherit an exact copy of the old cell's DNA.

The analogy between information-encoding biopolymers and a Turing machine, or a finite automata scanning a data tape is inescapable and has inspired several designs for DNA computers. The energy efficiency of a DNA computer is 2×10^{19} operation per Joule, nine orders of magnitude higher than that of classical computers. DNA capacity for information storing is also off the scale, 5 grams of DNA contain 10^{21} bases. The speed of a DNA processor is in the range of 500–5000 pairs/second, but the slow speed is compensated for by the massive parallelism possible with DNA circuits.

Several commercially available enzymes are used to carry out the basic operations required by a DNA computer: *nuclease*—enzyme capable of cleaving the phosphodiester bonds[4] between the nucleotide subunits of nucleic acids; *ligase*—enzyme capable of catalyzing the joining of two large molecules by forming a new chemical bond; *polymerase*—enzyme that catalyzes the formation of a long-chain molecule by linking smaller molecular units, as nucleotides with nucleic acids; *exonuclease*—enzyme capable of detaching the terminal nucleotide from a nucleic acid chain.

The transformation of the DNA necessary to carry out the operations of a DNA computer are: cutting, linking, replication, and destruction. The enzymes used to carry out these operations are: restriction endonuclease, ligase, polymerase, and exonuclease, respectively.

In a seminal paper, Leonard Adleman reported in 1994 the results of an experiment when a small graph was encoded in DNA molecules and the "computations" were carried using standard protocols for DNA manipulation. He reports solving a 7-point Hamiltonian path problem [6].

A directed graph G has a *Hamiltonian path* between two vertices v_{in} and v_{out} iff there exists a directed path consisting of one-way edges $e_1, e_2, \ldots, e_n$ from v_{in} to v_{out} in which each edge is traversed exactly once. The directed Hamiltonian path problem has been proven to be NP complete. A nondeterministic algorithm for solving this problem consists of the following steps:

---

[4]The phosphodiester bond is the linkage between the $3'$ carbon atom of one sugar molecule in one nucleotide and the $5'$ carbon atom of a sugar molecule in another nucleotide, deoxyribose in DNA, and ribose in RNA are the pentose monosaccharides molecules.

1. generate random paths through the graph;
2. keep only those paths which begin with v_{in} and end with v_{out};
3. if the graph has n vertices, then keep only those paths which enter exactly n vertices;
4. keep only those paths which enter all of the vertices of the graph at least once; and
5. if any paths remain, a Hamiltonian path between v_{in} and v_{out} exists.

In the implementation described in [6], each one of the five steps processed the product of the previous one. In Step 1 each vertex of the graph is associated with a random 20-mer[5] sequence of DNA [6]. In Step 2 the product is amplified by polymerase chain reaction (PCR)[6] and only DNA fragments corresponding to paths starting at v_{in} and ending at v_{out} are selected. In Step 3 the product is run on an agarose gel to measure the length of DNA molecules. The smaller molecules travel faster in an electric field and, as a result of the electrophoresis process, DNA fragments with 30 base pairs are isolated.

Each vertex was encoded as 6 base pairs and there were 5 vertices between v_{in} and v_{out} thus, only DNA fragments with 30 base pairs were selected. Then the product is PCR amplified and in Step 4 it was affinity purified using a biotin avidin magnetic beads system to select DNA fragments corresponding to paths entering each vertex exactly once. Finally, the product is PCR amplified, run on a gel, and sequenced in Step 5.

The complexity of the Hamiltonian path increases exponentially with the number of vertices of the graph. The amount of DNA for a graph with 200 vertices is larger than the mass of the Earth [111]. Moreover, as the length of the strands increases, the statistical errors grow significantly, more operations are necessary, more DNA is used, and the cost of the experiments increases. Applications of DNA computing to combinatorial problems proves to be challenging.

A DNA-based simulation of Boolean circuits is discussed in [179]. The inputs, and the AND and the OR gates are encoded as DNA sequences and the operations on them are carried out by standard techniques, such as ligations,

---

[5]"-mer," from Greek "meros," meaning "part," specifies the length of an oligonucleotide.
[6]In PCR a single copy or a few copies of a piece of DNA is amplified to generate millions of copies of the DNA sequence. PCR alternates between separating DNA into single strands using heat and conversion into double strands using primer and polymerase reactions.

separations by size, amplifications, cleavage, and detection by size. The runtime slowdown of large semi-bounded fan-in[7] Boolean circuits[8] is proportional with the logarithm of the maximum fan-out of the circuit and the space complexity is proportional with the product of the circuit size and the maximum fan-out. The *size of a Boolean circuit* is given by the number of gates and the *depth* is the length of the longest directed path in it.

A programmable molecular computing machine composed of enzymes and DNA molecules was announced in 2002 [32]. The hardware consists of a restriction nuclease and ligase. The software and the input are encoded by double-stranded DNA and programming amounts to choosing appropriate software molecules. The system processes the input molecule via a sequence of restriction, hybridization, and ligation cycles, and creates an output molecule that encodes the result.

A polynomial-time DNA computing solution for the bin-packing problem based on a sticker model is presented in a 2009 paper [196]. The solution involves the set of biological operations known as the *Adleman-Lipton model*:

- *extract*—given a test tube T and a sequence S, generate two tubes: +(T; S) with all the sequences in T that had S as a subsequence, and −(T,S) with the remaining sequences of T;
- *merge*—given T1 and T2, generate a new tube with the content of both;
- *detect*—given T return the logic value *yes* if there is at least a DNA molecule in it, and *no* otherwise;
- *discard*—discard tube T;
- *amplify*—given T, *amplify*(T, T1, T2) produces two identical copies of T, as test tubes T1 and T2 and then empty T;
- *append*—given T and a sequence S, *append*(T,S) affixes S at the end of each sequence in T.

An enhanced language on a multiset of finite strings over the alphabet $\{A, C, G, T\}$ consisting of four operations, combine, separate, set, and clear, is used to express the algorithm.

---

[7]*Fan-in* is the number of inputs a gate can handle and the *fan-out* of a logic gate output is the number of gate inputs it can connect to.
[8]A semi-bounded fan-in Boolean circuit with n inputs is a direct acyclic graph with labeled nodes and $2n$ nodes with in-degree zero.

A research group from CalTech reported in 2011, results related to the manufacturing of nucleic-acid-based integrated circuits [190]. The authors use a "seesaw" gate that makes use of a reversible strand displacement. Seesawing is the reversible reaction that exchanges the activity of DNA signals, allowing signal amplification and signal isolation. A pair of seesaw gates can perform AND or OR operation, sufficient for universal Boolean function evaluation.

2.7 QUANTUM INFORMATION PROCESSING SYSTEMS

Quantum is a Latin word meaning "some quantity." In physics it is used with the same meaning as the word *discrete* in mathematics; it refers to a quantity or variable that can take only sharply defined values, as opposed to a continuously varying quantity. Quantum mechanics is a mathematical model of the physical world. This model allows us to specify states, observables, measurements, and the dynamics of quantum systems. Quantum computing and quantum information theory are concerned with the transmission and processing of quantum states and the interactions of quantum information with the "classical" one. Classical information is carried by physical processes obeying the laws of classical physics. Classical physics does not use the quantization paradigm and includes classical mechanics and relativity.

Quantum computers are stochastic systems because the state of a quantum system is uncertain and therefore, a certain probability is associated with any possible state the system can be in. The output states of a stochastic engine are random: the label of the output state cannot be discovered. All we can do is to label a set of pairs consisting of an output state of an observable (a characteristic or attribute of the system) and a measured value of that observable. In quantum mechanics, we say that each pair consists of an eigenstate of a Hermitian operator and its eigenvalue. The following presentation is based on [156, 160].

Qubits. A quantum bit, called a *qubit*, is a quantum system used to store information. As opposed to a classical bit, which can be in one of the two states 0 and 1, a qubit can exist in a continuum of states. Moreover, *we can measure the value of a bit with certainty and without affecting its state, while the result of measuring a qubit is nondeterministic and the measurement alters its state.* While a classical bit can be in one of two states, 0 or 1, the qubit can be in states $|0\rangle$, and $|1\rangle$ called *computational basis states* and also in any state that is a linear combination of these states. This phenomenon is called *superposition*. Mathematically, the state, $|\psi\rangle$, of a *qubit* is represented

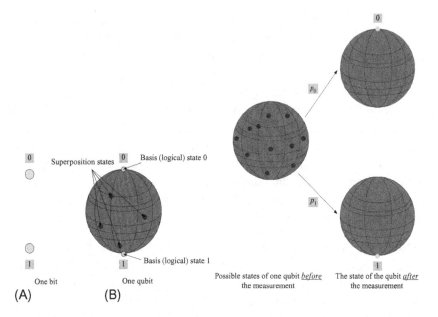

(A)   (B)

Fig. 2.2 (Left) Bit versus qubit. The state of a qubit can be represented as a vector from the origin to a point on the Bloch sphere. A qubit can be in a basis state, $|0\rangle$ or $|1\rangle$, or in a superposition state $|\psi\rangle = \alpha_0|0\rangle + \alpha_1|1\rangle$ with $|\alpha_0|^2 + |\alpha_1|^2 = 1$. A bit can be in one of two states, 0 or 1. (Right) A measurement forces a qubit in a superposition state to one of the two basis states, $|0\rangle$ with probability $p_0 = |\alpha_0|^2$ and $|1\rangle$ with probability $p_1 = |\alpha_1|^2$, respectively.

as a vector in a two-dimensional complex vector space. The Bloch sphere is a geometrical representation of the state of a qubit. Fig. 2.2 illustrates the difference between classical and quantum information.

Consider now a system consisting of n particles whose individual states are described by vectors in the two-dimensional vector space. In classical physics, the individual states of particles combine through the Cartesian product. The possible states of the quantum system of n particles form a vector space of 2^n dimensions; given n bits, we can construct 2^n n-tuples and describe a system with 2^n states. Individual state spaces of n particles combine quantum mechanically through the tensor product. If X and Y are vectors, then their tensor product $X \otimes Y$ is also a vector, and its dimension is $\dim(X) \times \dim(Y)$. For example, if $\dim(X) = \dim(Y) = 10$, then the tensor product of the two vectors has dimension 100.

The state space of a quantum system having n qubits has 2^n dimensions. There are 2^n *basis states* forming a computational basis and there are *superposition states* resulting from the superposition of basis states. The catch is that even though one quantum bit, a system with 2^1 basis states, can be in one of infinitely many superposition states, when the qubit is measured, the measurement changes the state of the quantum system to one of the two basis states. *From one qubit we can only extract a single classical bit of information.* In quantum systems, *the amount of parallelism increases exponentially with the size of the system*, thus it increases exponentially with the number of qubits. This means that the price paid for an exponential increase in the power of a quantum computer is a *linear increase in the amount of matter and space* needed to build the larger quantum computing engine. Adding a single qubit doubles the power of a quantum computer. For example, a quantum computer with 11 qubits has twice the computational power of a quantum computer with 10 qubits.

Quantum gates. The *quantum circuit model* expresses the transformations required by a quantum computation as a sequence of quantum gates [72]. A quantum gate is the quantum analog of a classic gate, it performs one or more logical transformations. A quantum gate is reversible, while classical gates with the exception of the NOT gate are not reversible. The transformation carried out by a quantum gate is expressed by an operator. For example, the most important one-qubit quantum gates are:

1. I—the identity gate leaves a qubit unchanged

$$I = \begin{pmatrix} 1 & 0 \\ 0 & 1 \end{pmatrix}. \tag{2.20}$$

2. X or NOT gate transposes the components of a qubit

$$\sigma_x = X = \begin{pmatrix} 0 & 1 \\ 1 & 0 \end{pmatrix}. \tag{2.21}$$

3. Y gate multiples the input qubit by i and flips the two components of the qubit

$$\sigma_y = Y = \begin{pmatrix} 0 & -i \\ i & 0 \end{pmatrix}. \tag{2.22}$$

4. Z gate changes the phase, flips the sign, of a qubit

$$\sigma_z = Z = \begin{pmatrix} 1 & 0 \\ 0 & -1 \end{pmatrix}. \tag{2.23}$$

5. Hadamard gate H

$$H = \frac{1}{\sqrt{2}} \begin{pmatrix} 1 & 1 \\ 1 & -1 \end{pmatrix}. \tag{2.24}$$

The transformation matrices of the first four gates, I, X, Y, and Z are the identity matrix I and the *Pauli matrices* $\sigma_x, \sigma_y, \sigma_z$, respectively. The output $|\varphi\rangle$ of these gates for a given input $|\psi\rangle = \alpha_0|0\rangle + \alpha_1|1\rangle$ is shown next.

$$|\varphi\rangle = I|\psi\rangle = \begin{pmatrix} 1 & 0 \\ 0 & 1 \end{pmatrix} \begin{pmatrix} \alpha_0 \\ \alpha_1 \end{pmatrix} = \begin{pmatrix} \alpha_0 \\ \alpha_1 \end{pmatrix} \quad \text{or} \quad |\varphi\rangle = \alpha_0|0\rangle + \alpha_1|1\rangle.$$
(2.25)

$$|\varphi\rangle = \sigma_x|\psi\rangle = \begin{pmatrix} 0 & 1 \\ 1 & 0 \end{pmatrix} \begin{pmatrix} \alpha_0 \\ \alpha_1 \end{pmatrix} = \begin{pmatrix} \alpha_1 \\ \alpha_0 \end{pmatrix} \quad \text{or} \quad |\varphi\rangle = \alpha_1|0\rangle + \alpha_0|1\rangle.$$
(2.26)

$$|\varphi\rangle = \sigma_y|\psi\rangle = \begin{pmatrix} 0 & -i \\ i & 0 \end{pmatrix} \begin{pmatrix} \alpha_0 \\ \alpha_1 \end{pmatrix} = i\begin{pmatrix} -\alpha_1 \\ \alpha_0 \end{pmatrix} \quad \text{or} \quad |\varphi\rangle = -i\alpha_1|0\rangle + i\alpha_0|1\rangle.$$
(2.27)

$$|\varphi\rangle = \sigma_z|\psi\rangle = \begin{pmatrix} 1 & 0 \\ 0 & -1 \end{pmatrix} \begin{pmatrix} \alpha_0 \\ \alpha_1 \end{pmatrix} = \begin{pmatrix} \alpha_0 \\ -\alpha_1 \end{pmatrix} \quad \text{or} \quad |\varphi\rangle = \alpha_0|0\rangle - \alpha_1|1\rangle.$$
(2.28)

$$|\varphi\rangle = H|\psi\rangle = \frac{1}{\sqrt{2}} \begin{pmatrix} 1 & 1 \\ 1 & -1 \end{pmatrix} \begin{pmatrix} \alpha_0 \\ \alpha_1 \end{pmatrix} \quad \text{or} \quad |\varphi\rangle = \frac{\alpha_0}{\sqrt{2}}(|0\rangle + |1\rangle) + \frac{\alpha_1}{\sqrt{2}}(|0\rangle - |1\rangle).$$
(2.29)

The Hadamard gate, H, when applied to a pure state, $|0\rangle$ or $|1\rangle$, creates a superposition state,

$$|0\rangle \mapsto \frac{1}{\sqrt{2}}(|0\rangle + |1\rangle) \quad \text{and} \quad |1\rangle \mapsto \left(\frac{1}{\sqrt{2}}\right)(|0\rangle - |1\rangle). \tag{2.30}$$

It follows that the transformation of a qubit $|x\rangle$, with $x = 0$ or $x = 1$, carried out by a Hadamard gate can be expressed as

$$|x\rangle \mapsto \frac{1}{\sqrt{2}}\left(|0\rangle + (-1)^x|1\rangle\right). \tag{2.31}$$

CNOT is a two-qubit gate with two inputs, the *control qubit*, $|\psi\rangle$ and the *target qubit*, $|\varphi\rangle$. The two outputs are the *control qubit* and the *target qubit*. The classical equivalent of a quantum CNOT gate is the XOR gate: its output is the sum modulo two ($\oplus$) of its two inputs. The target output of the classical CNOT gate is equal to the target input if the control input is 0, and flipped if the control input is 1. Flipping a classical bit a means complementing it, transforming it to $\bar{a}$: if $a = 0$, it becomes 1 and vice versa. *Flipping a qubit*

$|\psi\rangle = \alpha_0|0\rangle + \alpha_1|1\rangle$ results in $|\varphi\rangle = \alpha_1|0\rangle + \alpha_0|1\rangle$, where the projections on the two basis vectors are swapped.

Informally, the operation of the CNOT quantum gate is described as follows: the control input is transferred directly to the control output of the gate. The target output qubit is equal to the target input qubit if the control input is $|0\rangle$ and it is flipped if the control input is $|1\rangle$. The input and the output qubits of a CNOT quantum gate can be represented as vectors in a four-dimensional Hilbert space $\mathcal{H}_4$. If

$$|\psi\rangle = \alpha_0|0\rangle + \alpha_1|1\rangle \quad |\varphi\rangle = \beta_0|0\rangle + \beta_1|1\rangle. \qquad (2.32)$$

then the input vector of the quantum CNOT gate is the tensor product of the two vectors

$$|V_{\text{CNOT}}\rangle = |\psi\rangle \otimes |\varphi\rangle = \begin{pmatrix} \alpha_0 \\ \alpha_1 \end{pmatrix} \otimes \begin{pmatrix} \beta_0 \\ \beta_1 \end{pmatrix} = \begin{pmatrix} \alpha_0\beta_0 \\ \alpha_0\beta_1 \\ \alpha_1\beta_0 \\ \alpha_1\beta_1 \end{pmatrix}. \qquad (2.33)$$

The components of the input vector are transformed by the CNOT quantum gate as follows

$$|00\rangle \mapsto |00\rangle \quad |01\rangle \mapsto |01\rangle \quad |10\rangle \mapsto |11\rangle \quad |11\rangle \mapsto |10\rangle. \qquad (2.34)$$

The transformation matrix G_{CNOT} of the CNOT quantum gate can be written as a sum of outer products of the basis vectors [156]

$$G_{\text{CNOT}} = |00\rangle\langle00| + |01\rangle\langle01| + |11\rangle\langle10| + |10\rangle\langle11| = \begin{pmatrix} 1 & 0 & 0 & 0 \\ 0 & 1 & 0 & 0 \\ 0 & 0 & 0 & 1 \\ 0 & 0 & 1 & 0 \end{pmatrix}. \qquad (2.35)$$

Two qubits can be in a superposition state of close coupling with each other, in an intimately fused state known as an *entangled state,* a state with no classical analogy. *Entanglement* is the exact translation of the German term *Verschränkung,* used by Schrödinger, who was the first to recognize this quantum effect. It means that the state of a two-particle quantum system cannot be written as a tensor product of the states of the individual particles. The state of an entangled system cannot be decomposed into contributions of individual particles.

Implementation of quantum information processing systems. The implementation efforts for quantum information processing systems are guided by a set of five requirements for quantum computers and two for transfer of information formulated by DiVincenzo in 2000 [73] and reformulated in 2010 for systems with low level of decoherence.

1. *The physical system has well-characterized qubits and is scalable.* The embodiment of a qubit is a quantum two-level system, such as the two spin states of a spin-1/2 particle, or the ground and some excited state of an atom, or the vertical and horizontal polarization of a single photon. The qubits can be in superposition states and/or entangled states and these unique quantum mechanical characteristics are associated with the enormous computational power of quantum computing devices. These characteristics can be effective only if the qubits are well isolated from the environment; the process of decoherence due to the possible interaction with the environment must be very slow.

   The physical parameters of a well-characterized qubit must be accurately known and include: the internal Hamiltonian (it determines the energy eigenstates of the qubit); the presence of other states of the physical qubit besides the two characteristic (basis) states and the couplings among them; the interactions with other qubits; and the couplings to external fields that might be used to manipulate the qubit. In general, the qubit has other (higher) energy levels than the two basis states and the probability of the transitions to such states from the characteristic states must be very low and under the control of the physical system.

   Some of the proposed qubit implementations are based in atomic physics, such as pairs of energy levels of ions confined in a linear electromagnetic trap [50], Zeeman-degenerate ground states used in the NMR approach [59], or atomic energy levels of neutral atoms [41, 127]. Other qubits are implemented as the position of atoms in a trap or lattice, the presence or absence of a photon in an optical cavity, or the vibrational quanta of trapped electrons, ions, or atoms.

   Some of the physical implementations based on solid state, such as impurities in solids and the quantum dots, take advantage of the fact that they have well-characterized discrete energy levels that can be controlled through the manufacturing processes. The qubits in solid-state systems include spin states or charge states of quantum dots, quantized states of superconductive devices, localized Cooper-pair charge.

2. *The physical system must be able to have the state of the qubits initialized to a known low-entropy state, such as $|000 \ldots\rangle$, as in classical computation.* The initial state of the qubits can be prepared by "cooling," which can be either natural cooling (when the state of interest is the ground state of the qubit Hamiltonian), or by projecting the system into the state of interest through the appropriate measurement. The natural cooling

method is used in the case of electron spin resonance techniques: the electrons are placed in a strong magnetic field and their spins are allowed to align with it while interacting with a heat bath (natural thermalization). The state projection method is associated with laser cooling techniques which are applied to cooling ion states to near the ground state in a trap [50], and are usually accompanied by fluorescence detection used to measure the state of these ions (state projection). The cooling times by state projection could be much shorter than by natural relaxation. The state initialization time becomes an important factor, if this time is relatively long compared with the gate operation time, and/or repeated initialization is required by say, quantum error correction.

3. *The decoherence times of the physical system implementing the qubit must be much longer than the quantum gate operation time.* The deco-herence of a quantum system is due to thermodynamically irreversible interactions with the environment; it represents the principal mechanism for the transition from quantum to classical behavior. The evolution of a quantum system in contact with its environment is characterized by various decoherence times; each decoherence time is related to a different degree of freedom of the system.

   The decoherence times relevant for a quantum computer are associated with the degrees of freedom that characterize the physical qubits; they also depend on the specifics of the qubits' couplings to these degrees of freedom. For example, the decoherence time of the spin of an impurity in a perfect semiconductor depends on its location, whether it is in the bulk of the solid, or near the surface of the device, and how close it is to the structures used to manipulate its quantum state [73]. The decoherence times must be long enough to allow the quantum system to evolve undisturbed until the computation is complete. No physical system can be completely free of decoherence, but decoherence times of the order of $(10^4 - 10^5) \times$ (*gate operation time*) are considered acceptable for fault-tolerant quantum computation,[9] in which case the error probabilities are lower than a critical threshold. The reality is that quantum systems with long decoherence times of the order mentioned above are relatively hard to find.

4. *A physical system as the embodiment of a quantum computer must have available a "universal" set of quantum logic gates.* A quantum computer executes a sequence of unitary transformations $U_1, U_2, U_3, \ldots, U_n$, as

---

[9]*Gate operation time*, the time for the execution of an individual quantum gate represents the *clock time* of a quantum computer.

specified by a quantum algorithm, with each transformation acting on one, two, or, at most three, qubits. All these unitary operations are implemented by a "universal" set of quantum gates; a convenient set of universal quantum gates contains one two-qubit gate plus a set of one-qubit gates.

5. *The physical system must have a qubit-specific measurement capability.* At the end of a computation, the result is read out by specific measuring qubits. The measurement represents an interaction between qubits and the measurement apparatus and this is an irreversible process. Realistic measurements of quantum systems are expected to have very low quantum efficiencies ($\ll 100\%$); the probability of obtaining a certain value for an output qubit as a result of one measurement is very low. The efficiency of a measurement of a quantum computer output could be "increased" either by rerunning the computation for a number of times, or by copying the value of a single read-out qubit[10] to several ancilla qubits using CNOT gates and measuring each of them.

6. *The system must have the ability to interconvert stationary and flying qubits.* The term "flying qubits" refers to the physical qubits that are transmitted from place to place while the "stationary qubits" represent the physical qubits for reliable local computation. The qubits encoded either in the polarization or in the spatial wave function of photons are the preferred flying qubits at this time. The light transmission through optical fibers is a well-developed technology and reliable enough for the transmission of qubits, even at relatively long distance. Qubits unloading from the quantum computer into a transmission system, and loading them up through a reversed process presents technical difficulties.

7. *The flying qubits must be transmitted between specified locations without affecting their state.* The preservation of the photon quantum state during transmission through optical fibers or through atmosphere has been the main concern of many experiments in quantum cryptography [122], but not of quantum computing yet.

General criteria for systems with low level decoherence. The original criteria of DiVincenzo cannot be easily applied to some of the new emerging concepts; they can be rephrased [145] into three more general criteria based on the assumption that these can be achieved if the decoherence is kept at a small enough level. These new criteria are (i) scalability, (ii) universal logic, and (iii) correctibility.

---

[10] The state of a qubit cannot be copied, but the value of a qubit in a given basis can be copied.

Scalability is achieved by adding new, well-characterized qubits. *Universal logic* criterion requires the system to have a finite set of control operations. In the case of qubits, the set of universal logic gates may include nearly analogue single-qubit gates (such as spin-qubit arbitrary rotations) and any digital two-qubit entangling logic operation, such as the CNOT gate. *Correctability* requires that any quantum error correction protocol devised for any physical implementation should be able to maintain the desired state of the system by eliminating unwanted entropy introduced from the environment into the quantum computer, while adding/dropping qubits required by encoding/decoding operations. That can be done through a combination of efficient state initialization and measurement.

2.8 MEMBRANE COMPUTING

Membranes play an important role in the biochemical processes in living organisms. A cell is separated from its environment by a membrane, the nucleus of a cell where the genetic material resides is surrounded by a membrane, and various regions of a cell where specific biochemical processes take please are also surrounded by membranes. The transfer of molecules from one region of a cell to another is controlled by membranes and, often the chemical reactions that take place in a cell are catalyzed by proteins bounded on the membranes. The transport of molecules from lower to higher concentrations is also controlled by membranes.

Membrane computing (MC) is biologically inspired; it is a generalization of DNA computing, but it is a computational rather than a biological model. In MC, transformation rules allow objects encapsulated into compartments defined by membranes to evolve. In this evolution compartments communicate among themselves and with the environment. The structure of a P-system, as MC is named after its inventor, Gheorghe Paun, could be a hierarchical arrangement of membranes, as in a cell, or a net of membranes as in a tissue or a neural net. A membrane can be viewed as an abstraction, a separator of two regions of the Euclidean space, a finite "inside" and an infinite "outside," able to communicate among themselves [185].

Chemicals are modeled by symbols, or by strings of symbols, collectively called objects. A region defined by a membrane can contain other symbols or strings or other membranes. A P-system has one outer membrane, called the skin membrane, and a hierarchical relationship governing all its membranes under the skin membrane (see Fig. 2.3).

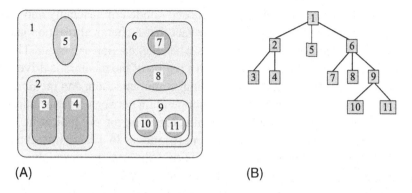

Fig. 2.3 (A) A membrane structure with 11 regions, each one surrounded by its own membrane. The membrane of the outer structure, structure 1, separates the structure from its environment. (B) The tree description of the membrane structure.

MC works with *multisets,* sets of objects whose multiplicities matter, to model biochemical processes in a cell where concentration, the number of molecules, is important. As customary in genetics, MC adopts a string representation of multisets, e.g., $aaabbc \rightarrow accccc$ is another representation for the transformation $a^3 b^2 c \rightarrow ac^5$ and means that three copies of a, two copies of b, and one copy of c are transformed in one copy of a and five copies of c. This transformation could represent a cellular chemical reaction in which b behaves as a catalyst and to produce five molecules of c and one molecule of a we need three molecules of a, two molecules of the catalyst, and one molecule of c.

Formally, a P-system of degree m is a construct of the form [184]

$$\Pi = (O, C, \mu, w_1, w_2, \ldots, w_m, R_1, R_2, \ldots R_m, i_o), \qquad (2.36)$$

where:

1. O is a finite and nonempty alphabet of objects,
2. $C \subset O$ is a set of catalysts,
3. μ is a membrane structure, consisting of m membranes, $1, 2, \ldots, m$,
4. $w_1, w_2, \ldots, w_m$ are strings over O representing multisets of objects in the regions $1, 2, \ldots, m$ of the membrane structure,
5. $R_1, R_2, \ldots, R_m$ are finite sets of evolution rules associated with the regions $1, 2, \ldots, m$ of the membrane structure, and
6. i_o is either one of the labels $1, 2, \ldots, m$ and then the respective region is the output region of the system, or it is 0, and then the result of a computation is collected in the environment of the system.

In P-systems rules and objects are chosen nondeterministically and parallelism occurs naturally mimicking the fact that a chemical reaction takes place for all molecules of two chemicals when the reaction can occur. Three types of local rules, each associated with a region of the membrane drive the evolution of the objects, multiset rewriting, communication, and membrane handling rules. There are also rules for cooperation between regions indicating the target of objects produced by a rule, e.g., *here, in, out* indicating that the object (a) remains in the same region, (b) moves to a randomly chosen directly lower membrane, and (c) moves into the region surrounding the membrane, respectively. For example, the rule $aaabbc \rightarrow accccc$ could be specified as $aaabbc \rightarrow (a, here)(c, out)(c, here), (c, in), (c, here)(c, here)$. Such rules are executed in parallel whenever the number of objects allow it.

2.9 CAN THERE BE A DEUS EX MACHINA IN COMPUTING?

According to the Merriam Webster Dictionary *Deus Ex Machina* is "a character or thing that suddenly enters the story in a novel, play, or movie, and solves a problem that had previously seemed impossible to solve." In Greek tragedies actors playing characters sent by Gods to solve hopelessly lost causes were brought to the stage by mechanical contraptions; this is the origin of the expression *Deus Ex Machina*. The ploy was used since ancient times by writers from Euripides to Shakespeare, and then to H.G. Wells[11] to introduce in their plays or novels minor miracles allowing the good and light to triumph over the bad and darkness.

Unquestionably, there is no *Deus Ex Machina* in science,[12] the progress of the plot is deliberate and strenuous with small steps in pushing forward the frontier of human knowledge; no miracles are ever present! Time and over again new theories that seemed far fetched, counterintuitive

---

[11] After Jason abandons Medea and their two children she kills her children; Euripides saves *Medea* in his play by sending a chariot commission by the Sun God to take her to a safe place in Athens. In *Pericles* and several other plays, Shakespeare introduces a character who breaks the flow of action and rewrites the ending of the play. Wells brings in bacteria to kill the Martians who triumphed over humanity in the *War of the Worlds*.

[12] Sensational discoveries are reported from time to time only to be debunked sooner or later. In recent years reports of cold fusion were discredited as the results reported could not be replicated. Starting in the Middle Ages perpetual motion devices were proposed and, in spite of the fact that the Second Law of Thermodynamics shows that perpetual motion is not possible, inventors do not seem to be deterred in their search for a *perpetuum mobile*.

and abstract, prove to be more refined and accurate reflections of the physical reality, rather than bursts of miracles. Quantum mechanics and general relativity theory whose predictions regarding gravitational waves were recently confirmed by elaborate experiments, are perfect examples of such disruptive theories.

As Moore's Law is approaching its inevitable end-of-life moment, quantum computing and, to a lesser extent DNA computing, have raised high expectations that soon we will be able to compute incredibly faster and with minimal energy costs and, at the same time, find effective ways to store large volumes of information. Quantum information processing seems to offer a magical solution for the future of computing and communication. Indeed, quantum key distribution protocols can ultimately guarantee secure communication and has already been demonstrated over distances of a few hundred kilometers. On the other hand, though considerable progress has been made in several technologies such as quantum dots, trapped ions in a cavity, or NMR, an experimental quantum computer with thousands of qubits is probably years away.

There is no better source of inspiration on managing complexity than nature; therefore, the investigation of complex structures and complex phenomena in nature is extremely valuable and helpful in understanding the challenging faced by man-made systems. None of the concepts discussed in this chapter provides magical and universally applicable solutions for the design and implementation of complex computing and communication systems. What we observe in nature must be adapted to the environment of a particular application. Consider, for example, epidemic algorithms used to disseminate topological information in communication networks. To limit the overhead due to such messages the life-time or number of hops traveled by each message must be limited.

Rather than replicating processes in nature we should discover useful analogies and shape them for particular applications. Take for example the selection process in the evolution of species. *Time* is the critical ingredient for self-organization and adaptation in nature. It took millions of years for biological species to adapt to natural conditions; only the members of a species with desirable traits survived and passed their genes to their descendants. It seems thus, hopeless to allow a man-made system to self-organize, manage, and repair itself, unless we understand that the time can be compressed as suggested by Heinz von Forester, see Section 1.9.

The rate of events that change the state in computer clouds and other large-scale systems is extremely high. This gives us the opportunity of embedding sophisticated learning algorithms in the systems to determine the essential characteristics of the environment after shorter periods of time. Knowledge accumulated in hours, days, or weeks can then be used to adapt to the environment and optimize the performance of the system. Of course, this applies only to ergodic processes,[13] but we have no reasons to believe that we are dealing with nonergodic processes for most systems of interest such as computer clouds.

Selecting the markers of adaptation is at the heart of evolution, as we have seen in Section 2.3. New ideas introduced by mixability theory [152] challenge the traditional concept of fitness. Profits and energy consumption seem to be good indicators of fitness for computer clouds. The choice of adaptation mechanisms is very challenging and it seems that market mechanisms are likely to fare better than the ones inspired by nature, as we shall see in the last chapter of this book.

2.10 MAJOR CONTRIBUTIONS AND FURTHER READINGS

John von Neumann is known not only for his work in self-replicating systems [236], but also for seminal contributions to game theory [237], computer architecture [233], reliability theory [235], ergodic theory [231, 232], and quantum mechanics [234].

Richard Feynman got the Noble Prize in Physics in 1965 for contributions to quantum electrodynamics. He is known for the Feynman diagrams, the Feynman Lectures on Physics, participation to the Manhattan Project and the investigation of the Challenger disaster, and also for his wit. He was the first to conclude that quantum systems cannot be exactly simulated with classical computers [80] and 3 years later he suggested that a computer exploiting the physical properties of quantum systems could be built [81]. In the late 1980s he played an important role in the development of a massively parallel computer, the Connection Machine. He once said "For a successful technology, reality must take precedence over public relations,

---

[13]A stochastic process is ergodic if the statistical properties of a set of realizations of the process can be deduced from a single, sufficiently long, random sample of the process.

for nature cannot be fooled." The Feynman Lectures on Computation [82] were published in 1996.

Leonard Adleman is known for his pioneering work on DNA computing [6, 7]. He got the Turing Award in 2002 for the 1978 RSA encryption system named after its creators Rivest, Shamir, and Adleman [193].

Rolf Landauer [146], Charles Bennett [33–35], David Deutsch [41, 71], Peter Shor [205–208] as well as experimentalists such as David DiVincenzo [72, 73], Ignacio Cirac and Peter Zoller [50, 51] have major contribution to the field of quantum computing. Books such as [156, 160, 175] cover the field.

Genetic algorithms were introduced in 1975 by John Holland [117]. A widely cited reference on GA is the comprehensive tutorial [247]. Ant optimization algorithms were proposed in the dissertation of Marco Dorigo [74] and further developed in [75, 76]. Swarm intelligence is analyzed in [53, 133]; more information at http://www.particleswarm.info/. MC was proposed by Gheorghe Paun in 1998 [184]. A book [185] and several conferences are dedicated to P-systems.

A 2007 survey of the field of natural computing is presented by [131] and a series of lectures on the same topic is available at [111]. Insights useful for understanding epidemic algorithms are provided by [42].

Next chapter is focused on how to manage complexity of large-scale cyber-physical systems.

CHAPTER 3

Managing Complexity of Large-Scale Cyber-Physical Systems

A large-scale system[1] has a very large number of interconnected hardware components running under a complex software system. Large-scale systems are now ubiquitous. The Internet is an example of a large-scale system that has become critical for the economic and social infrastructure of the modern society. The Internet connects more than one billion hosts and consists of millions of routers interconnected by communication links and running under sophisticated communication software. Large-scale sensor networks introduced in Section 3.11 are another example of complex systems. Computer clouds discussed in Chapters 4 and 5 are also complex systems with millions of multicore, multithreaded processors interconnected by a hierarchy of networks. The software stack distributed on all components enables such complex systems to operate reliably and effectively.

3.1 CYBER-PHYSICAL SYSTEMS

Most large-scale systems are cyber-physical systems integrating computation, communication, sensing, and physical processes. For several decades, we have designed and built systems with an increasingly larger numbers of components interacting with one another in intricate ways. In this section we examine the technological developments and the forces pushing integration of complex cyber-physical systems in the critical infrastructure of the society.

Breakthroughs in virtually all computing and communication technologies have made possible the design and implementation of increasingly more complex computing and communication systems. We have witnessed the unprecedented pace of evolution in processor architecture and solid-state technologies, optical storage technologies, wireless and fiber optics

---

[1] The term Ultra-Large-Scale system ULS is also used; a ULS is a "software intensive systems with unprecedented amounts of hardware, lines of source code, numbers of users, and volumes of data."

Complex Systems and Clouds. http://dx.doi.org/10.1016/B978-0-12-804041-6.00003-7

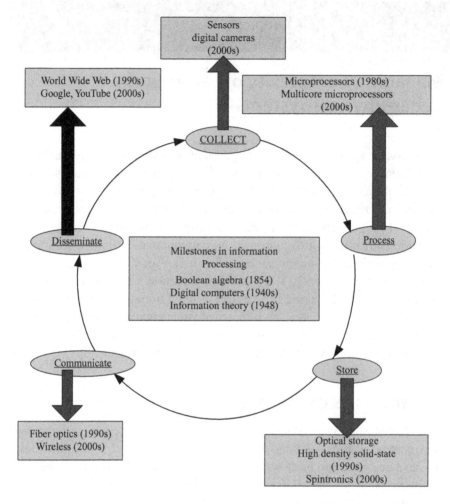

Fig. 3.1 Our ability to process, store, communicate, collect, and disseminate information due to breakthroughs in several technologies have enabled the design and implementation of increasingly more complex systems.

communication, sensors, and software (see Fig. 3.1). Advances in each of these areas increased the pressure for technological innovations, either directly or indirectly, in related areas.

The microprocessor technology put pressure on storage and communication technologies which, in turn, led to today's Internet. Sensors are now ubiquitous and enable the collection of large volumes of data. Every day, we generate 2.5 quintillion bytes of data, so much that 90% of all data in the world has been created in the last 2 years alone, according to [124].

The World Wide Web and social networks allow information collected by cameras embedded in our mobile devices, or generated by other data sources, to be stored and shared world-wide.

This evolution process continues to this day and it is unlikely to slow down any time soon [216]. Some of the forces pushing this evolution are illustrated in Fig. 3.2. The use of computing systems in virtually every area of human endeavor has reinforced the need for interconnectivity which, in turn, has hastened the support of mobile devices. Interconnectivity and mobility demand a continuous transformation of the Internet and the development of a vast array of wireless and cellular networks. The communication systems run under the control of real-time software.

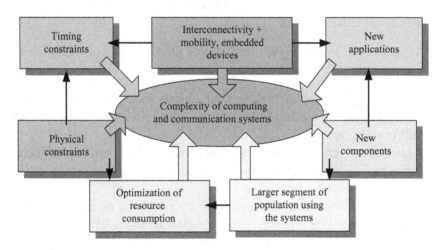

Fig. 3.2 Factors contributing to an ever increasing complexity of cyber-physical systems and the interactions among them.

The need to minimize power consumption is particularly critical for mobile devices with limited power reserves. It is also critical for large data centers, whose power consumption represents an increasingly larger fraction of the energy consumption in developed countries; such centers are expected to reduce energy consumption and shrink their carbon footprint. The constraints imposed by the laws of physics, such as heat dissipation and finite speed of light, make it harder and harder to increase the clock rate of processors.

Smaller and more energy efficient system components have become available and are embedded in many systems. Timing and physical constraints force us to increase the complexity of the software. Real-time software controls the behavior of multifunctional mobile devices such as the smartphones. Embedded microprocessors optimize the fuel consumption of cars and increase the energy efficiency of home appliances and of heating and cooling systems. To facilitate easier access to information technology for an increasingly larger segment of the world population, intelligence is built into the systems increasing the complexity of the system software.

Virtualization adds to the complexity of the system software. Resource virtualization abstracts the underlaying resources and simplifies their use, isolates users from one another, and supports replication which, in turn, increases the elasticity of the system. Virtualization is a critical aspect of cloud computing [214], equally important for the providers and the consumers of cloud services.

Virtualization simulates the interface to a physical object by any one of four means:

1. *Multiplexing*—create multiple virtual objects from one instance of a physical object. For example, a processor is multiplexed among a number of processes, or threads.
2. *Aggregation*—create one virtual object from multiple physical objects. For example, a number of physical disks are aggregated into a RAID system.
3. *Emulation*—construct a virtual object from a different type of a physical object. For example, a physical disk emulates Random Access Memory.
4. *Multiplexing and emulation*. Examples: virtual memory with paging multiplexes real memory and disk, and a virtual address emulates a real address; the TCP protocol emulates a reliable bit pipe and multiplexes a physical communication channel and a processor.

In 1992, Gordon Bell suggested the need of computing for the masses [31] and indeed, computer clouds have revolutionized the manner in which individuals, as well as organizations large and small, compute and store their data. Anyone with a credit card could use resources previously available only to those with access to supercomputers, or to the data centers of large organizations.

New applications take advantage of the new technological developments. For example, one of the fastest growing areas of cloud computing applications is data analytics, the process of extracting useful information from massive amounts of raw data. Data stored on computer clouds is accessible to hundreds of millions of mobile device users. The software stack of cloud servers is more complex in order to support resource virtualization, as well as effective and secure resource sharing.

It did not take a long time until *vehicular clouds* using onboard computing resources of vehicles became part of the conversation [16]. The concept of Smart Cities has captured the imagination of those concerned with life in large metropoles. In a smart city, large numbers of sensors and communication and computing systems work in concert to reduce pollution, minimize energy consumption, optimize city traffic, and prevent catastrophic failures of the distribution systems for water, gas, and electricity.

Cyber-physical systems based on technologies such as smart grids, smart homes, intelligent transportation, and smart cities allow direct integration of the physical world into computer-based systems, and lead to improved efficiency, accuracy, and economic benefit. The Internet of Things (IoT) is a global network of physical objects with embedded sensors and actuators. It is forecast that 6.4 billion connected things will be in use worldwide in 2016 and will reach 20.8 billion by 2020. In 2016, 5.5 million new things will get connected every day and their number will increase 30% in 2016 compared to the previous year (http://www.gartner.com/newsroom/id/3165317, accessed on January 2016).

Complex systems are now a critical element of the societal infrastructure and challenge our ability to build efficient and dependable large-scale systems. The complexity of the elements of the critical infrastructure is undeniable, yet their design was and still is, based on the traditional, mostly deterministic, system organization, and resource management.

3.2 SYSTEM COMPOSABILITY AND THE ROLE OF SOFTWARE

Composability is a system design principle focused on the relationships among system components. Composability of analog systems is limited by the laws of physics. Noise, power dissipation, and heat removal are some of the factors limiting the composability of analog systems.

Software has pushed the limit of composability of digital systems [194]. Software complexity is a function of the scale of the system, and thus, software complexity of a large-scale system is extreme. The question we examine next is how to assess software complexity. Software engineering uses several measures for software complexity. *Cyclomatic complexity* is a measurement of the extent of the control flow in the source code; the more conditional the logic, the more difficult to understand a piece of code is. Another measure, the *Halstead volume*, relates to the data flow; it quantifies the amount of information in the source code, how many variables are used, how often they are used, how many operators, how many functions, and how many variables they use. Yet another, more empirical measure is the *maintainability index* which measures the number of lines of code and how well commented the code is. This measure is based on the assumption that the larger the number of lines of code, the more difficult it is for a human to fully understand the code.

While these measures of software complexity may be useful for a sequential code, concurrency adds a new dimension to software complexity. Concurrent code is difficult to write, verify, and debug. Race conditions, deadlocks, and other synchronization anomalies, are only some of the problems faced when debugging concurrent code. Real-time adds yet another dimension to software complexity. The code for real-time systems has to be carefully crafted; moreover, it is designed for a particular hardware, and cannot be ported to a different one. Our use of the term *software complexity* implies all the elements mentioned above.

Communication among the components of large-scale systems is critical. In fact, computing and communication are deeply intertwined, whether the ultimate function of the system is computing, as in the case of computer clouds, communication, as in the case of the Internet, or sensing, as in the case of sensor networks. In a communication system, the routers are software-controlled, real-time, dedicated computer systems. The effectiveness of packet-switched networks depends on the ability of routers to effectively process very large numbers of data packets every second. In a computer cloud, a hierarchy of communication networks allow servers to communicate with one another and to give an end-user the impression of an infinite pool of resources. At the present time, the latency and the bandwidth of the interconnection networks of a computer cloud are an important factor limiting the performance of Big Data applications.

The autonomic computing initiative has encouraged research on self-management and self-organization. Some of the research has lead to industrial products; this is the case of the self-management via utility function [136]. The critical test for the viability of self-management and self-organization concepts and ideas is *scalability*. Unfortunately, few of the existing research results in autonomic computing can be applied to large-scale systems. Many of the existing proposals require intensive communication among system components and, when applied to large-scale systems, their effectiveness drops dramatically.

Practical means to support self-organization and self-management could lead to more efficient and more reliable large-scale systems. To contrast the manner in which self-organization and self-management can be approached, we discuss two cases, self-organization of a very large sensor network in Section 3.11 and a cloud reservation system based on coalition formation and combinatorial auctions in Chapter 5. In the first case the emphasis is on communication, how a very large number of sensors without a MAC address or any other built-in identity can communicate with one another and organize themselves as a system capable to collect and process sensed data. The cloud reservation system is a primitive form of self-organization. The history-based approach allows autonomous servers to organize themselves in coalitions based on information from previous combinatorial auctions. In time, this information is increasingly more accurate and the system is able to better predict the needs of the cloud user community.

3.3 MANAGING COMPLEXITY

A recent textbook on principles of computer systems design [194] devotes its first chapter to system complexity and to the means to manage complexity, including modularity, layering, and hierarchical organization. Layering and hierarchy have been present in social systems since ancient times. For example, the Spartan Constitution, called Politeia, describes a Dorian society based on a rigidly layered social system and a strong military. Nowadays, in a modern society, we are surrounded by organizations structured hierarchically.

Modularity is a technique to build a systems from a set of interacting components assembled and tested independently. Modularity has been used extensively since the industrial revolution for building every imaginable product, from weaving looms to steam engines, from watches to automobiles, and from electronic devices to airplanes. Individual modules are often made of subassemblies; for example, the power train of a car includes the engine assembly, the gear box, and the transmission. In computer architecture, pipelined processors have multiple functional units.

Modularity can reduce the cost for the manufacturer and for the consumers. The same module may be used by a manufacturer in multiple products; to repair a defective product, a consumer only replaces the module causing the malfunction, rather than the entire product. Modularity encourages specialization, as individual modules can be developed by experts with deep understanding of a particular field. It also supports innovation; it allows a module to be replaced with another one, possibly a more performant one, without affecting the rest of the system.

Since the early days of computing large programs have been split into modules, each one with a well-defined functionality. Modules with related functionalities have then been grouped together into numerical, graphical, statistical, and many other types of libraries. A strong requirement for modularity is to clearly define the interfaces between modules and enable the modules to work together.

Layering is a particular form of modularity when the functions of the system are ensured by modules with a well-defined communication pattern; logically, the modules are stacked on top of one another and each module, except the top and the bottom one, communicate only with the one above and the one below it. This restrictive communication pattern simplifies the design of the interfaces of each module and makes testing and debugging the system easier. Layering helps us in dealing with complicated problems when we have to separate concerns that prevent us from making optimal design decisions. To do so, we define layers that address each concern and design clear interfaces between the layers.

Communication protocols are layered. The TCP/IP network architecture accommodates a variety of physical communication channels that carry electromagnetic, optical, or acoustic signals, thus, there is the need for a *physical layer* whose function is to transport physical signals. The next concern is how to transport frames consisting of a number of bits, rather than signals, between two nodes linked to one another by a communication channel, thus, the need for a *data link layer*. The Internet is a network of networks; data packets have to traverse a set of networks and a chain of intermediate routers from the source to the destination; the concern of the *network layer* is to forward the data packets from one intermediate node to the next. The source, as well as the recipient of information, are outside the network and they are not interested in how the information crosses the network, but want the information to reach its destination unaltered; the *transport layer* is responsible for data segments delivery from the source to the destination. Finally, the information sent and received has a meaning only in the context of an application and this is the function of the *application layer*. Layering gives us insights into where to place the basic mechanisms for error control, flow control, and congestion control in the protocol stack.

Layering could also affect the performance; it could prevent optimizations. Then the rigorous communication patterns demanded by layering are sacrificed in favor of performance. For example, cross-layer communication allows wireless applications to take advantage of information available at the Media Access Control (MAC) sublayer of the data link layer.

There are systems for which it is difficult to envision a layered organization because of the complexity of the interactions among the individual modules. Consider, for example, a typical operating system with well-defined functional components:

- Processor management responsible for processor virtualization, scheduling, interrupt handling, execution of privileged operations and system calls, and multithreading.
- Virtual memory management responsible for translating virtual addresses to physical addresses.
- Multilevel memory management responsible for transferring storage blocks between different memory levels, most commonly between primary and secondary storage.
- I/O responsible for transferring data between the primary memory, I/O devices, and network interfaces.

There are multiple interactions among these components, therefore it seems unlikely that a strictly layered OS organization is feasible. An interesting question with practical implications for the future development of computing clouds is if a layered software architecture for computer clouds can be designed. One could argue that it may be too early for such an endeavor, that we need time to fully understand how to better organize a cloud infrastructure and we need to gather data to support the advantages of one approach over another.

Hierarchical organization. Herbert Simon defines a hierarchic system [210] as follows: "By a hierarchic system, or hierarchy, I mean a system that is composed of interrelated subsystems, each of the latter being, in turn, hierarchic in structure until we reach some lowest level of elementary subsystem."

We can distinguish two types of interactions in a hierarchically organized system, interactions among the subsystems and interactions within the subsystems. Typically, these interactions often are of different orders of magnitude. According to Herbert Simon, *nearly decomposable systems* have two properties [209]: "(a) in a nearly decomposable system, the short-run behavior of each of the component subsystems is approximately independent of the short-run behavior of the other components; (b) in the long run, the behavior of any one of the components depends in only an aggregate way on the behavior of the other components."

Hierarchical organization is a common approach to accommodate the complexity of many large-scale social, economical, computer, and communication systems. Hierarchical organization restricts the communication pattern between the system components; the system is organized as a tree. In a hierarchical organization, information about the state of the system flows from the leaves toward the root of the tree; management decisions flow in a reverse pattern, from the top to the bottom. Typically, each node manages the subtree rooted at that node. In practice, a more involved communication pattern may exist, a child node may have multiple parents.

Many large-scale computing systems are organized hierarchically; in each cluster, a *leader* is responsible for monitoring and controlling the activity of the cluster nodes and interacts with other cluster leaders to achieve common system objectives. Such an organization is more efficient as communication delays are shorter and the overhead for resource management is lower.

Layering and hierarchical organization have their own problems, could negatively affect the society, impose a rigid structure and affect social interactions, increase the overhead of activities, and prevent the system from acting promptly when such actions are necessary. In the case of computing and communication systems, layering typically affects performance.

3.4 CHALLENGES SPECIFIC TO LARGE-SCALE SYSTEMS

The computing and communication infrastructure is increasingly more complex as new technologies become available and require the software to support new functions and to interact with an increasingly more demanding environment. For example, support for mobility is now ubiquitous due to advances in wireless communication and cellular networks. Advances in sensor technology led to the ability to collect vast amounts of data and, in turn, the need for processing these data poses significant challenges to computer clouds. Another challenge is the integration in large-scale systems of an the increasingly growing population of embedded systems.

Several factors affect the complexity of modern computing and communication systems:

1. *The rapid pace of technological developments and the availability of relatively cheap and efficient new system components* such as multicore processors, sensors, retina displays, and high-density storage devices. The introduction of new technologies rapidly changes both the systems and the environment they operate in and often forces the system designers to further increase software complexity to accommodate the new technology.

    Retina displays increase the power consumption and force the system designers to compensate this increase by reducing the power consumption of other system components. The replacement of mechanical disk drives with solid-state drives considerably reduces the access time and the power consumption and increases the system reliability; it requires new software and, at the same time, invites the development of new applications.

    IBM announced recently the successful development of the 7 nm (nanometers) technology expected to replace in the next few years the 14 nm, the highest density technology used today. This new solid-state technology will be used for the production of processors and memory chips. Processors have dramatically increased their processing power. Increasing the density of transistors on a chip enabled the development of multicore processors, as well as the implementation of sophisticated architectural enhancements supporting Instruction Level Parallelism (ILP). The Instructions per Cycle (IPC) has increased steadily due to techniques such as pipelining, dynamic instruction scheduling, and speculative execution.

    The power dissipation of processors increases with the clock rate; for the current solid-state technologies, this increase is proportional to the clock rate to the power of two or three, i.e., when the clock rate doubles, the energy dissipation could increase as much as eight times.

Heat removal becomes problematic and this has forced the manufacturers to transition to multicore processors rather than increasing the clock rate.[2]

2. *New technologies required by large-scale systems are developed at a different pace.* This reality can only be accommodated by increasing the system complexity and, in particular, the complexity of the software controlling the system. But the software development technologies have not kept pace with the needs of large-scale systems, especially in the area of AI support.

There are other significant discrepancies, e.g., the processing power of modern processors had increased faster than the ability to communicate effectively. Thus, the performance of large-scale computing systems has not been able to take full advantage of the throughput of modern processors. Now processors in the same rack of a cloud infrastructure are connected by 10 Gbps Ethernet (10 GE). It is expected that 100 GE will replace them in the coming years. The multiple layers of the software stack of TCP/IP-based communication architecture is also a limiting factor of the communication speed for sensor and mobile applications.

3. *We are now faced with a paradigm shift in software development.* To exploit the computing power of multicore processors we have to rely on parallel software, which is difficult to implement and debug. This transition is necessary to exploit task-level parallelism rather than rely solely on ILP. Embedded systems are now ubiquitous and require concurrent, real-time software.

There are additional elements of computing and communication systems reflecting phenomena specific to complex systems [1]:

- The behavior of the systems is controlled by phenomena that occur at multiple scales/levels. As levels form or disintegrate, phase transitions and/or chaotic phenomena may occur.
- Systems have no predefined bottom level; it is never known when a lower level phenomena will affect how the system works.
- Systems are entangled with their environment. A system depends on its environment for its persistence, therefore, it is far from equilibrium. The environment is man-made and the selection required by the evolution can either result in innovation, or generate unintended consequences, or both.

---

[2]For example, Intel released Pentium 4 chips clocked at 3.6 GHz in 2006; at the end of 2013 the fastest Intel Haswell Core i7 CPUs ran at 3.9 GHz. Haswell is a microarchitecture developed by Intel aiming to optimize the energy consumption; it is based on a 22 nm process.

Other aspects of complexity are side-effects of the organization, management, and the operations of the systems, or of unrealistic assumptions about the system models:

- Abstractions of the system useful for a particular aspect of the design may have unwanted consequences at another level.
- Systems are expected to function simultaneously as individual systems and as groups of systems (systems of systems) [168].
- Typically, the systems are both deployed and under development at the same time.

A conclusion is that the design of large-scale systems should be focused on high-level policies rather than on the mechanisms for the implementation of the policies. This would allow the system to be more resilient to changes in the technologies and the environment. The policies should favor cooperation between autonomous entities and assume that individual components follow high-level policies, but make their decisions based on local information, rather than insisting on centralized or distributed control. Autonomy of individual components is critical due to the size of the system.

3.5 AUTONOMIC COMPUTING

The management and control of large-scale systems is extremely challenging. As the system complexity grows due to technological advances and under pressure from the user community, the system becomes unmanageable, less reliable due to the very large number of components, less secure, and more difficult to maintain due to the complexity of the software. These facts were recognized and, in early 2000, IBM advanced the idea of autonomic computing [85, 134].

The 2003 autonomic computing manifesto [134] proposed embedding complexity in the system infrastructure. Since then, a significant body of research was devoted to autonomic computing. Over 8,000 papers, nearly 200 conferences, and some 200 issued patents and more than 100 pending patents, are some of the results of a decade-long research effort in this field [137]. Some of these efforts have resulted in commercial products, such as the Tivoli software produced by IBM Cloud and Smarter Infrastructure Division. Some of the traits of autonomic computing, including self-optimization, self-configurations, and continuous monitoring, appear in database management systems (DBMS) such as DB2 [69]. DB2 supports disaster recovery and autonomic index determination.

Autonomic systems are expected to make decisions on their own based on high-level policies; such systems attempt to optimize their state and to adapt to changing conditions of the environment and of the internal state of the system. Four aspects of autonomic computing are identified in [134]:

1. Self-configuration—automated configuration of components and systems follows high-level policies, the entire system adjusts automatically and seamlessly.
2. Self-optimization—the components and systems continually seek opportunities to improve their own performance and efficiency.
3. Self-healing—the system automatically detects, diagnoses, and repairs localized software and hardware problems.
4. Self-protection—the system automatically defends against malicious attacks or cascading failures. It uses early warning to anticipate and prevent systemwide failures.

The goal of autonomic computing is to manage complexity, reduce cost of ownership, and enhance the quality of the software. Complexity should be managed by exploiting technological advances, including those in several areas of Artificial Intelligence. Autonomic computing requires software and hardware capable to ensure that the system is self-aware and, at the same time, aware of the environment [181]. The systems should be able to monitor and analyze internal events, as well as events caused by the interaction between the environment and the system. Machine-learning techniques, feedback control, planning and optimization techniques are some of the means to support system awareness.

An autonomic system should be supported by policy-based management and effective negotiations between system components. A policy defines the high-level objective driving the response of the system to internal changes of state and to changes in the environment. Different mechanisms for the implementation of policy-based management for large-scale systems exist, see Section 4.6.

A policy can specify the action to be taken or can define a goal state to be reached. In both cases, it is necessary to know the current state of the system as well as the state to be reached. Knowing with any degree of accuracy the global state of a large-scale system is a very challenging proposition. Equally challenging is the determination of the path leading to a desirable state.

The concept of *utility* is based on the principle of rational choice, i.e., a component of a complex system will choose the most beneficial course of action. Policies based on utility seem suitable for large-scale systems. The utility is a real number measuring the system's benefit of being in a certain state. For a system with a very large number of autonomous components, each one of the components is able to accurately determine its state and its utility. Determining the utility of the entire system requires a global resource manager tasked to collect information from all system components filtered by objective analyzers and then determine the course of action. The decision-making process involves an upwards flow of utility information followed by downwards flow of decisions.

This is the case of the Tivoli Intelligent Orchestrator (TIO) where the objective analyzers process utility information from groups of nodes [136]. This form of self-management is unlikely to be effective for systems with millions of components with rapidly changing states. The information used by the objective analyzers and by the global resource manager will inherently be obsolete. A significant fraction of the communication bandwidth of the system will be used in the process. In Chapter 5, we discuss the results of a simulation experiment comparing hierarchic control with market mechanisms. The results confirm that monitoring the states of individual system components does not always effectively support self-management.

The scalability of TIO self-management is questionable. According to [136]: "... Models are essential for relating higher-level metrics to lower-level system control parameters. In our data center example, we were able to tap into a queuing model that could predict what would happen if the amount of resource changed." Developing such models for large-scale systems is extremely challenging.

The decisions made by self-management must take into account, not only changes in the internal system configuration, but also the interactions with the environment [2, 5]. Some of these interactions affect the system resources, others reflect the service demands placed by the user community. Changes in the internal system configuration are due to predictable phenomena, such as individual server failures, or to unpredictable ones, such as power failures affecting a number of servers. Maintaining a history of such events helps in determining the failure rate and the actions to be taken in each case. This approach reflects the principle of embedding complexity in the system itself. Complex phenomena require a long history, thus, the self-management system should be able to learn and improve in time.

Service-level agreements (SLA) should spell out the interactions with the users which are part of the system environment. For example, the SLA should specify the type of workload. Rapid varying workloads, such as those generated by transaction processing systems, are more difficult to handle than batch processing.

3.6 SCALABLE SYSTEM ORGANIZATION

Scalability is a critical concern as the systems are increasingly more complex, e.g., social networks such as Facebook are projected to reach one billion users in several years. Today's computer networks connecting hundreds of millions of computers, computer clouds with millions of servers, the future smart power grid infrastructure expected to have a very large number of nodes including customers, power generators, and transmission lines, are only a few examples of systems expected to have properties invariant to the scale of the system, in other words, to be *scale-free*.

Graphs are mathematical structures used to model pairwise relations between objects and to study system organization. Several models of graphs have been investigated starting with the Erdös-Rény model [78], where the number of vertices is fixed and the edges connecting vertices are created randomly. This model produces a homogeneous network with an exponential tail; connectivity follows a Poisson distribution peaked at the average degree $\bar{k}$ and decaying exponentially for $k \gg \bar{k}$.

An evolving network, where the number of vertices increases linearly and a newly introduced vertex is connected to m existing vertices according to a preferential attachment rule, is described by Barabási and Albert in [9, 10, 29]. Regular graphs, where a fraction of edges are rewired with a probability p, have been proposed by Watts and Strogatz and called small worlds networks [244]. Networks whose degree distribution follows a Power Law are called scale-free networks. The four graph models are sometimes abbreviated as: ER (Erdös-Rény), BA (Barabási-Albert), WS (Watts-Strogatz), and SF (scale-free) models, respectively. We use the terms networks, nodes, and links when we discuss a physical system and the terms graphs, vertices, and arcs when we discuss the model of a system.

In a scale-free organization, the probability $p(k)$ that an entity interacts with k other entities decays as a Power Law discussed in Section 1.5

$$p(k) \approx k^{-\gamma}, \tag{3.1}$$

with γ a constant and k a positive integer. This probability is independent of the type and the function of the system, the identity of its constituents, and the relationships between them.

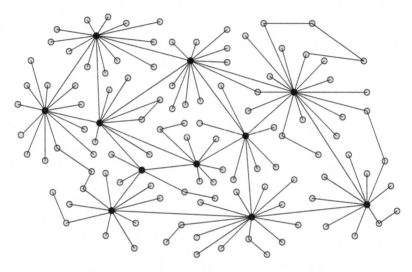

Fig. 3.3 A scale-free network is nonhomogeneous; the majority of the vertices of a graph model of a scale-free network have a low degree and only a few vertices are connected to a large number of edges; the majority of the vertices are directly connected with the vertices with the highest degree.

The graph of a scale-free network is *nonhomogeneous*, there are a few vertices with a high degree of connectivity and the majority of the vertices are only connected with few other vertices. In addition to scalability, scale-free networks have a significant number of other highly desirable properties discussed later in this section.

The degree distribution of scale-free networks follows a Power Law; we only consider the discrete case when the probability density function is $p(k) = af(k)$ with $f(k) = k^{-\gamma}$ and the constant a is $a = 1/\zeta(\gamma, k_{min})$ thus,

$$p(k) = \frac{1}{\zeta(\gamma, k_{min})} k^{-\gamma}. \tag{3.2}$$

In this expression k_{min} is the lowest degree of any node, and in our discussion we assume that $k_{min} = 1$; ζ is the Hurvitz zeta function[3]

$$\zeta(\gamma, k_{min}) = \sum_{n=0}^{\infty} \frac{1}{(k_{min} + n)^{\gamma}} = \sum_{n=0}^{\infty} \frac{1}{(1 + n)^{\gamma}}. \quad (3.3)$$

The high connectivity nodes of a scale-free network play the important role of hubs in communication and networking, a fact that can be exploited when designing efficient search algorithms [4].

Fig. 3.3 shows the graph of a scale-free network. The average distance d between the N nodes, also referred to as the diameter of the scale-free network, scales as $\ln N$; in fact it has been shown that when $k_{min} > 2$ a lower bound on the diameter of a network with $2 < \gamma < 3$ is $\ln \ln N$ [56].

A number of studies have shown that scale-free networks have remarkable properties, such as: (a) robustness against random failures [30]; (b) favorable scaling [9, 10]; (c) resilience to congestion [95]; (d) tolerance to attacks [223]; and (e) small diameter [56] and small average path length [29].

The moments of a Power Law distribution play an important role in the behavior of a network. It has been shown that the giant connected component (GCC) of networks with a finite average vertex degree and divergent variance can only be destroyed if all vertices are removed; thus, such networks are highly resilient against faulty constituents [54, 55]. These properties make scale-free networks very attractive for interconnection networks in many applications, including social systems [174], peer-to-peer systems, and sensor networks [147, 159].

Another important property is that the majority of the nodes of a scale-free network are directly connected with the nodes of higher degree (see Fig. 3.3). For example, in a network with $N = 130$ nodes and $m = 215$ links, 60% of the nodes are directly connected with the five nodes with the highest degree, while in a random network fewer than half, 27%, have this property [10]. Thus, the nodes of a scale-free network with a degree larger than a given threshold T could assume the role of "core nodes" and assume

---

[3] The Hurvitz zeta function $\zeta(s, q) = \sum_{n=0}^{\infty} \frac{1}{(q+n)^{s}}$ for $s, q \in \mathbb{C}$ and $\mathfrak{Re}(s) > 1$ and $\mathfrak{Re}(q) > 0$. The Riemann zeta function is $\zeta(s, 1)$.

management functions; the other nodes assume the role of computational and storage servers. This partition is autonomic; moreover, most of the server nodes are at distance one, two, or three from a core node which could gather more accurate state information from these nodes and with minimal overhead. In the next example if $k_{lim} = 4$ then 92.5% of the nodes are servers.

As an example, consider the case $\gamma = 2.5$ and the minimum node degree, $x_{min} = 1$; we first determine the value of the zeta function $\zeta(\gamma, x_{min})$ and approximate $\zeta(2.5, 1) = 1.341$ thus, the distribution function is $p(k) = k^{-2.5}/1.341 = 0.745 \times (1/k^{2.5})$, where k is the degree of each node. The probability of nodes of degree $k > 10$ is: $\text{Prob}(k > 10) = 1 - \text{Prob}(k \leq 10) = 0.015$. This means that at most 1.5% of the total number of nodes will have more than 10 links connected to them; we also see that 92.5% of the nodes have degree 1, 2, or 3. Table 3.1 shows the number of nodes of degrees 1 to 10 for a very large network, $N = 10^8$.

3.7 COMPLEX NETWORKS

Complex networks are ubiquitous. The nervous system, the Internet, and social networks are examples of complex networks. The study of complex networks focuses on three preeminent aspects, the small-worlds nature, clustering, and degree-distribution of such networks [11]. In this section we focus on the first two aspects.

Small-Worlds. In 1998, Watts and Strogatz published in the journal *Nature* an algorithm to produce graphs with short average path length l and high clustering C, two defining properties of graphs describing

Table 3.1 A Power-Law Distribution With Degree $\gamma = 2.5$; the Probability $p(k)$, and N_k, the Number of Nodes With Degree k, When the Total Number of Vertices Is $N = 10^8$

k	$p(k)$	N_k	k	$p(k)$	N_k
1	0.745	74.5×10^6	6	0.009	0.9×10^6
2	0.131	13.1×10^6	7	0.006	0.6×10^6
3	0.049	4.9×10^6	8	0.004	0.4×10^6
4	0.023	2.3×10^6	9	0.003	0.3×10^6
5	0.013	1.3×10^6	10	0.002	0.2×10^6

"small-worlds" [244]. This model is also known as *Six Degrees*, the title of the popular science book written by Watts. The "six degrees of separation" concept attributed to Milgram [170] is the most popular example of small worlds.[4] Next we present the Watts-Strogatz algorithm. We are given:

1. N—the desired number of nodes.
2. K—the mean degree, an even integer satisfying the condition

$$N \gg K \gg \ln(N) \gg 1. \tag{3.4}$$

3. $0 \le \beta \le 1$—a parameter which controls the shape of the graph.

The two limits, $\beta = 0$ and $\beta = 1$ correspond to a regular lattice and to an Erdös-Rényi random graph $G(n,p)$ with $n = N$ and $p = \frac{NK}{2\binom{N}{2}}$, respectively.

Two steps are required to construct an undirected graph with N nodes and $\frac{NK}{2}$ edges:

- Step 1: construct a regular ring lattice, a graph with N nodes each connected to K neighbors, $K/2$ on each side. If the nodes are labeled $n_0, \ldots, n_{N-1}$, there is an edge (n_i, n_j) if and only if

$$0 < |i - j| \mod \left(N - 1 - \frac{K}{2}\right) \le \frac{K}{2}. \tag{3.5}$$

- Step 2: for every node $n_i = n_0, \ldots, n_{N-1}$ take every edge (n_i, n_j) with $i < j$ and rewire it with probability β by replacing (n_i, n_j) with (n_i, n_k). Node n_k is chosen with uniform probability from all possible values avoiding:
  1. self-loops, $k \ne i$, and
  2. link duplication; no edge $(n_i, n_{k'})$ with $k' = k$ is allowed.

Properties of small-worlds are discussed in [25]. The number of nonlattice edges introduced by the Watts-Strogatz algorithm is about $\beta \frac{NK}{2}$. The average path length depends on the value of the parameter β, $l = l(\beta)$ and decreases fast when $\beta \to 1$ and the graph resembles a random graph. The average path length for $\beta = 0$ and $\beta = 1$ is

$$l(0) = \frac{N}{2K} \gg 1 \quad \text{and} \quad l(1) = \frac{\ln N}{\ln K}. \tag{3.6}$$

---

[4]Milgram concluded that there was a chain of acquaintances connecting most pairs of people.

Clustering. The clustering coefficient quantifies the tendency of the nodes of a complex graph to cluster together. This tendency is best exemplified by social networks where clusters of friends are present. If the k_i nearest neighbors of node n_i are part of the cluster there would be $N_i = k_i(k_i - 1)/2$ edges between them. The clustering coefficient of node i is

$$C_i = \frac{E_i}{N_i} = \frac{2E_i}{k_i(k_i - 1)} \tag{3.7}$$

with E_i the actual number of edges between these k_i nodes. For example, the clustering coefficient C of a small-worlds network depends of the value of β:

$$C(0) = \frac{3(K - 2)}{4(K - 1)}, \quad C(1) = \frac{K}{N} \quad \text{and} \quad C \to C(1) \quad \text{when} \quad \beta \to 1. \tag{3.8}$$

Empirical data confirm the existence of scale-free organization in complex networks. The power grid of the Western US has some 5,000 nodes representing power generating stations; in this scale-free network $\gamma \approx 4$. When the scale-free network is generated using the preferred attachment model [29] and when $\gamma \approx 3$, then the larger the number of nodes, the better it approximates the theoretical distribution.

Networks with a Power-Law distribution of node degrees may appear naturally in social networks and other virtual organizations. Such organizations are inherently heterogeneous, there are a few highly connected individuals and a very large number of individuals with few connections. Though sometimes the statistics used to identify the organization of a system as scale-free are questionable, several instances of virtual organizations, as well as man-made systems, seem to enjoy this type of organization.

For example, the collaborative graph of movie actors where links are present if two actors were ever cast in the same movie follows the Power Law with $\gamma \approx 2.3$ [244]. The average degree in the network of movie actors with $225,226$ nodes is $\bar{k} = 61$, the average path length is $l = 3.65$, and the clustering coefficient is $C = 0.79$, while the average path length and the clustering coefficient of a random graph of the same size and average degree are $l_{rand} = 2.99$ and $C_{rand} = 0.00037$, respectively [11]. We see that the average path length is close to that of a random graph with the same size and average degree, while its clustering coefficient is more than 100 times higher than a random graph.

Recent studies indicate that $\gamma \approx 3$ for the citation of scientific papers. A study of the papers in Medline[5] carried out in 2001 reported results regarding co-authorship in life sciences [174]. The average degree in the network of authors with 1,520,251 nodes is $\bar{k} = 18.1$, the average path length is $l = 4.4$, and the clustering coefficient is $C = 0.066$, while the average path length and the clustering coefficient of a random graph of the same size and average degree are $l_{rand} = 4.91$ and $C_{rand} = 1.1 \times 10^{-5}$, respectively [11]. This network, as well as similar networks of scientists in other fields, show a small average path length but a high clustering coefficient.

3.8 VIRTUALIZATION BY AGGREGATION: COALITION FORMATION

Virtualization by aggregation is the process of combining a set of physical resources into a single logical resource; this process aims to increase some capability of the system, e.g., the processing power, the processing speed, or the reliability. For example, Redundant Array of Independent Disks (RAID) combines multiple physical disk drives into a single logical unit to increase both the access speed and reliability by replicating the data on multiple physical disks. Some applications running on computer clouds may need resources that cannot be provided by a single server.

Informally, a *coalition* is a group of agents who cooperate to achieve a well-defined goal and expect to be rewarded for their accomplishments. An impressive array of real-world applications in several areas including economics, political, social, and computer science, motivate the vast body of research in coalition formation.

The emergence of robotics, sensor networks, computational grids, and computer clouds have amplified the interest in coalition formation when the agents are different embodiments of computer systems involved in task-oriented activities. There are several reasons for the coalition formation for task-oriented activities:

- The agents do not have enough resources to carry out the task on their own and need to combine their resources. This is the case of Big Data

---

[5]Medline is the bibliographic database of the U.S. National Library of Medicine with more than 22 million references to journal articles in life sciences.

cloud applications when only coalitions of multiple servers can supply the computing cycles and storage demanded by the application.

- The task requires agents, or coalitions of agents, with complementary abilities, as no agent or coalition has all the required expertise, and thus, they need to work in concert. This is the case when multiple CSPs join forces to create a *cloud federation*, or when the cloud infrastructure is required to carry out computations with a complex workflow and each phase requires a coalition with resources of different types or quantities.

A coalition could last for an extended period of time, or for a relatively short time; coalition stability is very important for the former, while the efficiency of coalition formation is critical for the latter. A coalition could be homogeneous or heterogeneous; in the first case, the agents are identical and perform similar tasks, in the second they are specialized to carry out different tasks required by a complex activity.

The need for cooperation and coalition formation arises in electronic markets, as well as in task-oriented domains. A combinatorial coalition formation problem related to electronic markets is discussed in [149]. The paper assumes that a seller has a price schedule for each item. The larger the quantity requested, the lower the price a buyer has to pay for each item; thus, buyers can take advantage of price discounts by forming coalitions.

A similar assumption is adopted by the authors of [148] who investigate systems where the negotiations among deliberate agents are not feasible due to the scale of the system. The paper proposes a macroscopic model and derives a set of differential equations describing the evolution in time of coalitions with a different number of participants. The results show that a low rate of leaving agents allows a coalition to achieve a steady state.

Coalition formation has been studied extensively over the years, see for example [129, 180]; more recent references are [8, 98, 176]. A vast literature is devoted to task-oriented coalition formation [148, 149, 200]. An interesting analysis of coalition formation with spatial and temporal constraints when the agents are robots is presented in [192]. Different aspects of resource management in computer grids, including load balancing, job-allocation, and scheduling, as well as revenue sharing when agents form coalitions or virtual organizations are analyzed in [44, 108, 138, 187, 219, 240]. Grid resource allocation is modeled as cooperative games [138] or noncooperative games [187]. Resource co-allocation is presented in [240].

Game theory provides the theoretical foundations of both topics covered in this chapter, coalition formation and combinatorial auctions. Game theory is a discipline pioneered by John von Neumann, who in 1927 published a seminal paper, "Theory of Parlor Games," including the proof of the Minmax theorem. His book first published in 1944 [237] addressed the question of coalition stability and introduced the concept of stable set, also called the Neumann-Morgenstern solution.

A *coalitional game* is a pair $\mathbb{G} = (\mathbb{A}, v)$, with $\mathbb{A}$ a set of players/agents and v a real-valued function associated with each coalition $\mathbb{C} \in \mathbb{A}$. The worth of a coalition, $v(\mathbb{C}) \in \mathbf{R}$, quantifies the benefits obtained by the players collaborating with one another. Coalition formation requires solutions to two problems: (a) the decision process for joining a coalition; (b) the policies and mechanisms for reward sharing among the members of a coalition.

The agents could play a noncooperative or a cooperative game when the goal is to optimize a common objective function. We shall only discuss *Transferable Utility* (TU) games. Utility is transferable if players can losslessly transfer utility to one another; this is possible only if a common currency equally valued by all agents exists. An example of a TU game is a voting game when a majority vote decides between two alternatives; if there are $n = 2k + 1$ agents and all vote, then the value of the winning coalition in this game is

$$v(\mathbb{C}) = \begin{cases} 1 & \text{if } |\mathbb{C}| > k, \\ 0 & \text{otherwise.} \end{cases} \qquad (3.9)$$

We now present the definitions of frequently used terms in coalition games. Consider a set $\mathbb{A}$ of agents $\mathcal{A}_i$ with $n = |\mathbb{A}|$; a *coalition* $\mathbb{C}$ is a nonempty set of $\mathbb{A}$. The entire set $\mathbb{A}$ is called the *grand coalition*.

A *coalition structure* is a *partition* of the set of all agents into disjoint, nonempty coalitions $\mathbb{S} = \{\mathbb{C}_1, \mathbb{C}_2, \ldots, \mathbb{C}_m\}$; thus

$$\bigcup_{i=1}^{m} |\mathbb{C}_i| = n \quad \text{and} \quad i \neq j \Rightarrow \mathbb{C}_i \cap \mathbb{C}_j = \emptyset. \qquad (3.10)$$

Call $\Pi(\mathbb{A})$ the set of all possible partitions of $\mathbb{A}$. $\pi(i) \in \Pi(\mathbb{A})$ means that coalition agent $\mathcal{A}_i$ belongs to partition π. Subsets of coalitions are called *blocks*.

Given two partitions $\pi_i, \pi_j \in \Pi(\mathbb{A})$ we say that π_i is a *refinement* of π_j if any block of π_i is contained in a block of π_j and write $\pi_i \leq \pi_j$. The algebraic structure $[\Pi(\mathbb{A}), \leq]$ is a lattice[6] called the *partition lattice* of $\mathbb{A}$. An example of a partition lattice when $n = 4$ is given in Fig. 3.4.

The value $v(i)$ of agent $\mathcal{A}_i \in \mathbb{A}$, measures the intrinsic worth of the agent. The *valuation/characteristic* function $v(\mathbb{C})$ measures the value of coalition $\mathbb{C}$. Given $\forall(\mathbb{C}_i, \mathbb{C}_j) \in \mathbb{A}$, $\mathbb{C}_i \cap \mathbb{C}_j = \emptyset$ we distinguish several types of coalitions:

- Additive when $v(\mathbb{C}_i \cup \mathbb{C}_j) = v(\mathbb{C}_i) + v(\mathbb{C}_j)$.
- Superadditive when $v(\mathbb{C}_i \cup \mathbb{C}_j) \geq v(\mathbb{C}_i) + v(\mathbb{C}_j)$.
- Subadditive when $v(\mathbb{C}_i \cup \mathbb{C}_j) \leq v(\mathbb{C}_i) + v(\mathbb{C}_j)$.

A related quantity is the *payoff*. The payoff $x(i)$ of agent $\mathcal{A}_i \in \mathbb{A}$ measures the benefit the agent has from joining the coalition; $x(\mathbb{C})$ measures the payoff of coalition $\mathbb{C}$, where

$$x(\mathbb{C}) = \sum_{\forall \mathcal{A}_i \in \mathbb{A}} x(i). \tag{3.11}$$

The pair $(x, \mathbb{C})$ is the *payoff configuration* for $\mathbb{C} \in \mathbb{S}$.

An agent $\mathcal{A}_i \in \mathbb{A}$ is *rational* when joining a coalition $\mathbb{C}$ improves her worth, i.e., its payoff is larger or equal to its valuation, $x(i) \geq v(i)$. *Group rationality* is defined as

$$x(\mathbb{C}) \geq v(\mathbb{C}), \quad \forall \mathbb{C} \in \Pi(\mathbb{A}). \tag{3.12}$$

The *payoff distribution* shows how the coalition worth is shared among the coalition members; if $x(i)$ is the payoff of agent $\mathcal{A}_i \in \mathbb{A}$, then the payoff distribution is the vector $x = (x(1), x(2), \ldots, x(n))$. A payoff distribution where no agent can improve its payoff without lowering the payoff of another agent is the *Pareto optimal*.

When $x(\mathbb{A}) = v(\mathbb{A})$ the payoff distribution covers the entire grand coalition and the payoff is said to be *efficient*. A payoff distribution efficient and rational for all agents is called an *imputation*. The *excess*, $e(\mathbb{C}, x) = v(\mathbb{C}) - x(\mathbb{C})$, corresponding to a payoff distribution $x(\mathbb{C})$ measures

---

[6]A lattice is an algebraic structure consisting of a partially ordered set when every pair of elements have unique supremum and infimum, or least-upper and greatest-lower bounds, respectively. For example, the natural numbers form a lattice with Least Common Multiple (LCM) and Greatest Common Divisor (GCD) the supremum and the infimum, respectively.

the total amount the agents gain or lose by forming a coalition $\mathbb{C}$. When the excess is positive, $e(\mathbb{C}, x) > 0$, the agents are motivated to leave their current coalitions and to form a new coalition $\mathbb{C}$

When the utility of an agent depends on the identity of the members of the coalition the coalition is called *hedonic*. Given a coalition structure $\mathbb{S}$ the preferences of agent $\mathcal{A}_i$ are represented by a transitive, complete, and reflexive relation over the set of coalitions $\mathbb{C}_k \in \mathbb{S}$ denoted as $\succeq_i$. The preference of agent $\mathcal{A}_i$ is *additively separable* if there exists a real-valued function $v : \mathbb{A} \to \mathbf{R}$ such that given any two partitions π_j, π_k

$$\pi_j \succeq_i \pi_k \Leftrightarrow \sum_{\mathcal{A}_l \in \pi_j} v_i(l) \geq \sum_{\mathcal{A}_l \in \pi_k} v_i(l). \tag{3.13}$$

Agents $\mathcal{A}_i \in \mathbb{A}$ rank all coalitions in $\Pi(\mathbb{A})$ via the relations $\succ_i$ and $\succeq_i$. When the condition $\mathbb{C} \succ_i \pi_k, \forall \mathcal{A}_i \in \mathbb{A}$ is satisfied all agents in $\mathbb{C}$ prefer being in coalition $\mathbb{C}$ than being in partition π_k; we say that coalition $\mathbb{C}$ *blocks* partition π_k. As an example consider three agents a, b, c with the following preference relations

$$1\ ab \succ_a ac \succ_a a \succ_a abc$$
$$2\ bc \succ_b ab \succ_b b \succ_b abc \tag{3.14}$$
$$3\ ac \succ_c bc \succ_c c \succ_c abc$$

It is easy to see that there is no core stable partition in this cyclic game, as all possible coalitions, abc, ab, ac, bc, a, b, c, are blocked:

$$
\begin{array}{ccccc}
1 & \Rightarrow & a & \text{blocks} & abc \\
1 & \Rightarrow & ab & \text{blocks} & ac, a \\
2 & \Rightarrow & bc & \text{blocks} & ab, b \\
3 & \Rightarrow & ac & \text{blocks} & bc, c
\end{array}
\tag{3.15}
$$

A partition π is *core stable* if there is no blocking coalition $\mathbb{C}$. The *core* of the game $(\mathbb{A}, v)$ includes all payoff distributions $x \in \mathbf{R}^n$ when x is a group rational imputation. An equivalent definition of the core is as the set of payoff distributions when the excess is not positive thus,

$$e(\mathbb{C}, x) \leq 0, \quad \forall \mathbb{C} \in \mathbb{A}. \tag{3.16}$$

Super additivity is implicitly assumed when the core is defined. The concept of *core* helps us analyze the stability of a coalition; a payoff distribution is in the core when no agent or group of agents reject the current payoff distribution and are willing to form other coalitions. Note that the core can be empty as illustrated by the example in Eqs. (3.15) and (3.16). The stability of hedonic coalitions is analyzed in [38].

A formula for a fair payoff distribution was proposed by Shapley in 1953 [201]. The *Shapley value* rewards agent $\mathcal{A}_i$ with payoff ϕ_i

$$\phi_i = \sum_{\mathbb{C} \subseteq (\mathbb{A} - \mathcal{A}_i)} \frac{|\mathbb{C}|!(n - |\mathbb{C}| - 1)!}{n!} (v(\mathbb{C} \cup \{\mathcal{A}_i\}) - v(\mathbb{C})) \qquad (3.17)$$

with the sum extended over all coalitions not including agent $\mathcal{A}_i$. The Shapley value given by Eq. (3.17) is the unique one satisfying the following three axioms

- A1: Symmetry—two agents should have equal rewards if they have identical contributions

$$\forall(\mathcal{A}_i \neq \mathcal{A}_j), \ \mathcal{A}_i \notin \mathbb{C}, \ \mathcal{A}_j \notin \mathbb{C} \quad v(\mathbb{C} \cup \mathcal{A}_i) = v(\mathbb{C} \cup \mathcal{A}_j) \Rightarrow x_i = x_j.$$
$$(3.18)$$

- A2: Rationality—agent $\mathcal{A}_i$ should enter coalition $\mathbb{C}$ only if it is granted at least the worth of the singleton, $v(\{i\})$. Reciprocally, agent $\mathcal{A}_i$ should be accepted in coalition $\mathbb{C}$ only if it adds to the value of the coalition more than $v(\{i\})$.
- A3: Additivity—if two agents get the payoffs x and y for two characteristic functions v and w, respectively, then their payoff should be $(x + y)$ when the characteristic function is $(v + w)$.

Interesting problems are posed by a *voting game* mentioned earlier. Formally, a game $(\mathbb{A}, v)$ is called a voting game when the characteristic function satisfies the following three conditions

$$v = \begin{cases} 1 & \text{for winning coalitions} \\ 0 & \text{otherwise} \end{cases};$$

$$v(\mathbb{A}) = 1 \text{ and } \forall(\mathbb{C}_i \subseteq \mathbb{C}_j) \in \mathbb{A} \Rightarrow v(\mathbb{C}_i) \leq v(\mathbb{C}_j). \qquad (3.19)$$

The last condition, often referred to as *monotonicity*, expresses the requirement that the addition of agents to coalition $\mathbb{C}$ does not change the outcome of the voting process from winning to losing.

A voting game is a *weighted voting game* $(\mathbb{A}, v, w, q)$ if

1. $w(w_1, w_2, \ldots, w_n)$ is a vector with w_i the weight of agent $\mathcal{A}_i$,
2. $v(\mathbb{C}) = 1$ iff $\sum_{\mathcal{A}_i \in \mathbb{C}} w_i \geq q$ with q a given threshold.

A weighted voting game is represented as $[q : w_1, w_2, \ldots, w_n]$. One answer to the question of how to measure the impact, or the power of agent $\mathcal{A}_i$ in a weighted voting game is given by the Shapley-Shubik power index [202], closely related to the Shapely value and expressed as

$$\phi_i = \frac{1}{n!} \sum_{\mathcal{A}_i \text{pivot} \in \mathbb{C}} (m - 1)!(n - m)! \quad \text{with} \quad m = |\mathbb{C}|. \tag{3.20}$$

The sum in Eq. (3.20) is over the coalitions for which agent $\mathcal{A}_i$ plays a pivotal role, in other words, it changes the final outcome of the voting. For example, given three agents a, b and c and the weighted voting game $[5; 3, 2, 1]$, the list of all possible coalitions given in Eq. (3.21) shows also the pivot as the underlined element

$$\begin{matrix} a\underline{b}c & b\underline{a}c & c\underline{a}b \\ ac\underline{b} & bc\underline{a} & c\underline{b}a \end{matrix} \tag{3.21}$$

Then $n! = 6$ and $\phi_a = \phi_b = 3/6 = 1/2$ and $\phi_c = 0$. Another example given in [217] discusses a four agent, a, b, c, d, weighted voting game $[6; 4, 3, 2, 1]$; then $\phi_a = 5/12, \phi_b = \phi_c = 3/12$ and $\phi_d = 1/12$.

The *Banzhaf index* introduced by Penrose and often referred to as Banzhaf-Coleman is given by

$$\beta_i = \frac{c_i}{\sum_{k=1}^{n} c_k} \tag{3.22}$$

with c_i the number of times voter i is critical.

3.9 COOPERATIVE GAMES FOR COALITION FORMATION

There are many instances when individual agents work together towards a common goal rather than being driven by their personal interest. This is true in the case of social activities and is also true for the autonomous servers of a cloud infrastructure. In Chapter 5 we present a reservation system based on coalition formation and combinatorial auctions. Coalitions are formed to create large pools of resources for Big Data applications. The common goal is to maximize the revenue of the cloud service provider.

Task-oriented coalition formation is often $\mathcal{NP}$ hard [99]. When all agents have the same ability to perform a single task, the problem is similar to the set partitioning problem, while in the case of agents able to perform multiple tasks the problem resembles the set covering problem [203].

Coalition formation as a cooperative game. The coalition formation is modeled as a cooperative game where the goal of all agents is to maximize the reward due to the entire set of agents. We consider a set of R servers $\{s_1, s_2, \ldots, s_R\}$, located in the same rack. In this case a *coalition* $\mathbb{C}_i$ is a nonempty subset of R.

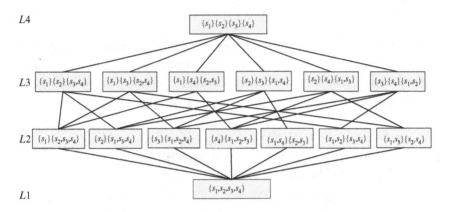

Fig. 3.4 *A lattice with four levels L1, L2, L3, and L4 shows the coalition structures for a set of four servers, s_1, s_2, s_3, and s_4. The number of coalitions in a coalition structure at level L_k is equal to k.*

Fig. 3.4 shows a lattice representation of the coalition structures for a set of four servers s_1, s_2, s_3, and s_4. This lattice has four levels, $L1$, $L2$, $L3$, and $L4$ containing the coalition structures with 1, 2, 3, and 4 coalitions, respectively. In general, the level k of a lattice contains all coalition structures with k coalitions; the number of coalitions structures at level k for a population of N agents is given by the Sterling Number of Second Kind:

$$S(N, k) = \frac{1}{k!} \sum_{i=0}^{k} (-1)^i \binom{k}{i} (k - i)^N. \qquad (3.23)$$

In the case illustrated in Fig. 3.4 $N = 4$ and the number of coalition structures at levels $L1 - L4$ are $1, 7, 6, 1$, respectively.[7] The total number of coalition structures with N agents is called the Bell number

---

[7]For $N = 5$ and $N = 6$ the Stirling Numbers of the Second Kind are respectively $1, 15, 25, 10, 1$ and $1, 31, 90, 65, 15, 1$.

$$B(N) = \sum_{k=0}^{N} S(N,k) = \sum_{k=0}^{N} \frac{1}{k!} \sum_{i=0}^{k} (-1)^i \binom{k}{i} (k-i)^N. \qquad (3.24)$$

The number of coalition structures increases exponentially with the number of agents. For example, for $N = 40$, a typical number of servers in a rack, the logarithm of the number of coalition structures is close to 10^{35} and $S(40, 14) = 3.585987225562180349142855410^{34}$.

Searching for the optimal coalition structure $\mathbb{C}$ is computationally challenging due to the size of the search space. The first step for determining the optimal coalition structure is to assign a *value* v reflecting the utility of each coalition. The second step is the actual coalition formation.

3.10 CYBER-PHYSICAL SYSTEMS AND THEIR SELF-ORGANIZATION SAGA

Complexity and self-organization have preoccupied the minds of the pioneers of computing, Turing [224] and von Neumann [235, 236]. The essence of self-organization is captured by Alan Turing's observation "Global order can arise from local interactions" [224].

Exploiting self-organization in the design and implementation of large-scale cyber-physical systems proves to be extremely challenging.

Self-organization implies that all individual components of a system respond to local stimuli, that there is a division of labor among the components, and the entire system adapts to reach common goals efficiently [57]. This implies that goal(s) must be defined, and the system interaction with the environment must be specified: there are stimuli/inputs, and the system produces some output. Each component has an internal state and this state changes as a function of the input and of the information about the states of other components. All units contribute to achieving the system's goal, no subset of units can achieve the goal, only the entire system as a whole can. Last, but not least, the system adapts and in time it achieves its goals more efficiently.

The design of all computing and communication systems aim to ensure robustness and graceful performance degradation when components fail. For example, routing in packet-switched networks is designed to maintain connectivity even when communication links and switches fail.

Communication protocols at the data link and transport layer transform error-prone communication channels into error-free ones.

A self-organizing system responds to changes of the environment through adaptation, anticipation, and robustness; the system reacts to changes in the environment, predicts changes, and reorganizes itself to respond to them, or is robust enough to sustain a certain level of perturbations. Self-organization and self-management of a man-made system imply that there is no centralized control and individual components organize and manage themselves to provide a function consistent with global system policies.

Consider, for example, the organization of the traffic lights in a large metropolis [88]. The system could be centralized, sensors placed in the vicinity of traffic lights send traffic data to a computer system which then uses a global optimization algorithm to minimize the waiting time of the vehicles to reduce pollution, and then sets up the traffic lights accordingly. In a self-organizing system, there is no central computer and each traffic light receives information from sensors in its proximity; the light turns red when there are only a few cars in the direction it controls and green when the converse is true. There is a negative feedback, if it stays on red for an extended period of time, the number of waiting cars increases and the light has to turn green. Multiple traffic lights are affected by the traffic flow in the direction they control thus have to coordinate their behavior.

Practical implementation of self-organization and self-management is challenging. Very few of the large-scale systems designed in recent years could claim some form of self-organization or self-management. This is in itself proof of the challenges faced by the designers of such systems. Some of these challenges are:

- The absence of a technically suitable definition of self-organization, a definition that could hint at practical design principles for self-organizing systems and quantitative evaluation of the results. Marvin Minsky [171] and Murray Gell-Mann [89] have discussed the limitations of core concepts in complex system theory, such as emergence and self-organization. The same applies to autonomic computing, there is no indication of how to implement any of the four principles and how to measure the effects of their implementation.
- A quantitative characterization of complex systems and of self-organization and self-management is extremely difficult. We can

only assess the effectiveness of a particular self-organization or self-management algorithm/protocol indirectly, based on some of the measures of system effectiveness, e.g., the savings in cost or energy consumption. We do not know how far from optimal a particular algorithm is.

- Large-scale systems exhibit the essential aspects of complexity; it is inherently difficult to control complex systems.

As pointed out in Chapter 1, complex systems: are nonlinear; operate far from equilibrium; are intractable at the component level; exhibit different patterns of behavior at different scales; require a long history to draw conclusions about their properties; scale well; exhibit complex forms of emergence; and are affected by phase transitions. For example, a faulty error recovery mechanism in the case of a power failure took down Amazon's East Coast Region cloud operations in 2013.

In contrast, simple systems are linear, operate close to equilibrium, are tractable at the component level, exhibit similar patterns of behavior at different levels, relevant properties can be inferred based on a short history, exhibit simple forms of emergence, are not affected by phase transitions, and do not scale well.

3.11 SELF-ORGANIZATION OF SENSOR NETWORKS

To illustrate that self-organization of cyber-physical systems is feasible, we now discuss a self-organizing sensor network. A *sensor network* consists of spatially distributed autonomous devices equipped with a radio transceiver or other wireless communication device, a micro-controller, a power source, and sensors which monitor temperature, sound, vibration, pressure, motion, chemical pollutants, radiation, or other physical characteristics of the environment. The software running on the nodes of a sensor network includes a network stack communicating with a middleware layer running on top of a real-time operating system.

Very-large sensor networks. We discuss self-organization principles to very large-scale sensor networks with applications in the area of climate changing, environment monitoring, or forest fire prevention. Typical applications could be studies of the temperature at the polar cap, of the sol humidity in a forest, or of the tremors in an earthquake prone or in a volcanic region. The area to be monitored by such applications is rather large, e.g., 1 mile^2, and for a density of 2 sensors per 100 ft^2 the total number of sensors is about 5×10^5. The sensors should be able to operate with their power reserves for a year or more. The maintenance, as well as the operation of the network, must be as inexpensive as possible.

The sensors are dropped from an aircraft or planted by a specialized device and are stationary or experience very limited mobility. An unmanned aircraft flies over the area and collects the information at predetermined time intervals. A more futuristic scenario involves sensors and actuators built into the variable geometry wing of a stratospheric aircraft. In a science fiction scenario, bio sensors attached to the molecules of a drug used for the treatment of a patient monitor the interaction of these molecules with the cells of the patient.

Energy efficiency is a major concern for mobile devices as they have limited power reserves and are able to recharge only after extended periods of time [107, 109, 252]. Communication among the mobile nodes is more energy-intensive than either computing or sensing; the energy to transmit 1 kB of data at a distance of 100 m is equal to the energy required by a processor using the year 2000 solid-state technology to execute 10^7 instructions [215]. The laws of physics limit the ability of new communication and energy storage technologies to match the sharp reduction of energy consumption per instruction we have witnessed throughout the last decades; we expect that communication efficiency will continue to be an important design goal for sensor networks.

The Organization, Routing, and Mobility (ORM) management of ad-hoc networks aim to maximize the throughput and minimize the delay, while the main objective of the ORM in a sensor network is to extend the lifetime of the network. A sensor network could have several orders of magnitude more nodes than a traditional ad hoc network and for economical reasons its nodes must be inexpensive. Even though technological advances translate into higher processing rates and storage capacity at lower costs, the nodes of future wireless sensor networks will be required to collaborate in order to accomplish any meaningful task.

Berkeley Motes and PicoNode, UCLA sensor nodes, and MIT AMPs are some of the devices used in sensor networks. For example, the MICA mote uses an 8-bit micro-controller with 128 kilobytes of flash memory and runs an operating system known as TinyOS [239]. Its radio has a range of several hundred feet and can transmit approximately 40,000 bits per second; it consumes less than 1 μA when it is off, 10 mA when it receives, and 25 mA when it transmits.

Self-organizing Sensor Network (SFSN) protocol. The self-organization strategy supported by the SFSN protocol guarantees that every node is connected with a limited number of nodes [159]. This means that a sensor $\sigma_i, 1 \leq i \leq N$ is able to construct a *proximity set*, $\mathcal{P}(\sigma_i)$, of neighboring sensors it communicates with. The network is scale-free, $|\mathcal{P}(\sigma_i)| \leq \mu$, regardless of the number N of sensors in the network; σ_i maintains a limited amount of state information regarding the sensors in $\mathcal{P}(\sigma_i)$. For example, the proximity set of sensor a, $\mathcal{P}(a)$, in Fig. 3.5 consists of a subset of sensors in the range of a; a must also be in the range of the sensors in $\mathcal{P}(a)$. The quantities μ, M and η, ν, κ in Figs. 3.5 and 3.6, respectively, are constants selected at the time the network is planned; see Table 3.2 for a summary of notations.

The *reciprocal* of event ϵ_k during the self-organization phase is the event $\epsilon_{\bar{k}}$ during an activity phase; the reciprocal index is $\bar{k} = \kappa - k - 1$. Reciprocal

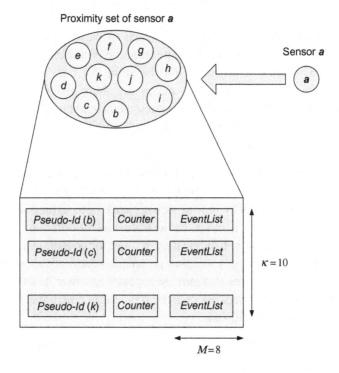

Fig. 3.5 *The sensors $b, c, d, \ldots, i, j, k$ are in the proximity set of sensor a, $\mathcal{P}(a)$, with $\mu = |\mathcal{P}(a)| = 10$. The entry for each sensor in $\mathcal{P}(a)$ consists of a unique pseudo identityPid, an EventList, and a Counter $\leq M$, the actual number of items in EventList. Each item in the EventList gives the index of the event when the sensor will wake up to receive and then transmit during the activity phase.*

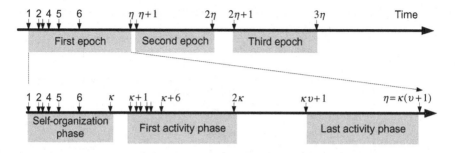

Fig. 3.6 Epochs, phases, and events. The number of events in an epoch is η and the number of events in a phase is κ. Each epoch consists of one self-organization phase followed by v activity phases. Thus, $\eta = \kappa(v + 1)$.

events occur in reverse order, if $k_1 \leq k_2$ then $\bar{k}_2 \leq \bar{k}_1$ and $\epsilon_{\bar{k}_2} \mapsto \epsilon_{\bar{k}_1}$. The ordering of events is $1 \mapsto 2 \mapsto 3 \ldots \mapsto \kappa - 1 \mapsto \kappa$ during the self-organization phase and $\bar{\kappa} \mapsto \overline{\kappa - 1} \mapsto \ldots \mapsto \bar{3} \mapsto \bar{2} \mapsto \bar{1}$ during an activity phase.

During the self-organization phase, a sensor σ_i assumes a globally unique pseudo-identity, $Pid(\sigma_i)$. Initially, the Pid of each sensor is set to zero. $Pid(\sigma_i) = k$, if during the self-organization phase σ_i *successfully transmits* during slot $(k - 1)$, possibly after a set of collisions, and wins the right to be the only sensor allowed to transmit at the beginning of slot k. The Pid is included in every message sent by σ_i during the self-organization phase to ensure that the proximity set does not grow beyond the limit imposed, $|\mathcal{P}(\sigma_i)| \leq \mu$ and also that σ_i does not appear multiple times in any proximity set $\mathcal{P}(\sigma_j)$. The Pid is available during the activity phase, but not used now.

The time evolution of the network consists of several *epochs*, each one starting with a *self-organization (set-up)* phase followed by a number v of *activity (steady-state)* phases (Fig. 3.6); the names of the phases are suggestive. We use the term *event* to describe a communication event, the transmission of a message at the beginning of a time slot; the index k of the event ϵ_k occurring at time t_k, the beginning at slot k, reflects the order of the event: if $k_1 \leq k_2$ then $\epsilon_{k_1} \mapsto \epsilon_{k_2}$ (ϵ_{k_1} before ϵ_{k_2}). All phases consist of the same number of events, κ. We can refer to an event by its global index, its index within an epoch, and its index within a phase, as in Fig. 3.7. The index k of ϵ_k is a global pointer into a random sequence of frequencies and time slots.

Table 3.2 The Notations Used for SFSN Protocol Description

σ_i	a sensor in the batch
$\mathcal{P}(\sigma_i)$	proximity set of σ_i
μ	maximal cardinality of the proximity set
μ_{actual}	actual cardinality of the proximity set
N	total number of sensors
M	maximum number of events in *EventList*
κ	number of events in a phase
ν	number of activity phases
η	number of events in one epoch
γ	transmission range
ρ	average sensor density
θ	standard deviation of sensor density
ϵ_k	kth event during the self-organization phase
$\epsilon_{\bar{k}}$	reciprocal event of ϵ_k during an activity phase
φ	parameter for synchronization
ζ	average nr. of sensors receiving a transmission
λ_k	carrier frequency in slot k
$\xi_j^{\lambda_k}$	hopping frequency around λ_k
E_o^t	energy for transmission during self-organization
E_o^r	energy for reception during self-organization
E_a^t	energy for transmission during activity
E_a^r	energy for reception during activity
$\mathcal{E}_{eff}$	energy efficiency of sensor network
ω	expected number of collisions in a CRI
δ	the duration of a micro-slot
$\Delta = n_\delta \delta$	the duration of a slot, $n_\delta = \mathcal{O}(10^3)$

The steps required by an informal high-level description of the self-organization algorithm are:

1. A specially configured node called the *sink*, initiates the self-organization process at the time t_1 of the first event ϵ_1 and requests to be included in the proximity set of one of the nodes in its vicinity and assumes a *Pid* of 1.

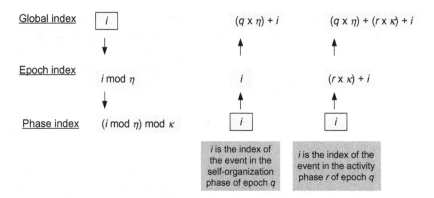

Fig. 3.7 Global, epoch, and phase indices of an event. If i is the global index then the epoch index is (i mod η) and the phase index is [(i mod η) mod κ]. If i is the index of an event in the self-organization phase of epoch q, then its phase index is i, and the global index is (q × η + i). If i is the index of an event in the rth activity phase of epoch q then its phase index is (r × κ + i), and the global index is (q × η + r × κ + i).

2. Multiple sensors receive the request and decide whether to respond or not; if more than one responds, a Collision Resolution Algorithm (CRA) is used and eventually sensor σ_i transmits successfully in the slot triggered by event ϵ_1 and wins the right to transmit at time t_2 of the second event, ϵ_2. Then σ_i assumes a *Pid* of 2, includes the *sink* in its proximity set, $\mathcal{P}(2)$, and records that during the activity phases must wake-up at reciprocal event $\bar{1}$ to receive a transmission from the *sink* and then transmit at reciprocal event $\bar{2}$ to a member of its own proximity set. At the time of the second event ϵ_2, the role of the *sink* is played by σ_i which sends a request to join the proximity set of one of its neighbors. Eventually, a sensor σ_j accepts; then σ_j assumes a *Pid* of 3 and includes σ_i in its proximity set, $\mathcal{P}(3)$. Later, when σ_j receives another request from $\sigma_i \in \mathcal{P}(3)$ it records only the index of the event in the *EventList* corresponding to *Pid* = 2.

3. The process continues and eventually the *sink* responds to a request from a sensor σ_k and includes σ_k in $\mathcal{P}(1)$. Recall that the *sink* has a *Pid* of 1 and each sensor assumes as *Pid* the index of the *first event* when it sends a request to join a proximity set.

4. The self-organization phase ends after κ events and an activity phase starts. During the activity phase, σ_i wakes up at the time of the events in its *EventList* to receive from one of the members of its proximity set and then transmit in the next slot to σ_j such that $\sigma_i \in \mathcal{P}(\sigma_j)$. At the end of each activity phase the sink reports to an external monitor.

In SFSN networks the total energy consumption during the self-organization and the ν activity phases are, respectively, $E_o = \omega \kappa (E_o^t + E_o^r)$ and $E_a = \nu \kappa (E_a^t + E_a^r)$, with $\omega > 1$ a factor depending upon the average number of collisions in a Collision Resolution Interval (CRI). The energy efficiency of the scheme is given by the following expression:

$$\mathcal{E}_{eff} = \frac{E_a}{E_o} = \frac{\nu(E_a^t + E_a^r)}{\omega(E_o^t + E_o^r)}. \tag{3.25}$$

We expect the energy for sending and receiving short control messages during the self-organization phase to be orders of magnitude lower than the one required for transmission during the activity phase, e.g., $(E_a^t + E_a^r) > 10^3 (E_o^t + E_o^r)$ then $\mathcal{E}_{eff} > 10^3 \nu/\omega$; thus, to increase the efficiency we should increase the number of activity phases and minimize the number of collisions.

The model of the scale-free sensor network. The model we propose is based upon the following assumptions:

1. The inexpensive sensors have "genetic information" including a random number generator, seeds, and other network parameters. During the fabrication process, the seeds are randomly chosen and the set of seeds is burned-in the read-only memory of all sensors in the batch. The sensors are tamper-proof, thus, it is unlikely to learn the genetic information by disassembling a sensor. The seeds $\alpha_q, 1 \leq q \leq 3$ are used as follows: α_1 to determine a random sequence of events occurring at time slots t_i; α_2 to determine a random sequence of carrier frequencies λ_i; and α_3 to determine a random hopping frequency $\xi_j^{\lambda_i}$ for each carrier frequency λ_i. The genetic material also includes: κ, the number of events in one phase and ν, the number of activity phases, as well as μ, the cardinality of the proximity set, M, the cardinality of the event index list used to keep track of transmission and receiving events, and φ, a parameter for synchronization.
2. The average transmission range of a sensor is γ and we expect to have on average ρ sensors per unit of the area covered by the network.
3. The network is dense; this means that $\zeta = \pi \times \gamma^2 \times \rho$, the average number of sensors that are able to receive the transmission of a sensor is at least $\zeta \geq p \times \mu$ with p a small integer, $4 \leq p \leq 6$ and μ the cardinality of the proximity sets.
4. The sink Σ has a larger power reserve and transmission range. It links the sensor network with the outside world and communicates with an

external controller (a satellite, a drone, or even a stationary device) to report relevant information. For now, we assume a unique sink, but fault-tolerance requires backup sinks that can take over if the original sink fails. Initially, all sensors are synchronized to the sink.

5. The sensors are *reactive* in terms of communication. A sensor responds to a successful transmission of another sensor after evaluating two *fitness functions f* and *g*; only if the value of the fitness function exceeds a certain threshold the sensor is allowed to transmit. This threshold depends on several parameters, including the strength of the incoming signal and the power reserve of the sensor. The fitness function and the determination of the threshold are fairly complex subjects and are not discussed in this section.

6. A sensor dwells φ micro-seconds on each frequency in a hopping sequence. When a sensor wakes up at the time of the event ϵ_i, its master clock is in one of the time slots t_{i-1}, t_i, or t_{i+1}. Each sensor knows the frequencies λ_{i-1}, λ_i, and λ_{i+1} on which the sender will dwell in the time slots t_{i-1}, t_i, and t_{i+1}. A strategy to allow synchronization in the presence of clock drift is: tune in, cyclically, to λ_{i-1}, λ_i, and λ_{i+1} spending $\varphi/3$ time units on each of them.

The expected duration of an epoch is application-dependent and it is controlled by η, the number of events per epoch. Some of the factors that affect the choice of η are: the duration of the deployment, the expected life-time of individual sensors, the intensity of communication during the deployment, and the frequency of topological changes. An epoch could last minutes for an intense and dynamic application when new sensors are added frequently and the life-time of sensors is very limited because they deplete their power at a high rate, e.g., monitoring and control of a forest fire. An epoch could be of the order of days, or even months for a low-intensity application with a relatively stable topology, e.g., long-term monitoring of volcanic activity. The expected duration of an epoch can be controlled by scaling the random numbers dictating the timing of events, e.g., using seconds, minutes, hours, and so on, as units of time.

An integrated Medium Access Control (MAC) and self-organization algorithm. There are two basic classes of strategies for sharing a communication channel: scheduled and nonscheduled multiple access. Both strategies are represented among the Medium Access Control (MAC) layer protocols for ad hoc and sensor networks. Among the strategies based upon scheduled access we mention: Code Division Multiplexing (CDMA) which employs spread-spectrum technology and a special coding scheme (where each transmitter is assigned a code) to allow multiple users to be multiplexed over the same physical channel; Time-Division Multiple Access (TDMA) divides access by time, while Frequency-Division Multiple Access (FDMA) divides it by frequency.

Several MAC-layer protocols for ad hoc networks avoid, or reduce collisions. A nonexhaustive list of such protocols includes: Medium Access Collision Avoidance (MACA) which uses Request to Transmit and Clear to Transmit (RTS/CTS) messages to avoid the *hidden node problem* [128]; Power Aware Multi Access protocol with Signaling for Ad Hoc Networks (PAMAS) which use one channel for control packets and one channel for data packets; Carrier Sense Medium Access with Collision Avoidance (CSMA/CA).

The SMACS (Self-organizing Medium Access Control for Sensor Networks) protocol [215] uses a TDMA-like frame combined with FDMA CDMA to avoid interference among nodes. The *organized* channel access method used by SMACS and SFSN protocols can be traced back to several papers [23, 91] which propose to form a hierarchical structure to localize groups of nodes and make the channel assignment easier.

Several other TDMA-based MAC protocols for sensor networks have been proposed, including WLC12-5 [188]. Sensor MAC (S-MAC) is a protocol inspired by PAMAS and implemented over Berkeley Motes [252]. The nodes listen and sleep periodically; the radio is set to sleep during transmissions of other nodes. Neighboring nodes form virtual clusters to auto-synchronize on sleep schedules. The protocol divides long messages into small segments and transmits all segments back to back; it uses RTS/CTS once per message but ACK for each segment. The energy savings are 2.5 times larger than for IEEE 802.11.

To increase the algorithm efficiency, the number of collisions experienced by a sensor when it transmits should be minimized and a sensor should be idle as long as feasible. Thus, it is highly desirable to integrate the MAC protocol/algorithm with the algorithm for self-organization which determines the schedule for communication. This requirement precludes the use of one of the existing MAC algorithms; we decided to adapt a known CRA and integrate it with our self-organization scheme.

A fair number of CRAs for random multiple access are extensively analyzed in the literature [83]. The basic idea of the algorithms is to split recursively the set of nodes involved in a collision on a multiple-access channel until the cardinality of the set is equal to one and a single node successfully transmits. This splitting is based upon the ternary channel feedback, "Success," "Collision," or "Idle Slot." *Blocking* algorithms forbid new nodes to join the set of nodes involved in a collision; newcomers have to wait until the original collision was resolved and only then transmit. *Nonblocking* algorithms allow newcomers to join a game in progress. The Stack Algorithm also known as CTM (Capetanakis-Tsybakov-Mihailov) [225], Fig. 3.8A, is nonblocking.

The model of the multiaccess channel suitable for a sensor network is slightly more complicated than the one considered by traditional CRAs. First, the transmission frequency changes, and, most importantly, not all sensors involved in a collision are able to hear the channel feedback. The transmission range of the sensors is normally distributed around γ. It is thus possible that two sensors b and c both transmit in response to a request from sensor a, but they are outside of the reception range of each other, a phenomenon encountered in wireless networks and called *the hidden node problem* [128]. The version of the stack algorithm (Fig. 3.8B) differs from the original CTM algorithm in several ways:

1. The algorithm is executed only during the self-organization phase when collisions may occur.
2. During the self-organization phase, the duration of a slot is $\Delta = n_\delta \delta$ with δ the duration of a micro-slot and $n_\delta = \mathcal{O}(10^3)$. The time t_k of the event ϵ_k is the starting time of slot k and of its first micro-slot. The time between two consecutive events is determined by the random number generator, and should be at least Δ ($t_{k+1} - t_k \geq \Delta$). We expect a collision in slot k to be resolved well before the event ϵ_{k+1} as ($n_\delta = \mathcal{O}(10^3)$).
3. Only one sensor is allowed to transmit in the first micro-slot of a slot: the *sink* transmits during the first slot; the "winner" of a collision resolution contest during slot $(k - 1)$, transmits in slot k.
4. The micro-slots are grouped in pairs. Collisions may occur only in the even micro-slots of a slot. Odd micro-slots are collision-free and used by the sensor which initiated the CRI to broadcast the channel feedback. This allows us to address the hidden node problem. Indeed, two sensors b and c may be in the range of sensor a and may attempt to responding to a in micro-slot $2k$, but they may be out of each other's range. To solve this problem, a will broadcast in micro-slot $2k + 1$ the channel feedback and in this case report a collision.

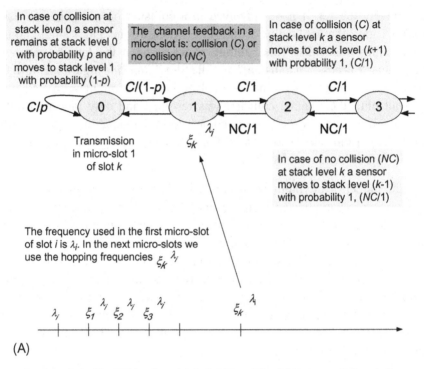

In case of collision at stack level 0 a sensor remains at stack level 0 with probability p and moves to stack level 1 with probability $(1-p)$

The channel feedback in a micro-slot is: collision (C) or no collision (NC)

In case of collision (C) at stack level k a sensor moves to stack level $(k+1)$ with probability 1, $(C/1)$

Transmission in micro-slot 1 of slot k

In case of no collision (NC) at stack level k a sensor moves to stack level $(k-1)$ with probability 1, $(NC/1)$

The frequency used in the first micro-slot of slot i is λ_i. In the next micro-slots we use the hopping frequencies $\xi_k \lambda_i$

(A)

Sensor **a** " wins"the CRI in micro-slot 6 of slot k and the right to transmit alone in the first micro-slot of slot $(k+1)$;then it conveys the channel feedback in odd micro-slots, 3, 5, 7, and 9. Collisions may occur only in even micro-slots; sensor **b** "wins" the CRI in the 8-th micro-slot of slot $(k+1)$and will transmit in micro-slot 1 of slot $(k+2)$

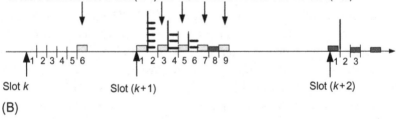

Slot k Slot $(k+1)$ Slot $(k+2)$

(B)

Fig. 3.8 (A) The stack collision resolution algorithm. Each sensor creates a virtual stack and once involved in a collision updates the stack based upon the channel feedback (collision/no-collision). Only sensors at stack level 0 are allowed to transmit during the collision resolution period. (B) Modified stack algorithm. The original sender conveys the channel feedback. In this case, sensor a transmits successfully in the 6th micro-slot of slot k and invites other sensors to transmit. Multiple sensors including b respond to the invitation; collisions involving sensor b occur in the micro-slots 2,4 and 6 of slot $(k + 1)$; finally, in micro-slot 8 sensor b is the only one allowed by the algorithm to transmit. Sensor a conveys the channel feedback in micro-slots 3,5,7, and in micro-slot 9 of slot $(k + 1)$ it announces that sensor b was successful and has won the right to transmit undisturbed in the first micro-slot of slot $(k + 2)$.

5. The algorithm is blocking, only the sensors involved in the initial collision are allowed to compete.
6. Each sensor involved in a collision maintains a counter of the micro-slots involved to determine the hopping frequency used to transmit in any micro-slot.

The algorithm is distributed in time and space; each sensor involved in a transmission maintains a virtual stack and updates it according to the channel feedback (Fig. 3.8A). The splitting algorithm guarantees that only one sensor can respond successfully in a CRI thus, the *Pid* of a sensor is unique. Only sensors at stack level 0 are allowed to transmit in any even micro-slot; initially, all sensors wishing to transmit in the second micro-slot of the slot k use frequency λ_k and set their stack level to 0. If there is a successful transmission (this happens when only one sensor transmits), then the CRI terminates after the sensor which transmitted in the first micro-slot announces the winner. If there is no transmission, one of the sensors sends a *ReqToForward* message in response to an "Idle Slot" channel feedback using the hopping frequency $\xi_1^{\lambda_k}$.

When multiple sensors transmit in one micro-slot, a collision occurs and all sensors update their stack as follows: remain at stack level 0 with probability p_s and move to stack level 1 with probability $(1 - p_s)$. It is likely that the cardinality of the set of sensors at stack level 0, allowed to transmit during the next pair of micro-slots will be smaller; these sensors use the first hopping frequency $\xi_1^{\lambda_i}$. The process continues; if a new collision occurs in the next pair of micro-slots, all sensors at stack level zero repeat the splitting process, while those at stack level 1 move to stack level 2 with probability one.

Self-organization phase. The role of the self-organization phase is to (a) allow all sensors to construct their proximity sets; and (b) establish the communication pattern between a sensor and the members of its proximity set during all activity slots.

Knowing the index k of the event ϵ_k does not mean that we know the time t_k of occurrence of the event. The times t_k are random, but all sensors can determine them, as they share the seeds for the random number generators used to calculate the times t_k.

During the self-organization phase, three types of messages are exchanged: *ReqToJoin* (RtJ), *ReqToForward* (RtF), and *AcceptToJoin* (AtJ). *ReqToJoin* expresses the desire of the sender to join the proximity set of one of its neighbors; *ReqToForward* signals that no neighbor is willing to accept the sender to join its proximity set and one of them forwards the message to others to keep the organization process going. A *ReqToForward* always contains the *Pid* of the originator of a *ReqToJoin* message, rather than the *Pid* of the sensor forwarding the message. An *AcceptToJoin* is sent in response to a *ReqToJoin*. Sensor σ_j uses two fitness functions f_j and g_j do determine how to respond to a successful transmission of a *ReqToJoin* from σ_i. f_j determines whether it should respond with an *AcceptToJoin* and g_j determines whether it should respond with a *ReqToForward*.

When σ_i includes in its proximity set a sensor with *Pid*=$\mathcal{I}_{sender}$ it also creates a counter of events when it has received messages from it, *Count*($\mathcal{I}_{sender}$), as well as an event index list *EventList*($\mathcal{I}_{sender}$), of size at most M (Fig. 3.5).

It follows that the storage requirements for control information for each sensor are: $\mu(2 + M)$ integers (Fig. 3.5). The self-organization algorithm followed by sensor σ_i with proximity set $\mathcal{P}(\sigma_i)$ and fitness functions f_i and g_i when σ_i observes a successful transmission in the slot of ϵ_k from $\mathcal{I}_{sender}$ is shown in Algorithm .

Occasionally, no sensor receiving a *ReqToJoin* is willing to respond (Fig. 3.9). In this example, sensor b responds to a *ReqToJoin* from a with an *AcceptToJoin* and a joins $\mathcal{P}(b)$ in slot k and b sends its own *ReqToJoin* in the first micro-slot of slot $(k + 1)$. After noticing an empty micro-slot in slot $(k + 1)$ sensor c which has its proximity set full, sends a *ReqToForward* which reaches sensor d; then d sends an *AcceptToJoin* and b joins $\mathcal{P}(d)$. Next d sends a *ReqToJoin* in slot $(k + 2)$ answered by e and the process continues, d joins $\mathcal{P}(e)$ and so on. This strategy allows the self-organization to continue even when sensors have their proximity sets full.

Activity phase. During an activity phase, the sensors carry out their monitoring function and report partial results. The schedule of events for each sensor, namely the slots when it transmitted successfully during the self-organization phase is known, and this knowledge allows each sensor to determine the slots during the activity phase when they have to wake-up to receive information and then transmit.

The event $\epsilon_{\overline{k}}$ in an activity phase is the reciprocal of the event ϵ_k in the self-organization phase; if sensor σ_i transmitted in the first micro-slot of slot k during the self-organization phase then it will be scheduled to wake-up and receive in slot $\overline{k-1}$ and then transmit in slot $\overline{k}$ where $\overline{k-1} = \kappa - k$.

Algorithm 3.1 The self-organization algorithm followed by sensor σ_i with proximity set $\mathcal{P}(\sigma_i)$

---

if f_i *returns True when receiving a message in one of the micro-slots of event k* **then**

    if $\mathcal{I}_{sender} \in \mathcal{P}(\sigma_i)$ **then**

        if $Count(\mathcal{I}_{sender}) \geq M$ **then**

            if *(g_i return True) and (no transmission at the first micro-slot of event $k+1$)* **then**

                broadcast RtF message at the second micro-slot of event $k+1$

            end

        else

            if *messageType is RtJ* **then**

                $Count(\mathcal{I}_{sender}) = Count(\mathcal{I}_{sender}) + 1$ insert k in $EventList(\mathcal{I}_{sender})$

            end

            transmit an AtJ message in the next micro-slot of slot k and follow the CRA **if** *transmission is successful* **then**

                add $\mathcal{I}_{sender}$ to $\mathcal{P}(\sigma_i)$, increment $Count(\mathcal{I}_{sender})$, insert k in $EventList(\mathcal{I}_{sender})$ broadcast RtJ message at the first micro-slot of event $k+1$

            end

        end

    else if $\mathcal{I}_{sender} \notin \mathcal{P}(\sigma_i)$ **then**

        if $|P(\sigma_i)| \geq \mu$ **then**

            if *(g_i return True) and (no transmission at the first micro-slot of event $k+1$)* **then**

                broadcast RtF message at the second micro-slot of event $k+1$

            end

        else

            transmit an AtJ message in the next micro-slot of event k and follow the CRA **if** *transmission is successful* **then**

                add $\mathcal{I}_{sender}$ to $\mathcal{P}(\sigma_i)$, increment $Count(\mathcal{I}_{sender})$, insert k in $EventList(\mathcal{I}_{sender})$ broadcast RtJ message at the first micro-slot of event $k+1$

            end

        end

    end

> **else if** f_i *returns False when receiving an incoming message* **then**
> > **if** *(g_i return True) and (no transmission at the first micro-slot of event $k + 1$)* **then**
> > > broadcast RtF message at the second micro-slot of event $k + 1$
> >
> > **end**
>
> **end**

The algorithm followed by sensor σ_i in the activity phase consists of the following steps:

- Compute the index of reciprocal events for all events included in the *EventList* for all members of $\mathcal{P}(\sigma_i)$.

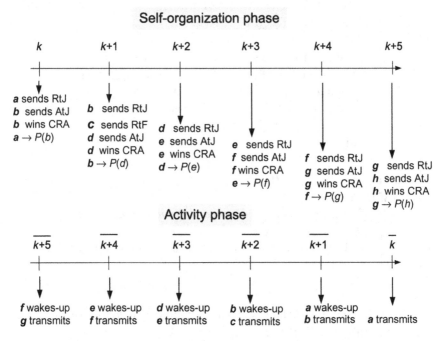

Fig. 3.9 *Handling of ReqToForward during the self-organization and activity phases. During the self-organization phase sensor b responds to a ReqToJoin from a with an AcceptToJoin and a joins $\mathcal{P}(b)$ in slot k and sends its own ReqToJoin in the first micro-slot of slot $(k + 1)$. After noticing an empty micro-slot in slot $(k + 1)$ sensor c which has its proximity set full, sends a ReqToForward which reaches sensor d; then d sends an AcceptToJoin and b joins $\mathcal{P}(d)$. Next d sends a ReqToJoin in slot $(k + 2)$ answered by e. During the activity phases sensors f, e, d, c, b, and a transmit in slots $\overline{k + 5}, \overline{k + 4}, \overline{k + 3}, \overline{k + 2}, \overline{k + 1}$, and $\overline{k}$, respectively, and the members of their respective proximity sets wake-up.*

- Construct an ordered list of reciprocal events.
- Determine the time of the next event when the sensor must wake up. Wake up and receive at that time. Compute the time of the next event and transmit at that time. Increment the count of events.
- Repeat the previous step until all reciprocal events, at most $\mu \times M$ of them, have been exhausted.

In the example in Fig. 3.9, during the self-organization phase the sensors a, b, c, d, e, f, and g transmit in slots $k, k + 1, k + 2, k + 3, k + 4$, and $k + 5$, respectively. During the activity phases sensors f, e, d, c, b, and a transmit in slots $\overline{k+5} = \kappa - k + 4, \overline{k+4} = \kappa - k + 3, \overline{k+3} = \kappa - k + 2, \overline{k+2} = \kappa - k + 1, \overline{k+1} = \kappa - k$, and $\overline{k} = \kappa - k - 1$, respectively, and the members of their respective proximity sets wake-up.

3.12 FURTHER READINGS ON LARGE-SCALE SYSTEMS AND SELF-ORGANIZATION

Alan Turing's seminal paper from 1952 [224] and John von Neumann's work on self-reproduced systems [235] provide insights in the self-organization process. Marvin Minsky [171] and Murray Gell-Mann [89, 90] have analyzed in depth the problems posed by self-organization of man-made systems.

The role of software as the "glue" for system composability is analyzed in [194] and system complexity metrics is discussed in [173]. Herbert Simon's contributions to the study of hierarchical organization are presented in [209, 210]. Autonomic computing principles have been formulated at IBM [134] and applied to the design of several systems, such as DB2 [69]. An analysis of the successes and problems faced by the autonomic computing movement can be found in [136, 137].

Theoretical studies of networks included the Erdös-Rény model [78], more recent work of Barabási and Albert in [9, 10, 29] and the discovery of Small-Worlds networks by Watts and Strogatz [244]. The "six degrees of separation" concept [170] is the most popular example of small-worlds. The properties of scale-free networks have been investigated in [54–56], [95], [223] and others.

Self-organization and its relation with coalition formation is discussed in [211]. Self-organization and its applications to computer systems are discussed in [93, 102, 103, 113, 114, 130]. Communication protocols used in mobile ah-hoc networks and in sensor networks are analyzed in [128].

The next chapter covers computer clouds, the challenges of resource management in systems consisting of millions of servers, current solutions, and self-management ideas for clouds.

CHAPTER 4

Computer Clouds

More than half a century ago, at the centennial anniversary of MIT, John McCarthy, the 1971 Turing Award recipient for his work in Artificial Intelligence, prophetically stated: "...If computers of the type I have advocated become the computers of the future, then computing may someday be organized as a public utility, just as the telephone system is a public utility...The computer utility could become the basis of a new and important industry." The McCarthy's prediction is now a technological and social reality.

In *utility computing* the hardware and the software resources are concentrated in large data centers and the users pay as they consume computing, storage, and communication resources. While utility computing often requires a cloud-like infrastructure, the focus of cloud computing is on the business model for providing computing services. Major IT companies such as Amazon, Google, IBM, Microsoft, Oracle, and others have been providing cloud computing services since 2006 when Amazon Web Services (AWS) services were offered for the first time.

The number of Cloud Service Providers (CSPs), the range of services offered by CSPs, and the number of cloud users have increased dramatically during the last few years. For example, in 2006 the EC2 (Elastic Cloud Computing) was the first service provided by AWS; 5 years later, in 2012, AWS was used by businesses in 200 countries. Another AWS service, S3 (Simple Storage Service), introduced also in 2006, has surpassed two trillion objects and routinely runs more than 1.1 million peak requests per second. The Elastic MapReduce has launched 5.5 million clusters since the start of the service in May 2010 (ZDNet 2013).

The infrastructure for supporting cloud services is continually growing. A recent posting on ZDNet reveals that in January 2012, EC2 was made up of 454,600 servers. When one adds the number of servers supporting other AWS services, then the total number of Amazon systems dedicated to cloud computing is much larger. An unofficial estimation puts the number of

Complex Systems and Clouds. http://dx.doi.org/10.1016/B978-0-12-804041-6.00004-9

servers used by Google in January 2012 close to 1.8 million; this number was expected to be close to 2.4 million by the early 2013.

Computer clouds are not usually considered to be cyber-physical systems, i.e., integrations of computation, networking, and physical processes, even though cloud applications as data streaming and cloud-based gaming have real-time constraints and may involve physical processes. It is not inconceivable that the range of cloud applications will, sooner rather than later, include cyber-physical systems, ubiquitous components of the Internet of Things. Applications in traffic management in smart cities, optimal energy management in smart power grids, carbon-emission and pollution control, or out-patient monitoring in health-care systems could also become part of the computing cloud ecosystem.

It seems obvious that managing such a complex infrastructure operating in a dynamic environment requires new thinking; traditional methods very successful for clusters and other small-scale assembly of systems cannot possibly be good enough. Self-organization seems to be one of the more promising alternatives to traditional, deterministic management mechanisms based on centralized or distributed control. How can self-organization be applied to computer clouds and why has it not been already implemented more than a decade after the autonomic computing manifesto? These are some of the questions addressed in this chapter.

4.1 A DOWN-TO-EARTH VIEW OF CLOUDS

Many CSPs are large IT companies actively involved in the development of new computing, storage, and communication technologies for many years. These companies use the latest technologies for their cloud infrastructure and motivate the other CSPs to follow suit. It is thus, fair to say that cloud computing is driven by the most recent advances in the field of computing and communication.

We now take a closer look at the defining attributes of the new philosophy for delivering computing services. Some of these attributes reflect the attractions of the new model for service delivery, others for the organization of the infrastructure which ensures the success of the business model. These attributes are:

- Cloud computing uses Internet technologies to offer elastic services.
- The resources used for cloud services are metered and the users are charged only for the resources they used.

- The maintenance and the security are ensured by service providers.
- Economy of scale allows CSPs to operate more efficiently due to specialization and centralization.
- To reduce maintenance costs, the cloud infrastructure typically uses the same family of hardware and similar software.
- Cloud computing is cost-effective due to resource multiplexing; lower costs for the service provider are passed on to the cloud users.
- The application data is stored closer to the site where it is used in a device- and location-independent manner.

The term "elastic computing" refers to the ability of dynamically acquiring computing resources and supporting a variable workload. A CSP maintains a massive infrastructure to support elastic services. Such a massive infrastructure requires a large initial investment, periodic updates of the servers and of the network components, and last, but not least, high electric bills and large maintenance costs, see Section 4.5.

Data replication increases reliability and security. Keeping the data close to the sites where it is needed lowers communication costs and the access time. Resource multiplexing can increase the average server utilization; the peak demands for CPU, memory, and I/O of several applications running on the same server typically occur at different times and lead to higher average server utilization.

Software and hardware *homogeneity* was typical for cloud infrastructure until recently. In the last few years, servers with attached co-processors such as GPUs (Graphic Processing Units) and FPGAs (Field-Programmable Gate Arrays) have been added to multicore processors. GPUs are particularly useful for multimedia applications, computational science, and engineering applications relying heavily on vector processing. Some of the servers use processors with multimedia extensions, e.g., AVX-512[1] to support vector processing. Increased cloud heterogeneity adds to the challenges faced by the Cloud Resource Management (CRM) system.

The ownership of the cloud infrastructure and the access to cloud services differ for public, private, hybrid, and community clouds. The infrastructure of *public clouds* is owned by an organization selling cloud services and it is made available to the general public and to large organizations.

---

[1] AVX-512 expands Advanced Vector Extension (AVX) to 512-bit support utilizing a new EVEX prefix encoding proposed by Intel in July 2013 and first supported by Intel with the Knights Landing processor scheduled to ship in 2015.

The infrastructure of *private clouds* is owned and operated solely by one organization and offers services only to the members of this organization. The organization could be a company, a research facility, or any other large institution with significant computing needs and sufficient resources to maintain the computing and communication infrastructure. *Hybrid clouds* consists of two or more private and public clouds sharing a set of common standards to support data and application portability. Lastly, the infrastructure of *community clouds* is shared by several organizations and supports a specific community of users.

Our discussion is focused on public clouds which offer services to a large user community. This is a pure form of utility computing where users have access to as much resources as they need and pay only for the resources they have consumed. This computing paradigm is extremely attractive for individual users. It is also attractive for large organizations as it frees them from maintaining their own IT infrastructure, a very costly proposition.

Fig. 4.1 presents the defining attributes, the resources, and the organization of the cloud infrastructure, as well as the cloud delivery models discussed in Section 4.2. The cloud infrastructure is distributed across multiple data centers. Resource virtualization discussed in Section 4.3 supports a more effective server sharing by allowing application migration,

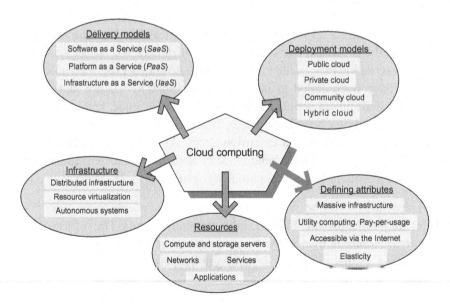

Fig. 4.1 Cloud computing: delivery models, deployment models, defining attributes, resources, and organization of the infrastructure. From D.C. Marinescu, Cloud Computing: Theory and Practice, Morgan Kaufmann, Waltham, MA, 2013.

and a better isolation of applications sharing a server. At the same time, virtualization negatively affects application performance and security and increases the complexity of the system software.

Cloud computing has changed the thinking about computing as discussed in Section 4.3. Still, major challenges for cloud computing exist in the area of security and resource management. In spite of low cost access to a large pool of computing resources, cloud computing requires a leap of faith; individuals and companies are sometimes reluctant to trust others with their data and proprietary information.

4.2 CLOUD DELIVERY MODELS

A cloud delivery model specifies the capabilities offered to users and the applications supported. There are three basic cloud delivery models, Software as a Service (*SaaS*), Platform as a Service (*PaaS*), and Infrastructure as a Service (*IaaS*).

SaaS clients use applications supplied by the service provider. *SaaS* does not allow any control of the cloud platform or the infrastructure. *PaaS* users can deploy consumer-created or acquired applications using programming languages and tools supported by the CSP. *IaaS* allows a more sophisticated user to deploy and run arbitrary software, including operating systems and applications. The internal organization of the cloud infrastructure is different for the three delivery models.

Fig. 4.2 represents the organization and the structure of the three delivery models, SaaS, PaaS, and IaaS, according to the Cloud Security Alliance (https://cloudsecurityalliance.org/). The system software for the *IaaS* delivery model is the most complex, but offers the highest degree of user flexibility and is useful for application developers, as well as users of existing applications. Its main appeal is access to a very large pool of computing resources needed for Big Data applications. On the other hand, *SaaS* does not require any computing skills. Many *SaaS* applications are online transaction processing systems (OLTP). Some store user information and have to use additional precautions to guard against unauthorized access. This is the case of email, banking, and other commercial applications.

SaaS—applications are supplied by the CSP. The applications are accessible from various client devices through a thin client interface, such as a web browser (e.g., web-based email). The user does not manage or control the underlying cloud infrastructure including network, servers, operating

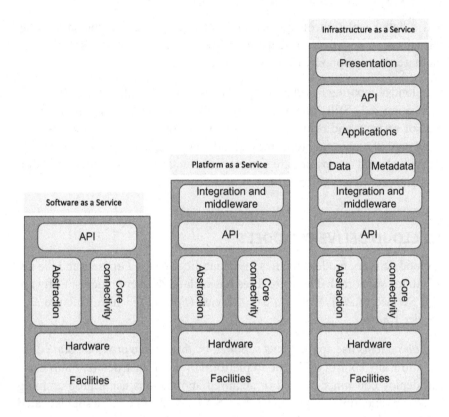

Fig. 4.2 The structure and the organization of the three delivery models, SaaS, PaaS, and IaaS [161]. SaaS services are accessed by using a thin client. PaaS supports applications designed and built under strict control of the CSP. IaaS offers a user-friendly and flexible access to computing resources. From D.C. Marinescu, Cloud Computing: Theory and Practice, Morgan Kaufmann, Waltham, MA, 2013.

systems, storage, or even individual application capabilities, with the possible exception of limited user-specific application configuration settings.

SaaS includes enterprise services such as workflow management, groupware and collaborative, supply chain, communications, digital signature, customer relationship management (CRM), desktop software, financial management, geo-spatial, and search. Another group of *SaaS* are Web 2.0 applications such as: metadata management, social networking, blogs, wiki services, and portal services. The most likely candidates for *SaaS* are applications when:

- Many competitors use the same product, such as email.
- Periodically there is a significant peak in demand, such as billing and payroll.

- There is a need for the web or mobile access, such as mobile sales management software.
- There is only a short-term need, such as collaborative software for a project.

PaaS delivery model is used for consumer-created or acquired applications using programming languages and tools supported by the provider. The end-user does not manage or control the underlying cloud infrastructure including network, servers, operating systems, or storage. The end-user has control over the applications at run time and, possibly, on the configuration of the execution environment. Such services include session management, device integration, sandboxes, instrumentation and testing, contents management, knowledge management, and Universal Description, Discovery, and Integration (UDDI), a platform-independent, Extensible Markup Language (XML)-based registry providing a mechanism to register and locate web service applications.

PaaS is not particularly useful when the application must be portable, when proprietary programming languages are used, or when the underlying hardware and software must be customized to improve the performance of the application. Its major application areas are in software development when multiple developers and users collaborate and the deployment and testing services are automated.

IaaS offers the ability to provision processing, storage, networks, and other fundamental computing resources; the consumer is able to deploy and run arbitrary software, which can include operating systems and applications. The consumer does not manage or control the underlying cloud infrastructure, but has control over operating systems, storage, deployed applications, and possibly limited control of some networking compo-nents, e.g., host firewalls. Services offered by this delivery model include: server hosting, web servers, storage, computing hardware, operating sys-tems, virtual instances, load balancing, Internet access, and bandwidth provisioning.

The *IaaS* cloud computing delivery model has a number of characteris-tics such as: the resources are distributed and support dynamic scaling, it is based on a utility pricing model and variable cost, and the hardware is shared among multiple users. This cloud computing model is particularly useful when the demand is volatile and a new business needs computing resources and it does not want to invest in a computing infrastructure, or when an organization is expanding rapidly.

4.3 HOW CLOUDS CHANGED OUR THINKING ABOUT COMPUTING

The infrastructure of computer clouds uses the latest computing and communication technology and, as expected, had a profound impact on both the hardware and the software developments in recent years. Our computing systems have evolved from single processors, to multiprocessors, to multi-core multiprocessors, clusters, and now Warehouse-scale Computers (WSC) controlled by increasingly more complex software stacks.

Built with inexpensive off-the-shelf components to deliver cheap computing cycles, the millions of servers operating in today's data centers are capable of delivering the computing power necessary to solve problems that previously could only be solved by large supercomputers assembled from expensive, one-of-a-kind components. The scale of the cloud infrastructure, combined with the relatively low mean-time to failure of the off-the-shelf components used to assemble a WSC, make the task of ensuring reliable services quite challenging.

At the same time, long-running cloud services require a very high degree of availability. For example, a 99.99% availability means that the services can only be down for less than 1 hour/year. Only a fair level of hardware redundancy combined with software support for error detection and recovery can ensure such a level of availability [110]. Software helps integrate a very large number of system components and contributes to the challenge of ensuring efficient and reliable operation as discussed in Section 3.2.

New services, which hide from the end-user some of the intricacies of parallel and distributed computing, facilitate access to cloud resources. For example, to deal with Big Data applications, new AWS services such as Map-Reduce and Elastic BeanStalk provide automatic support for concurrent execution and automate the execution of complex workflows.

Processor virtualization, running multiple independent instances of one or more Operating Systems (OS), pioneered by IBM in the early 1970s, was revived for computer clouds. Running multiple *Virtual Machines* (VMs) allows multiple applications to better share the resources of a server and achieve a better processor utilization. The instantaneous demands for resources of the applications running concurrently are likely to be different or complement each other, and the idle time of the server is reduced.

This form of processor virtualization by multiplexing is beneficial for both users and CSPs. Cloud users appreciate virtualization because it allows a better isolation of applications from one another than the traditional process sharing model. Another advantage is that an application developer can chose to develop the application in a familiar environment and under the OS of her choice. Virtualization also provides more freedom for the system resource management because VMs can be easily migrated. The VM migration proceeds as follows: the VM is stopped, its state is saved as a file, the file is transported to another server, and the VM is restarted.

On the other hand, virtualization contributes to increased complexity of the system software and has undesirable side effects on application performance and security. Processor sharing is now controlled by a new layer of software, the *Virtual Machine Monitor* (VMM), also called a *hypervisor*. It is often argued that a VMM is a more compact software with only a few hundred thousand lines of code versus the million lines of code of a typical OS, thus, it is less likely to be faulty. Unfortunately, though the footprint of the VMM is small, the server must run a management OS. For example, *Xen*, the VMM used by AWS and others, starts initially *Dom0*, a privileged domain that starts and manages the *DomU* unprivileged domains. *Dom0* runs the Xen management toolstack, is able to access the hardware directly, and provides Xen virtual disks and network access for guests.

Sharing has a negative effect on the application performance. System calls cannot be executed by the OS of a VM, but are trapped and executed only under the control of the VMM. Sharing has multiple effects on security. One of the more severe effects is that OS security patches cannot be applied to a VM archived as a file; when activated, the old version of OS will run. To make matters even worse, if the archived file is infected by a virus, then the virus will spread to other servers when the VM is activated.

Clouds support computing services for the masses. Anyone can have at her fingertips the massive computing infrastructure of the AWS, while only a few highly qualified individuals working on very important problems in science and engineering had access to supercomputers in the past. Moreover, a large segment of the population uses cloud services for electronic mail, or for data streaming. Indeed, several years ago, Netflix partnered with AWS to deliver content to millions of movie viewers.

Anyone with little or no knowledge about computing should be able to use *SaaS* cloud services; this is expected, the same way as few users

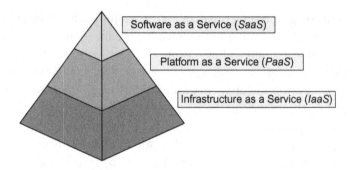

Fig. 4.3 Challenges posed by the three cloud delivery model and the control of cloud resources [161]. At the base of the pyramid, IaaS, is the most challenging, but offers the user the highest degree of control over cloud resources. The user is allowed to develop her own application and run it under the OS of her choice, provided that the OS is supported by the ISP. At the top of the pyramid SaaS is the least challenging, but does not offer any control over cloud resources, the user has access to a running application developed and installed by the CSP. From D.C. Marinescu, Cloud Computing: Theory and Practice, Morgan Kaufmann, Waltham, MA, 2013.

of the telephone system are experts in fiber optic communication or few drivers of cars with internal combustion engines understand the laws of thermodynamics. On the other hand, cloud computing poses serious challenges to software developers of applications using the *IaaS* cloud delivery model, e.g., AWS.

When we increased the computing power available to applications, at every step along the way we have also increased the complexity of the system, as well as that of the application software. Often, a cloud user is encouraged to develop new algorithms for data partitioning and concurrent processing. Fig. 4.3 allegorically depicts the three cloud delivery models and challenges they pose.

The software developers for cloud applications are faced with massive amounts of data and the need to process it in parallel to reduce the computing time. One of the greatest challenges is to optimize the application execution time without actually knowing the precise location where the instance or instances of the application run. The actual assignment of an instance is controlled by an automated component of the CRM system. This lack of transparency allows the system to optimize its overall performance, but at a price the users have to pay.

Cloud computing is a social and economic reality built on the belief that large-scale systems can deliver computing and storage services cheaply and operate securely and reliably. None of the components of this trust vector are fully supported by existing clouds; security incidents occur, data has been compromised, and cloud computing sites have been down for shorter or longer periods of time. Due to the scale of the system and the size of the user population, any security breach has devastating effects; the down time of a cloud infrastructure could affect millions of users. To ensure that computing clouds do not become victims of their own success, we should expect transformational changes in this field. One of these transformational changes could be application of self-organization principles to cloud computing.

4.4 HIERARCHICAL ORGANIZATION: WAREHOUSE-SCALE COMPUTERS

Cloud computing had an impact on the architecture of large-scale systems. The Warehouse-Scale Computers [27, 110] form the backbone of the cloud infrastructure of Google, Amazon, and other CSPs. WSCs are hierarchically organized systems with 50,000–100,000 processors capable of exploiting request-level and data-level parallelism.

Request-level parallelism is typical for transaction-oriented systems designed to support a very large user population, as well as requests rates of million transactions per second. Many interactive cloud applications such as email and a wide range of mobile applications, are based on the *SaaS* delivery model. Transactions are a form of request-response communication where a client generates the request, the request travels to the cloud, the cloud responds, and the response travels back to the client. *Data-level parallelism* is exploited by another important class of cloud applications. Data analytics and other batch applications based on the *IaaS* and *PaaS* delivery models process very large volumes of data. The data is partitioned in blocks which are then processed in parallel, see, for example, the Map-Reduce service [161] supported by AWS and others. The ability to effectively process both interactive and batch applications is critical for the cloud infrastructure.

At the heart of a WSC is a hierarchy of networks which connect the system components, servers, racks, and cells/arrays, together as in Fig. 4.4. Typically, a rack consists of 48 servers interconnected by a 48 port, 10 Gbps Ethernet (GE) switch. In addition to the 48 ports, the GE switch has two to eight uplink ports connecting a rack to a cell. Thus, the level of *oversubscription*, the ratio of internal to external ports, is between $48/8 = 6$ and $48/2 = 24$. This has serious implications on the performance of an

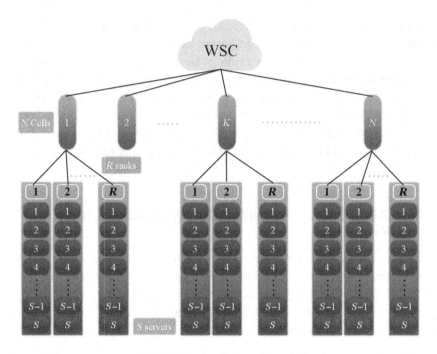

Fig. 4.4 The organization of a WSC with N cells, R racks, and S servers per rack.

application; two processes running on servers in the same rack have a much larger bandwidth and lower latency than the same processes running on servers in different racks.

The next component is a cell, sometimes called an array, consisting of a number of racks. The racks in a cell are connected by an array switch, a rather expensive communication hardware with a cost two orders of magnitude higher than that of the rack switch. The cost is justified by the fact that the bandwidth of a switch with n ports is of the order n^2 therefore, to support a 10 times larger bandwidth, for 10 times as many ports, the cost increases by a factor of 10^2. An array switch can support up to 30 racks.

WSCs support both interactive and batch workloads. The communication latency and the bandwidth within a server, a rack, and a cell are different, thus, the execution time and the costs for running an application is affected by the volume of data, the placement of data, and by the proximity of instances. For example, the latency, the bandwidth, and the capacity of the memory hierarchy of a WSC with 80 servers/rack and 30 racks/cell is shown in Table 4.1 based on the data from [27].

Table 4.1 The Memory Hierarchy of a WSC

Location	DRAM			Disk		
type	Latency	Bandwidth	Capacity	Latency	Bandwidth	Capacity
Local	0.1	20,000	16	10,000	200	2,000
Rack	100	100	1040	11,000	100	160,000
Array	3,000	10	31,200	12,000	10	4,800,000

The latency in microseconds, the bandwidth in MB/sec, and the capacity in GB. From L.A. Barossso, J. Clidaras, U. Hözle, The Datacenter as a Computer: An Introduction to the Design of Warehouse-Scale Machines, second ed., Morgan & Claypool, 2013.

The DRAM latency increases by more than three orders of magnitude, while the bandwidth decreases by a similar factor. The latency and the bandwidth of the disks follow the same trend, but the variation is less dramatic. To put this in perspective, the memory-to-memory transfer of 1,000 MB takes 50 msec within a server, 10 seconds within the rack, and 100 seconds within a cell, while the transfers between disks take 5, 10, and 100 seconds, respectively.

WSCs, though expected to supply cheap computing cycles, are by no means inexpensive; the cost of a WSC is of the order of $150 million, but the cost-performance is what makes them appealing. The capital expenditures for a WSC include the costs for servers, for the interconnect, and for the facility. A case study reported in [110] shows a capital expenditure of $167,510,000, including $66,700,00 for 45,978 servers, $12,810,000 for an interconnect with 1,150 rack switches, 22 cell switches, 2 layer 3 switches, and 2 border routers. In addition to the initial investment, the operation cost of the cloud infrastructure including the cost of energy is significant. In this case study the facility is expected to use 8 MW.

4.5 ENERGY CONSUMPTION, ELASTICITY, AND OVER-PROVISIONING

Cloud energy consumption is a complex subject extensively discussed in the literature [3, 15, 26, 28, 161, 230]. Some of the problems posed by the optimization of cloud energy consumption discussed in [165] are presented next.

The costs for maintaining the cloud computing infrastructure are significant. A large fraction of these costs are for data center heating and cooling, and for powering the servers and the interconnection networks.

It was predicted that by 2012 up to 40% of the budget of IT enterprise infrastructure would be spent on energy. While most of the power for large data centers, including cloud computing data centers, comes from power stations burning fossil fuels such as coal and gas, in recent years the contribution of solar, wind, geothermal, and other renewable energy sources has steadily increased.

Energy efficiency, the work done per Joule of energy affects the cost of cloud services. The energy costs are passed down to the users of cloud services and differ from one country to another and from one region to another. For example, the costs for cloud computing services in two AWS regions, US East and South America are, respectively: upfront for a year $2,604 versus $5,632 and hourly $0.412 versus $0.724. Higher energy and communication costs are responsible for the significant difference in this example; the energy costs for the two regions differ by about 40%.

Cloud elasticity and over-provisioning. One of the main appeals of the utility computing is cloud elasticity. *Elasticity* means that additional resources are guaranteed to be allocated when an application needs them and these resources will be released when they are no longer needed. The user ends up paying only for the resources actually used.

Elasticity is based on *over-provisioning* and on the assumption that there is an effective admission control mechanism. Another assumption is that the likelihood of all running applications dramatically increasing their resource consumption at the same time is extremely low. This assumption is realistic, though we have seen cases when a system is overloaded due to concurrent access by large crowds, e.g., the phone system in the case of a catastrophic event such as an earthquake. A possible solution is to request cloud users to specify in their service request the type of workloads and to pay for access accordingly, e.g., a low rate for slow varying and a high rate for workloads with sudden peaks.

Over-provisioning means that a CSP has to invest in a larger infrastructure than the *typical* cloud workload warrants. It follows that the average cloud server utilization is low [3, 37, 161]; the low server utilization negatively affects the common measure of energy efficiency, the performance per Watt of power, and the ecological impact of cloud computing. Over-provisioning is not economically sustainable [47].

Reduction of energy consumption thus, of the carbon footprint of cloud related activities, is increasingly more important for the society. Indeed, more and more applications run on clouds and cloud computing uses more energy than many other human-related activities. Reduction of the carbon footprint of large data centers can only be achieved through a comprehensive set of technical efforts. The hardware of the cloud infrastructure has to be refreshed periodically and new and more energy efficient technologies have to be adopted; the resource management software has to pay more attention to energy optimization.

Energy proportional systems and server utilization. In an ideal world, the energy consumed by an idle system should be near zero and should grow linearly with the system load. In real life, even systems whose power requirements scale linearly, when idle, use more than half the power they use at full load [3]. Indeed, a 2.5 GHz Intel E5200 dual-core desktop processor with 2 GB of RAM consumes 70 W when idle and 110 W when fully loaded; a 2.4 GHz Intel Q6600 processor with 4 GB of RAM consumes 110 W when idle and 175 W when fully loaded [28].

An *energy-proportional system* is one when the amount of energy used is proportional to the load of the system. Different subsystems of a computing system behave differently in terms of energy efficiency; while many processors have reasonably good energy-proportional profiles, significant improvements in memory and disk subsystems are necessary. The processors used in servers consume less than one-third of their peak power at very low load and have a dynamic range of more than 70% of peak power; the processors used in mobile and/or embedded applications are better in this respect.

The dynamic power range of other components of a system is much narrower [26]: less than 50% for DRAM, 25% for disk drives, and 15% for networking switches. The power consumption of such devices is: 4.9 kW for a 604.8 TB, HP 8100 EVA storage server, 3.8 kW for the 320 Gbps Cisco 6509 switch, 5.1 kW for the 660 Gbps Juniper MX-960 gateway router [28]. A number of proposals have emerged for energy proportional networks; the energy consumed by such networks is proportional with the communication load. For example, a data center network based on a flattened butterfly topology is more energy and cost-efficient [3].

Energy use and ecological impact of large data centers. The metric used to evaluate the energetic efficiency of a WSC or of a datacenter is the *power utilization effectiveness (PUE)*. PUE is the ratio of the total power utilized by the facility over the power used by the IT equipment.

A conservative estimation of the electric energy used now by the Information and Communication Technology (ICT) ecosystem is about 1,500 TWh of energy, 10% of the electric energy generated in the entire world. This includes energy used for manufacturing electronic components and computing and communication systems, for powering, heating, and cooling IT systems, and for recycling and disposing of obsolete IT equipment. ICT energy consumption equals the total electric energy used for illumination in 1985 and represents the total electric energy generated in Japan and Germany.

The energy consumption of large-scale data centers and their costs for energy used for computing and networking and for cooling are significant now and are expected to increase substantially in the future. In 2006, the 6,000 data centers in the United States reportedly consumed 61×10^9 kWh of energy, 1.5% of all electricity consumption in the country, at a cost of $4.5 billion [230]. The predictions were dire: the energy consumed by the data centers in the United States was expected to double from 2006 to 2011; peak instantaneous demand was expected to increase from 7 GW in 2006 to 12 GW in 2011, requiring the construction of 10 new power plants. The energy consumption of data centers and the network infrastructure is predicted to reach 10,300 TWh/year in 2030, based on 2010 levels of efficiency [230].

According to Moore's Law, the number of transistors on a chip thus, the computing power of microprocessors doubles approximately every 1.5 years. A recent study [140] reports that electrical efficiency of computing doubles also about every 1.5 years. Thus, performance growth rate and improvements in electrical efficiency almost cancel each out. It follows that the energy use for computing scales linearly with the number of computing devices.

The power consumption required by different types of human activities is partially responsible for the greenhouse gas emissions. The greenhouse gas emission due to the data centers is estimated to increase from 116 megatons of CO_2 in 2007 to 257 megatons in 2020 due primarily to increased consumer demand [230].

Energy-aware application scaling. Scaling is the process of allocating additional resources to a cloud application in response to a request consistent with the SLA. We distinguish two scaling modes, horizontal and vertical scaling. *Horizontal scaling* is the most common mode of scaling on a cloud; it is done by increasing the number of Virtual Machines (VMs) when the load of applications increases and reducing this number when the load decreases. Load balancing is critical for this mode of operation. *Vertical scaling* keeps the number of VMs of an application constant, but increases the amount of resources allocated to each one of them. This can be done either by migrating the VMs to more powerful servers, or by keeping the VMs on the same servers, but increasing their share of the server capacity. The first alternative involves additional overhead; the VM is stopped, a snapshot of the state of the VM is taken, the file is migrated to a more powerful server, and the VM is restarted at the new site.

The alternative to the wasteful resource management policy when the servers are *always on*, regardless of their load, is to develop *energy-aware load balancing and scaling* policies. Such policies combine *dynamic power management* with load balancing and attempt to identify servers operating outside their optimal energy regime, and decide if and when they should be switched to a sleep state or what other actions should be taken to optimize the energy consumption.

Energy optimization is an important policy for Cloud Resourced Management (CRM), but it cannot be considered in isolation, it has to be coupled with admission control, capacity allocation, load balancing, and quality of service. Existing mechanisms cannot support concurrent optimization of all the policies. Mechanisms based on a solid foundation, such as control theory are too complex and do not scale well, those based on machine learning are not fully developed, and the others require a model of a system with a dynamic configuration operating in a fast-changing environment. We believe that the most likely to succeed are market-based mechanisms discussed in Section 4.8.

4.6 CLOUD RESOURCE MANAGEMENT POLICIES AND MECHANISMS

The policies for CRM can be loosely grouped into five classes: (1) admission control; (2) capacity allocation; (3) load balancing; (4) energy optimization; and (5) quality of service (QoS) guarantees.

The explicit goal of an *admission control* policy is to prevent the system from accepting workload in violation of high-level system policies [102]. A system should not accept additional workload if this would prevent it from completing work already in progress or contracted. Limiting the workload requires some knowledge of the global state of the system.

Capacity allocation means to allocate resources for individual instances. An instance is an activation of a service on behalf of a cloud user. Locating resources subject to multiple global optimization constraints requires a search in a very large search space. Capacity allocation is more challenging when the state of individual servers changes rapidly.

Load balancing and *energy optimization* are correlated and affect the cost of providing the services; they can be done locally, but global load balancing and energy optimization policies encounter the same difficulties as the capacity allocation [144]. *Quality of service* (QoS) is probably the most challenging aspect of resource management and, at the same time, possibly the most critical for the future of cloud computing.

Resource management policies must be based on a disciplined approach, rather than ad hoc methods. The basic mechanisms for the implementation of these policies are:

Control theory. Control theory uses the feedback to guarantee system stability and to predict transient behavior [144], but can be used only to predict local, rather than global behavior; applications of control theory to resource allocation are covered in [77]. Kalman filters have been used for unrealistically simplified models as reported in [130].

Machine learning. A major advantage of machine learning techniques is that they do not need a performance model of the system. This technique could be applied for coordination of several autonomic system managers as discussed in [135].

Utility-based. Utility-based approaches require a performance model and a mechanism to correlate user-level performance with cost [136].

Market mechanisms. Auction models, such as the one discussed in [218], cost-utility models, or macroeconomic models are an intriguing alternative and have been the focus of research in recent years.

To our knowledge, none of the optimal or near-optimal methods to address the five classes of policies scale up, thus, there is a need to develop novel strategies for resource management in a computer cloud. Typically, these methods target a single aspect of resource management, e.g., admission control, but ignore energy conservation; many require very complex computations that cannot be done effectively in the time available to respond.

Performance models required by some of the methods are very complex, analytical solutions are intractable, and the monitoring systems used to gather state information for these models can be too intrusive and unable to provide accurate data. Many techniques are concentrated on system performance in terms of throughput and time in system, but they rarely include energy trade-offs or QoS guarantees. Some techniques are based on unrealistic assumptions; for example, capacity allocation is viewed as an optimization problem, but under the assumption that servers are protected from overload.

Virtually all mechanisms for the implementation of the resource management policies require the presence of a few systems which monitor and control the entire cloud, while the large majority of systems run applications and store data; some of these mechanisms require a two-level control, one at the cloud level and one at the application level. The strategies for resource management associated with *IaaS*, *PaaS*, and *SaaS* will be different, but in all cases the providers are faced with large fluctuating loads.

In some cases, when a spike can be predicted, `the resources can be provisioned in advance, e.g., for Web services subject to seasonal spikes. For an unplanned spike, the situation is slightly more complicated. Auto-scaling can be used for unplanned spike loads provided that: (a) there is a pool of resources that can be released or allocated on demand and (b) there is a monitoring system which allows a control loop to decide in real time to reallocate resources. Auto-scaling is supported by *PaaS* services, such as Google App Engine. Auto-scaling for *IaaS* is complicated due to the lack of standards; the Open Cloud Computing Interface (OCCI), an organization within Open Grid Forum (OGF) is involved in the definition of virtualization formats and APIs for *IaaS*. Challenges and opportunities for automated resource allocation in computer clouds are also discussed in [151, 220].

4.7 CLOUD RESOURCE MANAGEMENT SYSTEMS

In this section we review existing CRM systems used by several CSPs. Google uses systems such as Borg [226] and Omega [197] for cluster management in its cloud infrastructure. Amazon and Google support the creation of Docker-based containers which allow cloud users to run their applications in a resource-isolated manner.

Docker is an open-source, lightweight containerization platform that automates the process of deploying applications [14, 94]. Docker containers wrap up a software module in a complete filesystem that contains everything it needs to run: code, runtime, system tools, system libraries. This guarantees that it will always run the same, regardless of the environment it is running in. Containers have similar resource isolation and allocation benefits as VMs, but a different architectural approach allows them to be much more portable and efficient.

Kubernetes, is a system developed at Google for managing containerized applications across a cluster of nodes [143]. Twitter's infrastructure is managed by Mesos [116]. A storage management system used by VMware is described in [228].

A 12,000-server Google cluster, managed with the Borg system, achieves aggregate CPU utilization of 25–35% and aggregate memory utilization of 40% [70]. The aggregate CPU utilization of systems using Mesos is consistently below 20%, even though reservations reach up to 80% of system capacity. The Qasar system developed at Stanford University improves resource utilization in a 200-server EC2 cluster by 47% [70].

Existing systems can manage clusters with tens of thousands servers but the challenges outlined earlier in this chapter persist and motivate the search for effective and scalable policies and mechanisms for CRM [43, 46, 84, 150, 167, 176, 195, 245]. To respond to the needs of increasingly more complex applications consisting of multiple phases and requiring workflow management, CSPs are already offering workflow management services such as AWS Simple Workflow Management (SWS) and Elastic Bean Stock (EBS).

4.8 MARKET MECHANISMS FOR CLOUD RESOURCE MANAGEMENT

Many countries in the world enjoy a free-market economy where prices are based on unrestricted competition among independent suppliers and consumers of goods and services. Suppliers aim to maximize their profits and consumers look for the best quality at the lowest price. It was John Nash, who in 1951 established an important theoretical result for market economics, the *Nash equilibrium* [180]. Nash equilibrium states that in noncooperative games, a stable state occurs when no player has an incentive to deviate from her strategy after considering the choices of her opponents. This stable state may, or may not, exist and is different from a global optimal state. Noncooperative games model interactions in a market economy.

Market mechanisms are scalable and self-regulating. When the demand exceeds the supply, the price increases and when the supply is larger than the demand, the price of goods and services decrease. It is thus, not surprising that the application of market mechanisms to computer resource allocation has been researched since the early 1960s when large timeshared systems such as Multics [58] were designed. Initially, the goal of market mechanisms was to maximize the utilization of scarce computing resources. For many years the research continued to be focused on global optimization of system-centric metrics such as mean average job completion time, throughput, and system utilization [48].

The evolution of computing infrastructure from single timeshared systems to clusters, to grids, and now to clouds, increased progressively the level of resource sharing and broadened the scope of research in this area. The increased quantity of resources, the increased number of users, the broader spectrum of applications, all point out to more complex demands for market mechanisms. Cloud applications have different requirements, some applications have higher priorities than the others, users are willing to pay different prices for services, and resource management policies have to address complex social policies [204]. The interest in the application of market mechanisms for resource management in computer systems is illustrated by a substantial body of research including [48, 157, 158, 163, 204, 212, 218].

The following discussion is pertinent to *IaaS* cloud delivery model, where the user has some degree of control over the resources and to a lesser extent, to the *PaaS* cloud delivery model. All *SaaS* applications are supported by the CSP, the only choice a user has is to use or not use a particular application.

Market mechanisms should optimize not only system centric measures, but also user value. Utility computing and, implicitly cloud computing, have a clear advantage in this respect because the system does not have to infer what is the social value of resource consumption or whether an application is more valuable than another. The utility for the user is reflected by the price she agrees to pay for services. To ensure a fair market for a large user community, a cloud should offer different types of services at different prices.

Market mechanisms pose their own challenges to system designers. To avoid the tragedy of the commons [105] when one application's use of resources prevents others from running, the markets mechanisms should ensure *performance isolation*, a nontrivial, but necessary requirement. Occasionally, the demand could exceed the supply thus, *admission control* is also necessary to limit the access to services. Last, but not least, users may request *packages of resources* of different types and use them concurrently, or at different times.

When resources are independently controlled, as in the case of most computer grids, resource allocation leads to large combinatorial problems. The allocation of computer resources such as CPU cycles, primary memory, and secondary storage has to be balanced, but the balance differs from application to application. There are also limitations of the current system design that make integration of market mechanisms harder, such as the lack of user authentication and the kernel support for resource isolation.

A very difficult problem is predicting the resources required by a specific run. This is true for a newly developed application, as well as for an old one. The same application may use very different amounts of resources depending on the size of the input data. Practice shows that it is difficult to calibrate the resource needs based on the results of a test run. Changing the input data size may alter the execution flow, affect the spatial and temporal locality of the code, and increase the cache misses, as well as the I/O and communication intensity. The solutions to this problem adopted by computer clouds are elasticity and over-provisioning with the negative consequences discussed in Section 4.5.

Misestimation of application needs has negative consequences for reservations systems and it is even worse in the case of reservations based on bidding schemes. An underbid could increase the amount of resources needed to complete the task, the time to completion, and also the cost, because the application has to be rerun. An overbid also increases the cost, but there are means to address this problem as we shall see shortly. Periodic checkpointing is recommended in the case of long running batch workloads to ensure that any unplanned event such as a system failure or forced termination when the allotted time has expired, does not lead to a total waste of resources already consumed.

A major concern is how to allow cloud users to express their preferences regarding the five broad classes of CRM policies discussed in Section 4.6 and the relationships among them. This an important area that should receive more attention in the future. Achieving a good balance between accuracy of the specifications and user involvement, between the desire to offer multiple alternative and simplicity is a difficult task. An intelligent Graphics User Interface (GUI) should offer defaults based on history data on user preferences and application previous runs.

Market mechanisms have some advantage over the other mechanisms discussed in Section 4.6; they do not require a model of the system, are scalable, and last, but not least, do not require accurate information about the global state of the system. It is generally accepted that distributed systems which maintain state information are neither scalable nor robust; this is the reason why most Internet services are delivered by stateless servers. We have also known for some time that collecting state information consumes a significant share of system resources and that system management decisions based on obsolete state information are far from optimal. This knowledge is critical for the communication and computing infrastructure built around the Internet. In contrast, resource management in cloud computing is still based on hierarchical control models where state information is maintained at several levels.

We have also known that assembling large collections of systems each with a small, but finite probability of failure, requires novel design principles to guarantee system availability. New strategies, policies and mechanisms to implement these policies are necessary to: allow cloud servers to operate more efficiently; reduce costs for the CSPs; provide an even more attractive environment for cloud users; and support some form of interoperability. The pressure to provide new services, better manage cloud resources, and respond to a broader range of application requirements is increasing, as more US Government Agencies are encouraged to use cloud services.[2]

The choice of market mechanisms to support CRM policies is driven by the desire to support simple and effective means to implement them. Auctions seem well suited because they offer a straightforward manner to balance the demand and the supply. The next decision is who should participate at these auctions, who should represent the producers and the consumers. The physical organization of the cloud infrastructure and the accuracy of state information are the deciding factors for the choice of producers. In a hierarchic cloud organization, only the servers know

---

[2]See, for example, the November 6, 2014 memorandum "The DoD Cloud Way Forward" which stresses the need for the DoD to increase its use of cloud services.

precisely their state, the state information at higher levels of hierarchy is obsolete. Thus the servers, or as we shall see later, coalitions of servers should be able to place bids for service.

The consumers of services are cloud users or their proxies. Proxies have several advantages over direct user participation. Typically, auctions are organized periodically thus, the time when a service request is made and the time when the auction is conducted are different and requesting user's presence is undesirable. In addition, proxies can negotiate on behalf of users by combining specific options with history data about the application and past services. At the completion of the service the proxy can also negotiate returning the excess resources to the CSP.

Reservation systems are ubiquitous in many instances where a large population of clients compete for limited resources. Reservations allow a client to choose optimal packages and support efficient access to pools of resources, guarantee access, avoid overcommitting, and reduce the waiting time to service. Reservation systems have been used successfully by CSPs for some time in combination with spot resource allocations.

4.9 CLOUD FEDERATIONS AND SERVER COALITIONS

In large-scale systems, coalition formation supports more effective use of resources, as well as convenient means to access these resources [172]. It is therefore not surprising that coalition formation for computational grids has been investigated in the past. There is also little surprise that the interest in coalition formation migrated in recent years from computational grids to CRM. The interest in grid computing is fading away, while cloud computing is widely accepted today and its adoption by more and more institutions and individuals seems to be guaranteed at least for the foreseeable future.

Two classes of applications of cloud coalitions are reported in the literature:

1. Coalitions among CSPs for the formation of cloud federations. A *cloud federation* is an infrastructure allowing a group of CSPs to share resources; the goal is to balance the load and improve system reliability.
2. Coalitions among the servers of a data center. The goal is to assemble a pool of resources larger than the ones available from a single server. This topic will be discussed in depth in Section 5.3.

In recent years the number of CSPs has increased significantly. The question if they should cooperate to share their resources led to the idea of *cloud federations*, groups of CSPs who have agreed on a set of common standards and are able to share their resources. The infrastructure of individual CSPs consists of a hierarchy of networks and millions of servers thus, a cloud federation would indeed be a very complex system.

The vast majority of ongoing research in this area is focused on game-theoretic aspects of coalition formation for cloud federations [46, 167, 176], while coalitions among the servers of a single cloud has received little attention in the past [164]. This is likely to change due to the emerging interest in *Big Data* cloud applications which require more resources than a single server can provide. To address this problem, sets of identically configured servers able to communicate effectively among themselves form coalitions with sufficient resources for data- and computationally intensive problems.

Cloud coalition formation raises a number of technical, as well as nontechnical problems. Cloud federations require a set of standards. The cloud computing landscape is still evolving and an early standardization may slowdown and negatively affect the adoption of new ideas and technologies. At the same time, CSPs want to maintain their competitive advantages by closely guarding the details of their internal algorithms and protocols.

Reaching agreements on a set of standards is particularly difficult when the infrastructure of the members of the group is designed to support different cloud delivery models, see Section 4.2. For example, it is hard to see how the *IaaS* could be supported by either *SaaS* or *PaaS* clouds. Thus, in spite of the efforts coordinated by the National Institute of Standards (NIST), the adoption of inter-operability standards supporting cloud federations seems a rather distant possibility.

We have seen in Section 4.7 that resource management in one cloud is extremely challenging therefore, dynamic resource sharing among multiple cloud infrastructures seems infeasible at this time. Communication between the members of a cloud federation would also require dedicated networks with low latency and high bandwidth.

All these challenges make cloud federations a very appealing research area. A stochastic linear programming game model for coalition formation is presented in [176]; the authors analyze the stability of the coalition formation among CSPs and show that resource and revenue sharing are deeply intertwined. An optimal VM provisioning algorithm ensuring profit maximization for CSPs is introduced in [46].

A cloud federation formation described as a hedonic game and focused on the stability and the fairness of the game is discussed in [167]. The profit maximization for each federation is formulated as an integer programming problem (IP) and the game is augmented with a preference relation over the set of federations. The paper assumes that the VMs contributed by each CSP to a federation are characterized by a subset a of attributes from the set of the attributes $\mathcal{A}$, $a \in \mathcal{A}$, including the number of cores, the amount of memory and of secondary storage. The integer programming problem for CSP $\mathcal{C}_i$ in federation $\mathcal{F}$ is formulated as

$$\max \sum_{\mathcal{C}_i \in \mathcal{F}} \sum_{j=1}^{n} n_{i,j}(p_j - c_{i,j}), \qquad (4.1)$$

subject to the set of conditions

$$\sum_{j=1}^{n} q_j^a n_{i,j} \leq A_i, \quad \forall a \in \mathcal{A} \quad \text{and} \quad \sum_{\mathcal{C}_i \in \mathcal{F}} n_{i,j} = r_j, \qquad (4.2)$$

where $n_{i,j}$ is the number of VMs of type j, p_j is the price for a VM running an instance of type j, $c_{i,j}$ is the cost of an instance of type j provided by $\mathcal{C}_i$, q_j^a is the quantity of resource of type a in a VM of type j, A_i is the total amount of resource of type a offered by $\mathcal{C}_i$, and r_j is the number of VMs of type j requested. The paper adopts a payoff division based on the Banzhaf value [167].

Though of considerable theoretical interest, applications of game theory to the formation of cloud federation may not lead to practical realizations very soon. We have already mentioned that the development of interoperability standards faces major business as well as technical challenges. There is also another practical problem; the cloud users would expect that a federation would eliminate the negative consequences of vendor lock-in and, in particular, the impossibility to access their data in the case of a major event which takes down a cloud data center. But replicating data on multiple data centers could be prohibitively expensive.

Coalition formation based on cooperative games is another area of research. An algorithm to find optimal coalition structures in cooperative games by searching through a lattice like the one in Fig. 3.4, was introduced by [198]. A more refined algorithm is described in [191]; in this algorithm the coalition structures are grouped according to the so-called *configurations* reflecting the size of the coalitions.

4.10 AUCTIONS: CONCEPTS, RULES, AND ENVIRONMENTS

An *auction* is a public sale where the goods or services are sold to the highest bidder. A *combinatorial auction* is one where a buyer requires simultaneous access to a package of goods or, as is the case discussed in this chapter, a package of services. The bidders could be individuals, groups of individuals, organizations, corporations, robots, sensors, or autonomous servers in a large-scale system.

Auctions address fundamental questions in economics, the most important being who should get the goods offered and at what price. The environment where auctions are conducted and in particular, the size of the populations of sellers and buyers, the type and number of items auctioned, the private information shared among the participants, determine the type of auction and the rules of a particular auction. An auction is characterized by efficiency and the revenue it brings.

Among the numerous applications of auctions are: the auctioning of airport takeoff and landing slots, spectrum licensing by the Federal Communication Commission (FCC), and industrial procurement. In Chapter 5 we discuss auctions involving two distinct set of bidders, cloud users bidding for services and cloud servers bidding to provide services.

Auction theory has been one of the most intensively studied area of economics in the last half century. In 1961 Vickrey used game theory methods to study the dynamics of auctions [227]; this seminal paper marks the beginning of the auction theory.[3] In the *private value model* introduced in [227], each bidder has its own value for every package of goods and has no knowledge about the values of any other bidder; the individual values do not depend on the private information of other bidders. The paper shows that when each bidder pays the social opportunity cost of his winnings rather than his own bid, then truthful bidding is a dominant strategy.

---

[3]Vickrey got the Nobel prize for economics in 1996 for his contributions to the theory of incentives under asymmetric information; he died 3 days after the prize was announced.

The Vickrey-Clark-Groves (VCG) is an extension of the original Vickrey auction when bidders simultaneously submit sealed bids for the items they desire. The highest bid wins, but the winner pays the amount of the second-higher bid. It is obvious that a bidder does not have any incentive to bid anything else but the value she intends to pay. It is relatively easy to prove[4] that in a VCG auction, truthful reporting is a dominant strategy and optimizes the total value obtained as a result of the auction.

We now introduce several concepts from auction theory and refer to the auction participants as agents. First, auctions are *strategic* games, in other words, the choices of an agent are affected by the choices of the other participants in the game. A strategy is *dominant* if it allows an agent to gain a larger payoff than any other strategy, regardless of the choices made by other agents.

Price discovery allows all agents to gauge the eventual price an item will be auctioned at for multiple rounds auctions. The *deposit* is the amount of funds an agent wishing to participate at an auction is required to place with the auctioneer. The *reserve price* is the minimum price the seller is willing to accept for an item being auctioned. This price is only known to the seller, it is not made public.

Opportunity cost measures the benefits obtained by an agent who has two options and chooses one over the other. For example, the opportunity cost of getting an advanced degree requiring four years of study is the amount of money the student would have gotten should she have worked for four years instead. The *social opportunity cost* is the cost from the standpoint of all members of a society, rather than the cost of the individual placing the bid.

Utility, cost, revenue, and expenditure are important concepts in economy. *Marginal utility, cost, revenue, or expenditure* are concepts used in auction theory to describe the effect when the quantity increases by one unit. They are contrasted with their *global* counterparts; both marginal and global measures are function of the quantity of goods. The relation between total and marginal is the same for all these measures of economic activity.

The marginal utility is the rate at which total utility increases as quantity increases; it is the slope of the total utility curve, thus, it is high when the total utility increases sharply, negative when it decreases, and zero when it

---

[4]For the proof see, for example, page 19 of [61].

is constant. For example, the marginal utility of a service quantified by the number of vCPUs measures the increase in utility when instead of say 5 vCPUs the cloud user is allocated 6 vCPUs.

The *principle of declining marginal utility* reflects the fact that increasing the quantity leads to lower and lower increases of the marginal utility. Unfortunately, utility cannot be measured; what we can measure is the marginal value, e.g., what we gain when we use 6 vCPUs instead of 5. Goods are *complementary* when a set of them has a higher value than the sum of the individual value of the goods in set; for example, the value of a pair of socks is larger than the value of the left sock plus the value of the right one.

The first type of auction we discuss is the *simultaneous ascending auction* (SAA) developed in 1994 for FCC spectrum licensing and used since in the United States and abroad. In this auction all items are auctioned at the same time and the agents are allowed to bid on any item or on sets of items. The bidding terminates when none of the participating agents raises the bid for any item. Then, the highest bidder acquires an item or a set of items at the price of the bid.

The advantage of this scheme is its efficiency. An effective *price discovery* allows the agents to develop early in the auction the sense of what the final price for each item might be. Most such auctions allow the agents to withdraw their bids and thus, limit their exposure. The main disadvantage of SAA is that package bidding is not supported and agents may win some of the items in the set they desire, but not all.

The typical rules governing most auctions including the SAA are :

1. Activity rule—requires the agents to bid consistently. For example, agents desiring to acquire large quantities of goods at the end of the auction, thus, bidders in the last rounds when the prices are higher, are required to bid for large quantities at the beginning of the auction, when the prices are lower. This *monotonicity in quantity rule* increases the effectiveness of price discovery in SAA and other auctions.
2. Minimum bid increment rule—allows an auction to proceed efficiently rather than drag on for a long time; bid increments in the range 5–20% are typical.
3. Stopping rule—necessary to give the agents enough flexibility to pursue their strategy and eventually withdraw their bids.

4. Withdraw rule—specifies the conditions high bidders can withdraw their bid, typically subject to a withdraw penalty. There are additional penalties for withdrawing the highest bid. In such cases the second highest bidder is not responsible for her bid as she might have placed bids for other items instead. Often, the penalty for withdrawing the highest bid is the difference between the bid and the final sale prices of the items.
5. Payment rule—usually a refundable deposit is required before bidding and a final payment is due after the conclusion of the auction for the items won.
6. Bid information rule—typically full transparency is required; all agents are informed about the identity of all participating agents and the size of their deposits.
7. Quantity cap rule—limits the quantity of items an agent may win.

An alternative activity rule based on consumer theory is the *Revealed Preference Rule* (RP). Consider two instances in time, $t_1 < t_2$, and the corresponding prices, $p(t_1), p(t_2)$ and x_1, x_2, respectively, the size of the packages demanded by a particular agent. The corresponding values of the packages are $v(x_1)$ and $v(x_2)$, respectively. Then a sincere bidder prefers

$$x_1 \text{ to } x_2 \text{ when } v(x_1) - p(t_1) \cdot x_1 \geq v(x_2) - p(t_2) \cdot x_1$$

$$\text{and} \tag{4.3}$$

$$x_2 \text{ to } x_1 \text{ when } v(x_2) - p(t_2) \cdot x_2 \geq v(x_1) - p(t_1) \cdot x_2.$$

Adding the two inequalities we obtain the RP rule

$$(p(t_1) - p(t_2)) \cdot (x_2 - x_1) \leq 0. \tag{4.4}$$

4.11 COMBINATORIAL AUCTIONS: THE CLOCK-PROXY AUCTION

Auctions in which participants can bid on combinations of items or *packages* are called *combinatorial auctions*; such auctions provide a relatively simple, scalable, and tractable solution to cloud resource allocation [19, 238]. For example, the airways spectrum in the United States is auctioned by the FCC and communication companies bid for licenses. A package consists of multiple licenses; the quantities in these auctions are the bandwidth allocated times the population covered by the license. Individual bidders choose to bid for packages during the proxy phase and pay the prices they committed to during the clock phase. Two recent combinatorial auction algorithms are the *Simultaneous Clock Auction* and the *Clock Proxy Auction* [20]; the algorithm introduced in [218] is called *Ascending Clock Auction*.

Package bidding assumes that a seller offers $\mathcal{N}$ different types of items. A buyer bids for packages of items. A *package* is a vector of integers $\mathcal{Z} = \{z_1, z_2, \ldots, z_\mathcal{N}\}$ which indicates the quantity of each item in the package; the price of items is given by $\mathcal{M} = \{m_1, m_2, \ldots, m_\mathcal{N}\}$. Package bidding can be traced back to generalized Vickrey auctions based on the Vickrey-Clarke-Groves mechanisms [52, 100].

In an *ascending package auction* (APA) there are $\mathcal{K}$ participants identified by an index, $k = 0$ is the seller and $k = 1, 2, \ldots, \mathcal{K}$ are the buyers [18]. Each buyer has a *valuation* vector $v_i = (v_i(z), z \in [0, \mathcal{M}])$ where $v_k(z)$ represents the value of package z to the bidder k. In an ascending package auction, all bids are firm and a bid cannot be reduced or withdrawn. The auctioneer identifies after each round the set of the bids that maximize the total price, the *provisional winning bids*. The auction ends when a new round fails to elicit new bids; then the provisional winning bids become the winners of the auction.

A bidder can be deterred from bidding for the package she really desires by the threat that competitors could drive prices up; this would threaten the equilibrium of an ascending package auction. This problem does not exist in *ascending proxy auctions* when each bidder instructs a proxy agent to bid on her behalf [18]. The proxy accepts as input the bidder's valuation profile and bids following a "sincere strategy."

In an APA the bidders pass the information about quantities of items and prices to proxies which iteratively summit package bids designed to maximize the profits of the bidders. The auctioneer chooses as provisional winners the bids that maximize the revenue for the suppliers of the items. The process stops when the proxies do not submit new bids.

Clock auctions are combinatorial auctions designed for auctioning related items. In clock auctions the auctioneer announces prices for individual items and the agents specify the quantities of individual items they desire at the current price. When the demand for an item increases, so does its price until there is no excess demand (see Fig. 5.7). On the other hand, when the offering exceeds the demand, the price decreases [18]. The process stops when there are no more items with excess demand.

The *clock proxy auction* starts with a clock phase with multiple rounds until there is no excess demand for any of the items being auctioned. Next the agents pass to the proxy the information on items, quantities, and prices. During the proxy phase, the process continues as described above. During the clock phase, the cost of the package is computed as the sum of products of quantity and price per unit, the so-called *linear pricing* and the monotonicity in quantity rule applies. In practice, clock auctions use discrete rounds rather than continuous-time rounds. In such auctions the size of the bid increments is important. Large increments shorten the duration of the auction but introduce inefficiencies as well as the potential for gaming the system. The technique of *intra-round bids* allows a discrete-time clock auction to benefit from virtually all nice properties of continuous-time auctions.

This technique works as follows: the auctioneer defines end-of-round prices and the bidders express their price vectors in the range from start-of-the round to the end-of-the round prices. If during the round, which can last a relatively long time, tens of minutes, there is an excess supply for some item, the round ends with the current prices, otherwise the round ends with the end-of-round prices proposed by the auctioneer.

The clock phase ends when there is no excess demand for any of the items being auctioned and produces the information about all packages and the prices bid for each one of them throughout this phase. At the end of the clock phase, a significant excess supply for many items may exist and a strategy for maximizing the revenues could exploit this information. For example, one can find the position of the clock when the revenue was maximal and use the corresponding prices as the starting prices for the proxy phase.

4.12 FURTHER READINGS ON CLOUDS AND CLOUD RESOURCE MANAGEMENT

The interest in cloud computing is reflected by a very large number of publications covering different aspects of computer clouds. Existing CRM systems are presented [14, 94, 116, 143, 197, 226, 228].

CRM and economic models are discussed in [5, 47, 77, 86, 103, 126, 151, 161, 163, 165, 167, 176, 186, 195, 245]. Multiple aspects of cloud energy consumption are analyzed in [3, 15, 26, 28, 161, 165, 230]. Over-provisioning, server utilization, and their economic impact are discussed in [3, 37, 47, 161].

Coalition formation is covered in [172] and game-theoretic aspects of coalition formation for cloud federations are analyzed in [46, 167, 176]. A fair number of papers are dedicated to auctions [19, 20, 218, 227, 238].

The next chapter is focused on CRM for Big Data applications in science and engineering and the need for user-centric policies for resource allocation. Results of simulation experiments for market-oriented policies based on coalition formation and combinatorial auctions are reported.

CHAPTER 5

Cloud Self-Organization and Big Data Applications

From the early days of cloud computing it was evident that computer clouds provide an ideal environment for many enterprise applications. The success of cloud computing stimulated the interest in the new paradigm and, as a result, the pace of the development of the infrastructure and cloud services accelerated. In the second decade of the new millennium, more and more applications migrated to clouds, with the notable exception of Big Data scientific and engineering applications.

According to Gartner Research, "Big Data is high volume, high velocity, and/or high variety information assets that require new forms of processing to enable enhanced decision-making, insight discovery, and process optimization" (http://www.gartner.com/it-glossary/big-data/). Big Data applications demand massive computing resources including CPU cycles, primary and secondary storage, and network bandwidth. Only computer clouds and powerful supercomputers can supply such resources.

Existing data show that mobile applications, data analytics, and many Big Data enterprise applications perform well on the cloud as they exploit *request-level parallelism*. These applications take advantage of the low cost for cloud services. At the other end of the spectrum are applications in computational sciences, discussed in Section 5.1, computational finance, and computational engineering. The *data-level parallelism* of such applications is often *fine-grained* and they do not perform well on clouds.

It is likely that faster communication, more powerful processors, and new Cloud Resource Management (CRM) policies addressing the problems discussed in Section 4.7 will support a broader range of Big Data cloud applications. None of these improvements alone is sufficient and adopting all of them would significantly add to the costs of the cloud infrastructure. Indeed, faster interconnection networks are very expensive and they represent a significant fraction of a supercomputer cost. Such changes will also require extensive experimentation with new policies and mechanisms implementing the policies, a difficult proposition because it is infeasible to

Complex Systems and Clouds. http://dx.doi.org/10.1016/B978-0-12-804041-6.00005-0

experiment with systems on this scale. These facts alone might suggest that major changes in CRM should not be expected soon.

Scalability is a major challenge for autonomic computing and for the existing CRM policies. Big Data cloud applications and, in particular, applications in computational sciences and engineering, exacerbate these challenges, as we see in Section 5.2 in the discussion of tensor network contraction (TNC) with applications to condensed-matter physics. The performance of the TNC application, and possibly many others, is likely to be limited, not only by the relatively high latency and low bandwidth of cloud interconnection networks, but also by resource bundling, the fact that resources are offered in packages of predetermined configurations that may, or may not match the needs of the application. This should motivate the research community to investigate alternative cloud management for Big Data scientific applications, such as the ones discussed in this chapter.

The questions addressed in this chapter are: Can existing CRM policies and mechanisms for implementing these policies support an effective environment for the increasingly broader spectrum of applications migrating to clouds? Are there alternative mechanisms for CRM that can perform better than the ones in use nowadays? How do we evaluate new CRM policies and mechanisms and stimulate a smooth migration of research results to practice?

Providing convincing answers to these questions is far from trivial. The cloud computing landscape is very diverse and very dynamic, thus, we have to accept some compromises. Supporting elasticity and other desirable features of cloud computing will inevitably lead to suboptimal resource utilization and higher power consumption.

Market-oriented solutions give effective answers to some of the explicit goals of autonomic computing and self-management. Such solutions are scalable, adaptive, react to changes in the environment, and balance the supply and demands dynamically. A self-organized system based on market-oriented policies and mechanisms could have desirable properties such as high resource utilization and increased energy efficiency, while presenting a user-friendly cloud computing environment.

The discussion of alternative mechanisms for resource allocation for Big Data applications is focused on a reservation system based on server coalitions and combinatorial auctions. The model assumes a hierarchical organization of the cloud infrastructure and autonomous servers that cooperate to respond to the service requests of a large user community.

5.1 BIG DATA APPLICATIONS IN SCIENCE AND ENGINEERING

It should not be surprising that applications in computational physics, chemistry, biology, astrophysics, nanotechnology, civil engineering, computer-aided design, and many other areas of science and engineering do not perform well on clouds. These applications are CPU-, memory-, and I/O-intensive and run efficiently on systems with low-latency, high-bandwidth interconnection networks available on the most powerful supercomputers [222].

Clouds built with off-the-shelf components offer a cost-effective alternative to computing and it would be beneficial to make cloud computing an attractive choice for scientific and engineering applications. Overcoming the high cost and the limited availability of supercomputers would accelerate the discovery process in many areas of science and would also led to more aggressive designs of advanced systems.

In this section we discuss the astounding progress made by the infrastructure for cloud computing during the past few years. We also contemplate the difficult road ahead in the quest to allow applications in computational sciences and engineering that process data sets, ranging in size from petabytes to exabytes and beyond, to run efficiently on clouds. Such applications require:

1. An infrastructure with fast interconnects, faster processors, and high performance storage systems. Faster processors alone will only exacerbate the imbalance between computing and communication bandwidth.
2. Guaranteed access to large pools of resources for extended periods of time.
3. Support for complex workflows with specific resource demands for each phase of the workflow [86].
4. A fault-tolerant environment for long-running applications.
5. Stable and effective system software, including resource management.

A study carried out in the early days of cloud computing [126] reports on the results of a comparison of several supercomputers with the Amazon Web Services (AWS), vintage 2009–10. This study used the high performance benchmark discussed next.

High Performance Computing Challenge (HPCC). HPCC is a suite of seven synthetic benchmarks: three targeted synthetic benchmarks which quantify basic system parameters that individually characterize the computation and communication performance; four complex synthetic benchmarks which combine computation and communication and can be considered simple proxy applications. These benchmarks are:

- *DGEMM*—measures the floating point performance of a processor/core and the results are close to the theoretical peak performance of the processor, the memory bandwidth is not a factor and the code is cache friendly;
- *STREAM*—measures the memory bandwidth;
- *HPL*—a dense linear system in double precision arithmetic;
- *FFTE*—measures the floating point rate of execution of double precision complex one-dimensional Discrete Fourier Transforms;
- *PTRANS*—parallel matrix transpose, tests the total communications capacity of the interconnection network; and
- *RandomAccess*—measures the rate of integer random updates of memory (GUPS).

Table 5.1 The Results of the Measurements Reported in [126]

System	DGEMM (Gflops)	STREAM (GB/s)	Latency (μs)	Bndw (GB/s)	HPL (Tflops)	FFTE (Gflops)	PTRANS (GB/s)	RandAcc (GUP/s)
Carver	10.2	4.4	2.1	3.4	0.56	21.99	9.35	0.044
Frankl	8.4	2.3	7.8	1.6	0.47	14.24	2.63	0.061
Lawren	9.6	0.7	4.1	1.2	0.46	9.12	1.34	0.013
EC2	4.6	1.7	145	0.06	0.07	1.09	0.29	0.004

From K.R. Jackson, L. Ramakrishnan, K. Muriki, S. Canon, S. Cholia, J. Shalf, H. Wasserman, N.J. Wright, Performance analysis of high performance computing applications on the Amazon Web services cloud, in: Proceedings of IEEE Second International Conference on Cloud Computing Technology and Science, 2010, pp. 159–168.

Supercomputers versus AWS vintage 2010. The systems used for the comparison with cloud computing in [126] are:

1. *Carver*—a 400 node IBM iDataPlex cluster with quad-core Intel Nehalem processors running at 2.67 GHz and with 24 GB of RAM

(3 GB/core). A single Quad Data Rate IB link connects each node to a fat-tree network and a global two-dimensional mesh.

2. *Franklin*—a 9,660-node Cray XT4; each node has a single quad-core 2.3 GHz AMD Opteron processor with 8 GB of RAM (2 GB/core). Each processor is connected through a 6.4 GB/s bidirectional HyperTransport interface to the interconnect via a Cray SeaStar-2 ASIC. The SeaStar routing chips are interconnected in a tridimensional torus topology, where each node has a direct link to its six nearest neighbors.

3. *Lawrencium*—a 198-node (1,584 core) Linux cluster; a compute node is a Dell Poweredge 1950 server with two Intel Xeon quad-core 64 bit, 2.66 GHz processors with 16 GB of RAM (2 GB/core). A compute node is connected to a Dual Data Rate InfiniBand network configured as a fat tree with a 3:1 blocking factor. Codes were compiled using Intel 10.0.018 and Open MPI 1.3.3.

The *EC2* instance was a m1.large with four *Elastic Compute Units* (ECUs), two virtual cores with two ECUs each, and 7.5 GB of memory. In 2010 AWS used ECUs to measure the processor performance and in 2014 switched to the now ubiquitous vCPU. An ECU was approximately equivalent to a 1.0–1.2 GHz 2007 Opteron or 2007 Xeon processor. The nodes were connected with Gigabit Ethernet (GE).

The results in Table 5.1 give us some ideas about the characteristics of scientific applications likely to run efficiently on computer clouds. We see that communication intensive applications are significantly affected by the increased latency and lower bandwidth.

The 2016 AWS and scientific Big Data applications. The AWS infrastructure has benefited from new technologies and it is probably the most attractive and cost-effective cloud computing environment for scientific applications [13]. AWS offers several types of instances targeting different classes of applications:

- T2—provide a baseline CPU performance and the ability to exceed the baseline;
- M4 and M3—provide a balance of compute, memory, and network resources;
- C4—use high performance processors and have the lowest price/compute performance;
- R3—are optimized for memory-intensive applications;

- G2—target graphics and general-purpose GPU applications;
- I2—are storage optimized; and
- D2—deliver high disk throughput.

Each instance packages a different combination of processors, memory, storage, and network bandwidth. The number of vCPUs, as well as the type of processor, its architecture, and clock speed are different for different instance types. A vCPU is a virtual processor assigned to one virtual machine; AWS does not specify if a vCPU corresponds to a core of a multicore processor, though this is likely. The amount of memory per vCPU is the same for low- and high-end instances. The memory is sometimes measured in Gibibytes, 1 GiB = 2^{30} bytes or 1,073,741,824 bytes while 1 GB = 10^9 bytes.

The processors used by instances in Table 5.2 are Intel Xeon E5-2670 v3 running at 2.5 GHz for M4 instances, Intel Xeon E5-2666 v3 running at 2.9 GHz for C4 instances, and E5-2670 for G2. The first two processors support Advanced Vector Extensions AVX and AVX2. The two are extensions to the x86 ISA; the width of the SIMD register file is increased from 128 to 256 bits. The NVIDIA GPUs, for G2 instances each has 1,536 CUDA cores and 4 GB of video memory.

AVX2 has several additional features: expansion of most vector integer SSE and AVX instructions to 256 bits; three-operand general-purpose bit manipulation and multiply; three-operand fused multiply-accumulate support; gather support, enabling vector elements to be loaded from noncontiguous memory locations; DWORD and QWORD-granularity any-to-any permutes; and vector shifts.

Several operating systems, including Apple OS, Linux, Windows, FreeBSD, OpenBSD, and Solaris support AVX. Recent releases of the GCC compiler support AVX. Unfortunately, there are no recent benchmarks comparing the performance of systems on the top 500 list with some of the 2016 AWS instances presented in Table 5.2, see https://aws.amazon.com/ec2/instance-types/.

The floating point performance of C4 instances is impressive. For example, a c4.8xlarge instance with 2 Intel Xeon E5-2666 v3 processors running at 3.50 GHz, 18 cores, and 36 threads, with 32 KB x 9 L1 instruction and data caches, 256 KB x 9 L2 cache, 26.3 MB L3 cache, and 60 GB main memory delivers more than 61 Gflops from a multicore configuration according to http://browser.primatelabs.com/geekbench3/1694602 (see Fig. 5.1).

Table 5.2 **The Resources Offered by** M4, C4, **and** G2 **AWS Instances; the Number of vCPUs, the Amount of Memory, the Data Rates for Disk Access, and the Cost Per Hour**

Instance Type	vCPU	Memory (GiB)	EBS Throughput (Mbps)	Cost ($/h)
m4.large	2	8	450	0.12
m4.xlarge	4	16	750	0.239
m4.2xlarge	8	32	1,000	0.479
m4.4xlarge	16	64	2,000	0.958
m4.10xlarge	40	160	4,000	2.394
c4.large	2	3.75	500	0.105
c4.xlarge	4	7.5	750	0.209
c4.2xlarge	8	15	1,000	0.419
c4.4xlarge	16	30	2,000	0.838
c4.8-xlarge	36	60	4,000	1.675
g2.2xlarge	8	15	–	0.65
g2.4xlarge	32	60	–	2.60

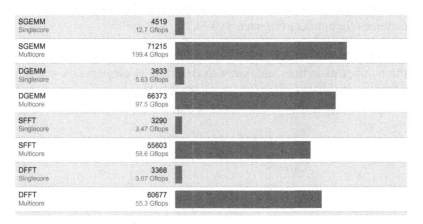

SGEMM Singlecore	4519 12.7 Gflops	
SGEMM Multicore	71215 199.4 Gflops	
DGEMM Singlecore	3833 5.63 Gflops	
DGEMM Multicore	66373 97.5 Gflops	
SFFT Singlecore	3290 3.47 Gflops	
SFFT Multicore	55603 58.6 Gflops	
DFFT Singlecore	3368 3.07 Gflops	
DFFT Multicore	60677 55.3 Gflops	

Fig. 5.1 The performance of a c4.8xlarge AWS instance.

The performance of G2 instances with attached GPUs is even more impressive. Results reported in [66] show the performance of CUDA 7.0 for several libraries including cuFFT, cuBLAS, cuSPARSE, cuSOLVER, cuRAND, and cuDNN. For example, cuBLAS supports all 152 standard routines and distributed computations across multiple GPUs with out-of-core streaming to CPU and no upper limits on matrix size supporting more than 3 Tflops in single precision and more than 1 Tflops in double precision (see Fig. 5.2).

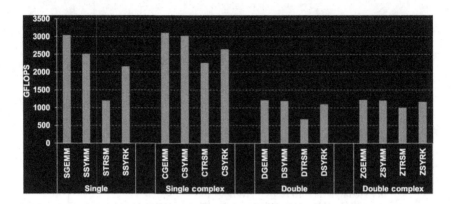

Fig. 5.2 The performance of CUDA 7.0 for several BLAS library routines. CUDA, CUDA 7.0 performance report, http://on-demand.gputechconf.com/gtc/2015/webinar/gtc-express-cuda7-performance-overview.pdf (accessed April 2016).

5.2 A CASE STUDY: TENSOR NETWORK CONTRACTION ON AWS

To illustrate the problems posed by Big Data, we discuss an application in the area of condensed matter physics and analyze different options offered by 2016 vintage AWS for running the application. M4 and C4 seem to be the best choices for applications such as TNC.

Tensor contraction. In linear algebra the *rank* $\mathcal{R}$ of an object is given by the number of indices necessary to describe its elements. A scalar has rank 0, a vector $a = (a_1, a_2, \ldots, a_n)$ has rank 1 and n elements, a matrix $\mathcal{A} = [a_{ij}], 1 \leq i \leq n, 1 \leq j \leq m$ has rank 2 and $n \times m$ elements

$$\mathcal{A} = \begin{bmatrix} a_{11} & a_{12} & \ldots & a_{1m} \\ a_{21} & a_{22} & \ldots & a_{2m} \\ \vdots & & & \\ a_{n1} & a_{n2} & \ldots & a_{nm} \end{bmatrix}. \tag{5.1}$$

Tensors have rank $\mathcal{R} \geq 3$; the description of tensor elements is harder. For example, consider a rank 3 tensor $\mathcal{B} = [b_{jkl}]$ with elements $b_{jkl} \in \mathbb{R}^{2 \times 2 \times 2}$. The eight elements of this tensor are: $\{b_{111}, b_{112}, b_{121}, b_{122}\}$ and $\{b_{211}, b_{212}, b_{221}, b_{222}\}$. We can visualize the tensor elements as the vertices of a cube where the first group of elements are in the plane $j = 1$ and $j = 2$, respectively. Similarly, the tensor elements $\{b_{111}, b_{211}, b_{112}, b_{212}\}$ and $\{b_{121}, b_{221}, b_{122}, b_{222}\}$ are in the planes $k = 1$ and $k = 2$, respectively, while $\{b_{111}, b_{121}, b_{211}, b_{221}\}$ and $\{b_{112}, b_{122}, b_{212}, b_{222}\}$ are in the planes $l = 1$ and $l = 2$, respectively.

Tensor contraction is the summation over repeated indices of the two tensors or of a vector and a tensor. Let $\mathcal{C}$ be the contraction of two arbitrary tensors $\mathcal{A}$ and $\mathcal{B}$. The rank of the tensor resulting after contraction is

$$\mathcal{R}(\mathcal{C}) = \mathcal{R}(\mathcal{A}) + \mathcal{R}(\mathcal{B}) - 2. \tag{5.2}$$

For example, when $\mathcal{A} = [a_{ij}]$, $\mathcal{B} = [b_{jkl}]$ and we contract over j we obtain $\mathcal{C} = [c_{ikl}]$ with

$$c_{ikl} = \sum_j a_{ij} b_{jkl}. \tag{5.3}$$

The rank of $\mathcal{C}$ is $\mathcal{R}(\mathcal{C}) = 2 + 3 - 2 = 3$. Tensor $\mathcal{C}$ has 8 elements

$$c_{111} = \sum_{j=1}^{2} a_{1j} b_{j11} = a_{11} b_{111} + a_{12} b_{211} \quad\Big|\quad c_{121} = \sum_{j=1}^{2} a_{1j} b_{j21} = a_{11} b_{121} + a_{12} b_{221}$$

$$c_{212} = \sum_{j=1}^{2} a_{2j} b_{j12} = a_{21} b_{112} + a_{22} b_{212} \quad\Big|\quad c_{222} = \sum_{j=1}^{2} a_{2j} b_{j22} = a_{21} b_{122} + a_{22} b_{222}$$

$$c_{112} = \sum_{j=1}^{2} a_{1j} b_{j11} = a_{11} b_{112} + a_{12} b_{212} \quad\Big|\quad c_{122} = \sum_{j=1}^{2} a_{1j} b_{j21} = a_{11} b_{122} + a_{12} b_{222}$$

$$c_{211} = \sum_{j=1}^{2} a_{2j} b_{j11} = a_{21} b_{111} + a_{22} b_{211} \quad\Big|\quad c_{221} = \sum_{j=1}^{2} a_{2j} b_{j21} = a_{21} b_{121} + a_{22} b_{221}$$

$$\tag{5.4}$$

Tensor networks and Tensor Network Contraction (TNC). A *tensor network* is defined as follows: let $[A_1], \ldots, [A_n]$ be n tensors with index sets $x^{(1)}, \ldots, x^{(n)}$ where each $\{x^{(i)}\}$ is a subset of $\{x_1, \ldots, x_N\}$ with N very large. We assume that the "big" tensor $[A]_{\{x_1,\ldots,x_N\}}$ can be expressed as the product of the "smaller" tensors $[A_1], \ldots, [A_n]$

$$[A]_{\{x_1,\ldots,x_K\}} = [A_1]_{\{x^{(1)}\}} \ldots [A_n]_{\{x^{(n)}\}}. \tag{5.5}$$

We wish to compute the scalar

$$Z_A = \sum_{\{x_1,\ldots,x_N\}} [A_i]_{\{x_1,\ldots,x_N\}}. \tag{5.6}$$

For example, $N = 7$ and $n = 4$ and the index set is $\{x_1, x_2, \ldots, x_7\}$ for the TNC in Fig. 5.3. The four "small" tensors and their respective subsets of the index set are

$$[A_1]_{\{x_1,x_2,x_5\}}, [A_2]_{\{x_2,x_3,x_4\}}, [A_3]_{\{x_3,x_4,x_6\}}, \text{ and } [A_4]_{\{x_5,x_6,x_7\}}. \tag{5.7}$$

The "big" tensor $[A]$ is the product of the four "small" tensors

$$[A]_{\{x_1,x_2,x_3,x_4,x_5,x_6,x_7\}} = [A_1]_{\{x_1,x_2,x_5\}} \otimes [A_2]_{\{x_2,x_3,x_4\}} \otimes [A_3]_{\{x_3,x_4,x_6\}} \otimes [A_4]_{\{x_5,x_6,x_7\}}. \tag{5.8}$$

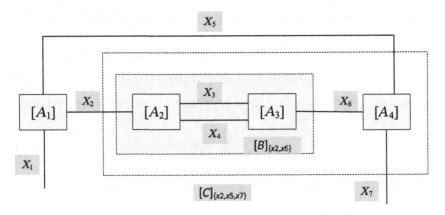

Fig. 5.3 The ordering of tensor contraction when the index set is $\{x_1, x_2, \ldots, x_7\}$ and the four "small" tensors are $[A_1]_{\{x_1,x_2,x_5\}}$, $[A_2]_{\{x_2,x_3,x_4\}}$, $[A_3]_{\{x_3,x_4,x_6\}}$, and $[A_4]_{\{x_5,x_6,x_7\}}$. Tensors [B] and [C] are the results of contraction of $[A_2]$, $[A_3]$, and $[A_4]$, [B], respectively.

To calculate Z_A we first contract $[A_2]$ and $[A_3]$ and the result is tensor $[B]$

$$[B]_{\{x_2,x_6\}} = \sum_{x_3} \sum_{x_4} [A_2]_{\{x_2,x_3,x_4\}} \otimes [A_3]_{\{x_3,x_4,x_6\}}. \qquad (5.9)$$

Next we contract $[B]$ and $[A_4]$ to produce $[C]$

$$[C]_{\{x_2,x_5,x_7\}} = \sum_{x_6} [B]_{\{x_2,x_6\}} \otimes [A_4]_{\{x_5,x_6,x_7\}}. \qquad (5.10)$$

Finally, we compute

$$Z_{\{x_1,x_7\}} = \sum_{x_2} \sum_{x_5} [A_1]_{\{x_1,x_2,x_5\}} \otimes [C]_{\{x_2,x_5,x_7\}}. \qquad (5.11)$$

TNC is CPU and memory intensive. If the tensor network has an arbitrary topology, TNC is considerably more intensive than in the case of a regular topology, e.g., a 2-D lattice.

An example of TNC. We now discuss the case of an application where the tensors form a 2-D, $L \times L$ rectangular lattice. Each tensor in the interior of the lattice has four indices each one running from 1 to D^2, while outer tensors have only three indices, and the ones at the corners have only two. The resulting tensors form a product of vectors (top and bottom tensors) and matrices (interior tensors) with vertical orbitals running from 1 to D^{2L}. The space required for TNC can be very large, we expect parameter values as large as $D = 20$ and $L = 100$. This is a Big Data application, 20^{200} is a very large number indeed!

Fig. 5.4 illustrates the *generic TLC algorithm* for $L = 8$. The first iteration of the computation contracts the left-most (1L) and the right-most columns (1R) of the tensor network. The process continues until we end up with the "big" vector after $L/2 = 4$ iterations. The left and right contractions (1L, 2L, and 3L) and (1R, 2R, and 3R) are mirror images of one another and are carried out concurrently.

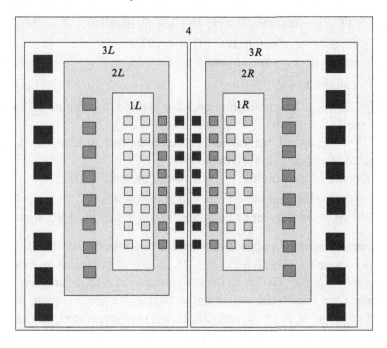

Fig. 5.4 Contraction when $L = 8$ and we have an 8×8 tensor network. The first iteration contracts columns 1 and 2 and columns 7 and 8, see 1L and 1R boxes. During the second iteration the two resulting tensors are contracted with columns 3 and 6, respectively, as shown by 2L and 2R boxes. During the third iteration the new tensors are contracted with columns 4 and 5, respectively, as shown by the 3L and 3R boxes. Finally, during the fourth iteration the "big" vector is obtained by contracting the two tensors produced by the third iteration.

TNC algorithm for condensed matter physics. In quantum mechanics, vectors in an n-dimensional Hilbert space describe quantum states, and tensors describe transformation of quantum states. TNC has applications in condensed-matter physics and our discussion is focused only on the algorithmic aspects of the problem.

The algorithm for TNC should be flexible, efficient, and cost-effective. Flexibility means the ability to run problems of different sizes, with a range of values for D and L parameters. An efficient algorithm should support effective multithreading and optimal use of available system resources.

The notations used to describe the contraction algorithms for tensor network T are:

- $N^{(i)}$—number of vCPUs for iteration i; $N = 2$ for all iterations of Stage 1, while the number of vCPUs for Stage 2 may increase with the number of iterations;
- m—the amount of memory available on the vCPU of the current instance;
- $\mathcal{T}^{(i)} = [\mathcal{T}_{j,k}^{(i)}]$—version of the $[T]$ after the ith iteration;
- $L^{(i)}$—the number of columns of $[T]$ at iteration i;
- $\mathcal{T}_{j,k}^{(i)}$—tensor in row j and column k of $\mathcal{T}^{(i)}$; $T_{j,k}^1 = T_{j,k}$;
- $\mathcal{T}_k^{(i)}$—column k of $\mathcal{T}^{(i)}$;
- $\mathbb{C}(\mathcal{T}_k^{(i)}, T_j), i > 1$—contraction operator applied to columns $\mathcal{T}_k^{(i)}$ and T_j in Stage 1;
- $\mathbb{V}(\mathcal{T}^{(L_{col})})$—vertical contraction operator applied to the "big tensor" obtained after L_{col} column contractions;
- μ—amount of memory for $T_{j,k}$, a tensor of the original T;
- $\mu^{(i)}$—storage for a tensor $\mathcal{T}_{j,k}^{(i)}$ created at iteration i;
- I_{max}—maximum number of iterations for Stage 1 of the TNC algorithm.

The *generic contraction algorithm* for a 2-D tensor network with L_{row} rows and L_{col} columns, $T = [T_{j,k}], 1 \le j \le 2L_{row}, 1 \le k \le 2L_{col}$ is an extension of the one in Fig. 5.4. TNC is an iterative process, at each iteration two pairs of columns are contracted concurrently. During the first iteration, the two pairs of columns of T, $(1, 2)$, and $(2L, 2L - 1)$ are contracted. At iterations $2 \le i \le L$ the new tensor network has $L^{(i)} = L - 2i$ columns. The contraction is applied to pairs of columns. The two columns resulting from the left and right contractions of the leftmost and rightmost columns at iteration $(i - 1)$ are now columns 1 and $L^{(i)}$. They are contracted with columns 2 and $L^{(i)} - 1$, respectively.

The TNC algorithm is organized in multiple stages with different AWS instances for different stages. Small to medium size problems need only the first stage to produce the results and use low-end instances with 2 vCPUs, while large problems must feed the results of the first stage to a second one running on more powerful AWS instances. A third stage may be required for extreme cases when the size of one tensor exceeds the amount of vCPU memory, some 4 GB at this time. The three stages of the algorithm are now discussed.

- *Stage 1*. An entire column of $\mathcal{T}^{(i)}$ can be stored in the vCPU memory and successive contraction iterations can proceed seamlessly when

$$L_{row}\left(2\mu + \mu^{(i-1)} + \mu^{(i)}\right) < m. \tag{5.12}$$

This is feasible for the first iterations of the algorithm and for relatively small values of L_{row}. Call I_{max} the largest value of i which satisfies Eq. (5.12).

Use a low-end M4 or C4 instance with 2 vCPUs, $N = 2$. The computation runs very fast with optimal use of the secondary storage and network bandwidth. Each vCPU is multithreaded, multiple threads carry out the operations required by the contraction operator $\mathbb{C}$ while one thread reads the next column of the original tensor network, $\mathcal{T}$ in preparation for the next iteration.

- *Stage 2.* After a number of iterations, the condition in Eq. (5.12) is no longer satisfied and the second phase should start. Now an iteration consists of partial contractions when subsets of column tensors are contracted independently. In this case the number of vCPUs is $N > 2$.
- *Stage 3.* As the amount of space needed for a single tensor increases and the vCPU memory cannot store a single tensor

$$\mu_i > m. \tag{5.13}$$

In this extreme case we use several instances with the largest number of vCPUs, e.g., either M4.10xlarge or C4.10xlarge.

5.2.1 Stage 1 TNC Algorithm
The algorithm is a straightforward implementation of the generic TNC algorithm:

1. Start an instance with $N = 2$, e.g., C4.large
2. Read input parameters, e.g., L_{row}, L_{col}
3. Compute I_{max}
4. First iteration
   a. vCP1—read T_1 and T_2, apply $\mathbb{C}(T_1, T_2)$; start reading T_3
   b. vCP2—read $T_{L_{col}}$ and $T_{L_{col}-1}$, apply $\mathbb{C}(T_{L_{col}}, T_{L_{col}-1})$, start reading $T_{L_{col}-2}$
5. Iterations $2 \le i \le \min[I_{max}, L_{col}]$. The column numbers correspond to the contracted tensor network with $L_{col}^{(i)} = L_{col} - 2(i - 1)$ columns
   a. vCP1—apply $\mathbb{C}(T_1^{(i)}, T_2)$; start reading T_3
   b. vCP2—apply $\mathbb{C}(T_{L_{col}^{(i)}}^{(i)}, T_{L_{col}^{(i)}-1})$; start reading $T_{L_{col}^{(i)}-2}$
6. If $L_{col} \le I_{max}$ carry out vertical compression of the "big tensor" and finish

a. Apply $\mathbb{V}(T^{(L_{col})})$
b. Write result
c. Kill the instance
7. Else prepare the data for the Stage 2 algorithm
   a. vCPU1—save $T_i^{(i)}$
   b. vCPU2—save $T_{L_{col}-i}^{(i)}$
   c. Kill the instance

5.2.2 Stage 2 TNC Algorithm

This stage starts with a tensor network $T^{(I_{max})}$ with $2(L_{col} - I_{max})$ columns and L_{row} rows. Multiple partial contractions will be done for each column of $T^{(I_{max})}$ during this stage.

The number of vCPUs for the instance used for successive iterations may increase. Results of a partial iteration have to be saved at the end of the partial iteration. The parameters for this phase are:

- $\mu_{pc}^{(i)}$—the space per tensor required for partial contraction at iteration i

$$\mu_{pc}^{(i)} = \mu + \mu^{(i-1)} + \mu^{(i)} \tag{5.14}$$

partial contraction increases the space required by each tensor
- $\mathbb{C}_{pc}\left(T_k^{(i)}, T_j, s\right)$—partial contraction operator applied to segment s of columns $T_k^{(i)}$ and T_j in Stage 2
- $n_r^{(i)}$—number of rows of a column segment for each partial contraction at iteration i given by

$$n_r^{(i)} = \left\lceil \frac{m}{\mu_{pc}^{(i)}} \right\rceil \tag{5.15}$$

- $p^{(i)}$—number of partial contractions per column at iteration i

$$p^{(i)} = \left\lceil \frac{L_{row}}{n_r^{(i)}} \right\rceil \tag{5.16}$$

The total number of partial contractions at iteration i is $2p^{(i)}$
- The number of vCPUs for iteration i is

$$N^{(i)} = 2p^{(i)} \tag{5.17}$$

- $L_{col}^{(i)}$—the number of columns at iteration i of Stage 2
- $I_{Max} = L_{col} - I_{max}$—the number of iterations of Stage 2 assuming that Stage 3 is not necessary

- $\mathbb{A}_{pc}\left(\mathcal{T}^i_{k,p^{(i)}}\right)$—assembly operator for the $p^{(i)}$ segments resulting from partial contraction of column k at iteration i

Stage 2 TNC consists of the following steps:

1. For $i = 1, I_{Max}$
   a. Compute $\mu_{pc}, n_r^{(i)}, p^{(i)}, N^{(i)}$
   b. If $N \leq 40$ start an instance with $N = N^{(i)}$; else start multiple C4.10xlarge instances to run concurrently all partial contractions
   c. For $j = 1, p^{(i)}$
      - $vCPU_j$
        - Read $\mathcal{T}^{(i)}_{1,j}$ and $T_{2,j}$ and apply $\mathbb{C}_{pc}\left(\mathcal{T}^{(i)}_{1,j}, T_{2,j}\right)$
        - Store the result $\mathcal{T}^{(i+1)}_{1,j}$
      - $vCPU_{j+p^{(i)}}$
        - Read $\mathcal{T}^{(i)}_{L^{(i)}_{col},j}$ and $T_{L^{(i)}_{col}-1,j}$ and apply $\mathbb{C}_{pc}\left(\mathcal{T}^{(i)}_{L^{(i)}_{col},j}, T_{L^{(i)}_{col}-1,j}\right)$
        - Store the result $\mathcal{T}^{(i+1)}_{L^{(i)}_{col},j}$
   d. Assemble partial contractions
      - $vCPU_1$
        - Apply $\mathbb{A}_{pc}\left(\mathcal{T}^i_1, p^{(i)}\right)$
        - Store the result $\mathcal{T}^{(i+1)}_1$
      - $vCPU_2$
        - Apply $\mathbb{A}_{pc}\left(\mathcal{T}^i_{L^{(i)}_{col}}, p^{(i)}\right)$
        - Store the result $\mathcal{T}^{(i+1)}_{L^{(i+1)}_{col}}$
2. If $i < I_{Max}$ proceed to next iteration, $i = i + 1$; else
   a. Apply $\mathbb{V}\mathcal{T}^{(I_{Max})}$
   b. Write TNC result
   c. Kill the instance

5.2.3 Stage 3 TNC Algorithm

The algorithm is similar with the one for Stage 2, but now a single tensor is distributed to multiple vCPUs.

An analysis of the memory requirements for TNC. Let us assume that we have L tensors per column and each tensor has dimension D. Consider the leftmost, or equivalently the rightmost column, and note that the number of bonds differs for different tensors, the top and the bottom tensors have

2 bonds and the other $L - 1$ have 3 bonds, so the total number of elements in this column is

$$\mathcal{N}_1^{(0)} = 2D^2 + (L - 2)D^3. \tag{5.18}$$

The top and bottom tensors of the next column have three bonds and the remaining $L - 2$ have four bonds, thus the total number of elements in the second column is

$$\mathcal{N}_2^{(0)} = 2D^3 + (L - 2)D^4. \tag{5.19}$$

After contraction the number of elements becomes

$$\mathcal{N}_1^{(1)} = 2D^3 + (L - 2)D^5. \tag{5.20}$$

Each tensor element requires two double precision floating point numbers thus, the amount of memory needed for the first iteration is

$$\mathcal{M}^{(1)} = 2 \times 8 \times [D^2 + (L - 2)D^3 + 2D^3 + (L - 2)D^4 + 2D^3 + (L - 2)D^5]$$
$$= 16 \times [2D^3 + (L - 2)D^4 + 2D^2(1 + D) + (L - 2)D^3(1 + D^2)]. \tag{5.21}$$

The amount of memory needed for iterations 2 and 3 are

$$\mathcal{M}^{(2)} = 16 \times [2D^3 + (L - 2)D^5 + 2D^3 + (L - 2)D^4 + 2D^4 + (L - 2)D^7]$$
$$= 16 \times [2D^3 + (L - 2)D^4 + 2D^3(1 + D) + (L - 2)D^5(1 + D^2)] \tag{5.22}$$

and

$$\mathcal{M}^{(3)} = 16 \times [2D^4 + (L - 2)D^7 + 2D^3 + (L - 2)D^4 + 2D^5 + (L - 2)D^9]$$
$$= 16 \times [2D^3 + (L - 2)D^4 + 2D^4(1 + D) + (L - 2)D^7(1 + D^2)]. \tag{5.23}$$

It follows that the amount of memory for iteration i is

$$\mathcal{M}^{(i)} = 16 \times [2D^3 + (L - 2)D^4 + 2D^{i+1}(1 + D) + (L - 2)D^{2i+1}(1 + D^2)]. \tag{5.24}$$

When $D = 20$ and $L = 100$ the amount of memory for the first iteration is

$$16 \times [2 \times 20^3 + 98 \times 20^4 + 2 \times 20^2 \times (1 + 20) + 98 \times (20^3 + 20^5)]$$
$$= 5,281,548,800 \text{ bytes.} \tag{5.25}$$

This example shows why only the most powerful systems with ample resources can be used for TNC. It also shows that an application has to adapt, the best it can, to the packages of resources provided by the CSP, while in a better world an application-centric view should prevail, and the system should assemble and offer precisely the resources needed by an application neither more nor less.

5.3 SERVER COALITIONS, COMBINATORIAL AUCTIONS, AND BIG DATA

A main advantage of computer clouds is that their infrastructure benefits from the latest hardware and software technologies. We have seen in Section 5.1 that cloud servers now use the most powerful processors with large caches and ample main memories and run sophisticated software capable of masking hardware failures. It is thus, the time to analyze if CRM policies can be adapted to the needs of high-impact applications. In this section we start our discussion of alternative CRM policies and their potential effect on Big Data applications in computational science and engineering.

Many existing and future cloud applications are likely to need computing cycles, main memory, disk space, and other resources well beyond those provided by a single server thus, the need for assembling coalitions of servers offering sufficient resources for data-intensive applications. At this time, Cloud Service Providers (CSPs) support a limited number of instances with a different number of vCPUs that may, or may not, match application needs.

Market mechanisms, such as coalition formation and combinatorial auctions can be very effective for the implementation of CRM policies for data-intensive applications. The case study presented in Section 5.2 is a perfect illustration of the need for alternative CRM of Big Data applications. The reservation system discussed in this chapter addresses the challenges posed by such applications. A reservation system based on coalition formation and combinatorial auctions achieves two objectives: *coalitions* of servers supply the resources demanded by the applications and *combinatorial auctions* deliver packages of coalitions, one coalition for each phase of the application workflow.

Two strategies for coalition formation are presented next. The first strategy, *History-Based (HB)* uses feedback and learning from past behavior, as shown in Fig. 5.5. HB exploits information from past auctions to determine the size of the coalitions formed in each rack. Then the coalitions selected based on historic data compete to satisfy the current user needs for service. It

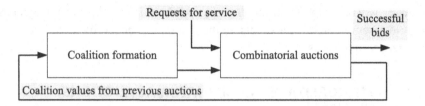

Fig. 5.5 A protocol with two stages; feedback about past values of individual coalitions is used to determine the value of individual coalition structures as shown in Section 5.4.

is very likely that over time, patterns of behavior will develop and it is beneficial to use information about coalitions that were successful in past auctions to drive the process of coalition formation as discussed in Section 5.4, and this would benefit a History-Based (HB) coalition formation process.

The second strategy, called *Just-in-Time (JST)*, is intuitive and straightforward, server coalitions are formed based on customer needs expressed at the time of the auction. JST implementation consists of several steps:

1. Examine the service requests and determine the type of servers and the size of the coalitions.
2. Send directives down the hierarchical structure of a WSC on the type of servers and the sizes matching the needs.
3. Servers form coalitions matching the service requests.
4. Coalitions compete for service requests.
5. Unsatisfied service requests are submitted again.

One is probably inclined to believe that JST coalition formation is a better choice because it seems more natural to respond to the current needs, rather than anticipate the needs. A counterargument is that in JST the two processes, the coalition formation and the combinatorial auctions are independent, thus, the goal of providing packages involving multiple coalitions is likely to involve additional overhead.

There are other reasons to be concerned about the effectiveness of JST coalition formation which requires information about the current state of the servers. Cloud data centers consist of multiple WSCs each with hundreds of thousands of servers interconnected by a hierarchy of networks. CRM policies relaying on state information collected through a monitoring process is rather inefficient compared with a trivial bidding process [163]. This motivates us to investigate market models for resource management based on coalition formation, but why combinatorial auctions?

A combinatorial auction is a market where the participants can place bids for *packages* of goods or services. Combinatorial auctions allow cloud users to acquire packages consisting of coalitions of servers with different types and amounts of resources. Combinatorial auctions are desirable because different phases of an application may require systems with different configurations or systems supporting different functions.

For example, the ubiquitous MapReduce applications illustrate the need for coalition formation and combinatorial auctions: coalitions of servers with attached GPUs are optimal for the computationally intensive Map phase, and coalitions of servers with solid-state secondary storage would be best for the Reduce phase. The two types of coalitions must be acquired at the same time; the results produced during the Map phase by the first coalitions should be stored during the Reduce phase on the systems in the second coalitions.

5.4 HISTORY-BASED RACK-LEVEL COALITION FORMATION

The organization of the cloud infrastructure should support a flexible environment. The resource management system should allocate resources in packages determined by the actual application needs, rather than providing a limited set of predefined packages. This objective can be best achieved by market-based self-organization and self-management mechanisms which are more efficient, agile, and user-friendly than the ones relying on hierarchical resource management.

The coalition formation process discussed next is based on concepts related to cooperative games presented in Section 3.8. A rack is homogeneous, all servers have the same architecture and identical configuration and are indistinguishable from one another. Rather than being selfish, the goal of all servers in a rack is to cooperate with one another and bring in a maximum benefit to the CSP. The homogeneity assumption simplifies considerably the search for an optimal coalitions structure (CS).

Spatial locality constrains. Communication is critical for the performance of a parallel application with a complex workflow, therefore mapping computations to processors should be very high on the priority list of any CRM system. The coalition members should be able to effectively communicate with one another and this condition should be of utmost concern for the coalition formation algorithms.

The infrastructure of cloud data centers is hierarchically structured and the communication latency among the servers in a rack is lower and the bandwidth is larger than communication with servers in another rack. The coalition formation should ensure *spatial locality* to minimize the communication overhead among the members of a coalition; it is therefore desirable to form coalitions among the tens of servers in the same rack of a WSC.

A rack consists of N powerful multicore servers capable of providing sufficient computing cycles, as well as, primary and secondary memory for virtually all Big Data applications. A rack is homogeneous as all servers have identical configurations. This realistic assumption simplifies considerably the complexity of the search for an optimal coalition structure as the servers are indistinguishable from one another.

Coalition lifetime and payoff distribution. In the applications discussed in the literature, coalitions have a rather long lifetime and coalition stability is of primary concern. This is not the case for the HB coalitions. The cloud model assumes slotted time and auctions organized at the beginning of each allocation slot. The coalitions have a short-lifetime; a coalition participates at an auction and, if successful, the coalition persists for the duration of the contract.

If a coalition is not successful during the auction organized in the current slot, the members are free to act alone. Some coalition members of an unsuccessful coalition may decide to offer their services for the current slot on the spot market, others may decide to stay idle for the current time slot and join a new coalition in the next allocation slot. Joining a coalition is not a long-term commitment, it is for a short time, and it is an ad hoc process.

The value of a coalition also reflects the length of time the coalition was active in response to a successful auction. The value attributed to a coalition of n servers is distributed equally among the members of the coalition. The value of a package of several coalitions auctioned successfully is divided among the coalitions based on the resource supplied by each one of them.

An algorithm for rack-level coalition formation. The S servers in a rack have a unique SId and are organized in a logical ring, SId^{i-1} and SId^{i+1} are the predecessor and, respectively, the successor of SId^i; SId^S and SId^2 are the predecessor and, respectively, the successor of SId^1.

Each server maintains a *coalition success record*, $\mathcal{R} = \{n, p, p_m\}$ with n the coalition size, p the probability of success, and p_m the probability that m copies of a coalition of size n were successful at an auction. All servers have the same information therefore, these records are identical. The probability of success p is the ratio of instances when a coalition consisting of n servers from this rack was matched with a service request and the number of instances this coalition size was offered but the bid was unsuccessful. When the system starts, $\mathcal{R} = \emptyset$ and the coalition sizes are randomly selected.

At the beginning of allocation slot k the role of *rack leader* is assumed by the server with $SId^j, j = k \mod S$. The rack leader communicates with the servers in the rack and with the WSC admission control process $\mathcal{A}$ which matches service requests with the set of coalitions proposed by all racks. The functions of the rack leader are:

1. Collect bids from servers ready to participate in coalition formation at the beginning of allocation slot k.
2. Select the set of coalitions most likely to be successful.
3. Send to $\mathcal{A}$ the set of proposed coalitions including the service type provided by the rack.
4. Receive from $\mathcal{A}$ the set of successful coalitions if any.
5. Form coalitions if the set of successful coalitions is not empty.
6. Broadcast data including: the set of proposed coalitions, the set of successful coalitions, and the servers in each coalition.
7. Get a confirmation that its successor in the ring is ready to assume the role of rack leader at the next allocation slot.

To select the set of coalitions most likely to be successful, the rack leader first determines the set of available servers N_k and then selects the clusters sizes n_i in the order of their probability of success such that the condition expressed by Eq. (5.26) is satisfied.

$$\sum_i n_i \leq N_k. \tag{5.26}$$

If this set does not include all N_k available servers then clusters of size one or two are added. For example, if $N_k = 19$ and the clusters of sizes $3, 5, 6$ have the largest probability of success then the list of coalitions proposed is $\mathcal{L} = \{1, 1, 1, 2, 3, 5, 6\}$.

A rack leader with SId^j conducts the coalition formation process as follows:

1. Order the set of successful coalitions based on the coalitions with the probability of success. Use the coalition size to break ties, larger coalitions being preferred.
2. Order the set of available servers based on their SId and the relative distance between them. For example, SId^{j+4} is placed before SId^{j+7}.
3. Allocate servers to coalitions based on the two ordered sets.

When the proposed coalition list is $\mathcal{L}\{1, 1, 1, 2, 3, 5, 6\}$, the ordered successful coalition list is $\mathcal{S} = \{3, (6, 1)\}$, and the available servers are at distance $D = \{3 - 5, 9 - 17, 20, 24 - 28\}$ from the current rack leader with SId^j, then the coalitions will be

$$\mathbb{C}_1 = \{SId^{j+3}, SId^{j+4}, SId^{j+5}\}.$$
$$\mathbb{C}_2 = \{SId^{j+9}, SId^{j+10}, SId^{j+11}, SId^{j+12}, SId^{j+13}, SId^{j+14}\}. \qquad (5.27)$$
$$\mathbb{C}_3 = \{SId^{j+15}\}.$$

5.5 A COMBINATORIAL AUCTION PROTOCOL

Several combinatorial auctions protocols discussed in Section 4.11 have been analyzed, but none is a good choice for CRM. In traditional applications of combinatorial auctions, the bidders are the consumers of resources, while in this particular application, there are two distinct competitions, one initiated by the providers and the other one by the consumers of services.

The protocol presented in this section primarily targets reservation systems for the *IaaS* cloud delivery model represented by AWS. Reservation and spot allocations are now offered by many CSPs. Reservations guarantee access for long-running enterprise applications, while spot allocations are used primarily by individual users for software development. This is the case of AWS where reservations are more costly than spot allocation.

The protocol is inspired by the clock-proxy auction [20]. This auction seems most suitable for cloud computing environments with a large population of both buyers and sellers. The clock-proxy auction has two phases:

1. A *clock* phase when the price discovery takes place.
2. A *proxy* phase, when the bids for packages are entertained.

Packages of services. The resources auctioned by the combinatorial auction protocol are supplied by coalitions of servers in different racks; the cloud users request packages of resources. The protocol supports auctioning packages consisting of combinations of services in one or more time slots.

The items sold are services advertised by coalitions of autonomous servers and the bidders are the cloud users. Each service is characterized by:

1. A *type* describing the resources offered and the conditions for service.
2. The time slots when the service is available.

A service S offered by a coalition is described by a relatively small number of *attributes*, $\{a_1, a_2, \ldots, a_i, \ldots\}$. Each attribute a_i can take a number of distinct values, $v_i = \{v_{i,1}, v_{i,2}, \ldots\}$. The first attribute is the coalition size or, equivalently, the number of vCPU provided. Other attributes could be the type of service, e.g., CPU-intensive, memory-intensive or data-intensive, the architecture, e.g., "32-bit" or "64-bit," the "server model," e.g., "vN" (von Neumann), "DF" (data-flow), or "vN-GPU" (vN with graphics co-processor).

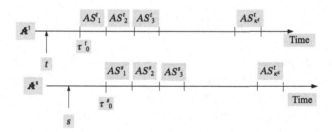

Fig. 5.6 *Auctions* $\mathbb{A}^t$ *and* $\mathbb{A}^s$ *conducted at times t and s, respectively.* τ_0^t *and* τ_0^s *are the start of the first allocation slots,* AS_1^t *and* AS_1^s *of the two auctions. The number of slots auctioned in each case are* κ^t *and* κ^s, *respectively.*

Terms used to describe the auction. An *allocation slot* (AS) is a period of fixed duration, e.g., 1 hour, that can be auctioned. An *auction*, $\mathbb{A}^t$, is organized at time t if there are pending reservation requests which require immediate attention. Fig. 5.6 shows two consecutive auctions at times t and s; during the first slot of auction $\mathbb{A}^t$ new reservation requests are received and the allocation slot AS_2^t is not fully covered; this slot becomes AS_1^s for $\mathbb{A}^s$.

Call $\mathcal{S}^t$ the set of services the clients want to reserve during auction $\mathbb{A}^t$

$$\mathcal{S}^t = \{S_1^t, S_2^t, \ldots, S_{\nu^t}^t\} \quad \text{with} \quad S_i^t = [SId, (a_j, v_{j,k})]. \tag{5.28}$$

A *reservation bundle*, $\alpha_{i,j}^t \subset \mathcal{S}^t$, is the set of services requested by client i in slot j of auction $\mathbb{A}^t$

$$\alpha_{i,j}^t = \{(S_{i,j,1}^t, r_{i,j,1}^t), (S_{i,j,2}^t, r_{i,j,2}^t), \ldots\}. \tag{5.29}$$

with $r_{i,j,l}^t$ a measure of the quantity; for example, if the attribute is "service intensity" the quantity is the number of vCPUs.

An *advertised bundle*, $\beta_{k,j}^t \subset \mathcal{S}^t$, is the set of services offered by coalition k in slot j of auction $\mathbb{A}^t$

$$\beta_{k,j}^t = \{(S_{k,j,1}^t, q_{k,j,1}^t, p_{k,1}^t), (S_{k,j,2}^t, q_{k,j,2}^t, p_{k,2}), \ldots\} \tag{5.30}$$

with $q_{k,j,l}^t$ a measure of the quantity of service l and $p_{k,l}$ the price per hour established by coalition k for service S_l^t. A *package*, $\mathcal{P}_i^t$ is a set of reservations for services requested by client i for slots $j_1, j_2, \ldots$ during auction $\mathbb{A}^t$.

$$\mathcal{P}_i^t = \{\alpha_{i,j_1}^t, \alpha_{i,j_2}^t, \ldots\}. \tag{5.31}$$

The clock phase. Fig. 5.7 illustrates the basic idea of a clock phase: the auctioneer announces prices and the bidders indicate the quantities they wish to buy at the current price. When the demand for an item increases, so does its price until there is no excess demand; on the other hand, when the offering exceeds the demand, the price decreases.

During the clock phase of auction $\mathbb{A}^t$ the price discovery is done for each time slot and for each type of service; a clock runs for each one of the κ^t slots and for each one of the ν^t services. Next the clock phase for service S_l^t in slot j is discussed. Assume that there are n coalitions $\mathbb{C} = \{\mathbb{C}_1, \mathbb{C}_2, \ldots, \mathbb{C}_n\}$ offering the service and m service requests from clients $\mathbb{D} = \{\mathbb{D}_1, \mathbb{D}_2, \ldots, \mathbb{D}_m\}$.

A clock auction starts at clock time $t = 0$ and at price per unit of service for S_l

$$p_l^0 = \min_{\mathcal{C}_k}\{p_{k,l}\}. \tag{5.32}$$

Call $\mathcal{C}_0$ the available capacity at this price and $\mathcal{D}_0$ the demand for service S_l^t offered at price p_l^0 in slot j

$$C_0 = \sum_{k=1}^{n} q_{k,j,l}^t \quad \text{and} \quad \mathcal{D}_0 = \sum_{i=1}^{m} r_{i,j,l}^t. \tag{5.33}$$

If $\mathcal{C}_0 < \mathcal{D}_0$ the clock c advances and the next price per unit of service is

$$p_l^1 = p_l^0 + \mathcal{I} \tag{5.34}$$

with $\mathcal{I}$ the price increment decided at the beginning of auction. There is an ample discussion in the literature regarding the size of the price increment; if too small, the duration of the clock phase increases, if too large, it introduces incentives for gaming the auction [20].

The process is repeated at the next clock value starting with the new price. The clock phase for service S_l^t and slot j terminates when there is no more demand.

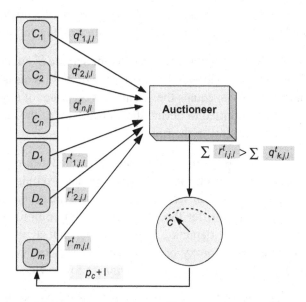

Fig. 5.7 *The clock phase for service S_l^t and slot j. The starting price is p_l^0 given by Eq. (5.32). The clock advances and the price increases from p_c to $p_c + \mathcal{I}$ when the available capacity at that price given by Eq. (5.33) is exhausted; the demand is given by Eq. (5.33).*

The proxy phase. In a traditional clock-proxy auction, the bidders do not bid directly, they report the price and the quantity of each item in the package they desire to a proxy. Then the proxy bids in an ascending package auction.

The proxy phase of the auction consists of multiple rounds. The auction *favors bids for long runs of consecutive slots* for services provided by the same coalition. This strategy is designed to exploit *temporal* and *spatial locality* and minimize the overhead for resource allocation, and reduce communication, as well as the execution time.

The auction starts with the longest runs and the lowest price per slot and proceeds with increasingly shorter runs and diminished incentives. Once a run of consecutive slots is the subject of a provisional winning bid, all shorter runs of slots for that particular service are removed from the coalition offerings.

During the first round, only the longest run of consecutive slots for each one of the services offered by the participating coalitions is auctioned and only bidders that have committed to any of the slots of the run are allowed to bid. The price per slot for the entire run is the lowest price for any slot of the run the bidder has committed to during the clock phase of the auction. If there are multiple bids for services, S_l^t the *provisional winner* is the one providing the largest revenue for the coalition offering the service.

If κ_l^t is the longest run of consecutive slots for service S_l^t auctioned in the first round then, in the second round, a shorter run of $\kappa_l^t - 1$ slots is auctioned. The price for the entire run equals the second lowest price for any slot of the run the bidder has committed to during the clock phase of the auction times the number of the time slots in the run.

The length of the consecutive slot runs auctioned decreases and the incentives diminish after each round. The preliminary rounds end with the auction of a single slot for each service. At the end of the preliminary round, each bidder is required to offer the price for the slot committed to during the clock phase. Fig. 5.8 depicts a plausible snapshot at the end of the preliminary rounds of the proxy phase when four services S_1, S_2, S_3, and S_4, are offered and shows the provisional winners for service S_4.

During the final round, the bidders reveal the packages they want to reserve; these packages include only the provisional winners from the preliminary slots. Once all provisional winning bids for services in a reservation request are known, the auctioneer chooses the package that best matches the consumer's needs and, at the same time, maximizes the profit for the CSP. The *coalition* for a reservation request consists of the set of coalitions that provide the services in the winning package.

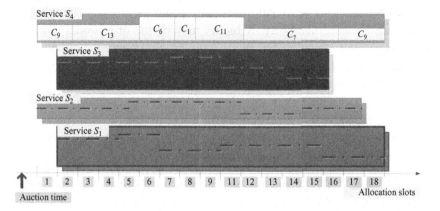

Fig. 5.8 A snapshot at the end of the preliminary rounds of the proxy phase when there are four services offered and the auction covers 18 allocation slots. Dotted lines represent the quantity of service with provisional winners. Only the provisional winners for S_4 are shown, the clients are labeled as $C_9, C_{13}, C_6, C_1, C_{11}, C_7,$ and C_9.

In this auction all bids are firm, they cannot be withdrawn. The auction is monotonic, the length of runs of consecutive slots auctioned decreases continually; this guarantees that the auction eventually terminates. Linear pricing guarantees that the price of any package can be computed with ease.

Effectiveness metrics. The effectiveness of the protocol is captured by several metrics:

1. The *customer satisfaction index*—percentage of reservation requests fully or partially satisfied in each allocation slot.
2. The *service mismatch index*—percentage of services requested but not offered in each allocation slot.
3. The *service success index*—percentage of services successfully auctioned.
4. The *capacity allocation index*—percentage of the capacity offered but not auctioned in each allocation slot.
5. The *overbidding factor*—percentage of slots with a provisional winner that have not been included in any package.
6. The *temporal fragmentation index*—percentage of services successfully auctioned in nonconsecutive slots given all services successfully auctioned.
7. The *additional profit index*—percentage of additional profit of coalitions involved in the auction, the difference of the actual price obtained at the auction and the price demanded by the coalition relative to the price demanded by the coalition.

Limitations and vulnerabilities. The protocol is fairly complex and has at least one vulnerability. A bidder may be the provisional winner of services in slots not included in its winning package; such services will remain unassigned during the current auction. A solution is to penalize *excess bidding activity* and charge the bidder a percentage of the costs for these services. Another alternative is to include in a reservation request a set of "substitute services" for a service S_i. Then, during the last round of the proxy phase, the auctioneer could try to match services having provisional winners with unsatisfied requests for services.

The capacity offered, but not auctioned, in each slot is available for *spot allocation* thus, it has the potential to be used, rather than being wasted. The capacity of a coalition left uncommitted at the end of the auction $\mathbb{A}^t$ for AS_1^t, the first slot of the auction (see Fig. 5.8), is then available for *spot allocation* at a price equal to $p_{k,l}$, while the free capacity in slots starting with AS_2^t can be offered at the next auction if this auction takes place before the beginning of the slot. This capacity is measured by the *spot allocation opportunity index.*

5.6 EVALUATION OF CLOUD POLICIES AND MECHANISMS

The question we address now is how to experiment with new cloud policies and mechanisms implementing these policies. Experimentation with a realistic cloud infrastructure is not feasible as such systems cannot be shut down, reconfigured, and their behavior and performance under new policies cannot be thoroughly investigated. Analytical studies are unrealistic due to the scale and the complexity of the system.

It is always tempting to conduct experiments on a testbed system, but there is no guarantee, in fact it is unlikely, that the results will hold for a large-scale system. New phenomena and different system behavior is expected when a system scales up, as we have seen in Chapters 1 and 3. As pointed out in [27] "... the WSCs are a new class of large-scale machines driven by new and rapidly evolving sets of workloads. The size alone makes them difficult to experiment with, or to simulate effectively..."

One expects to learn useful lessons from the successful methodology used for the development of other complex, man-made systems designed to perform under different operating conditions. This is the case of modern microprocessors, aircraft, or space exploration systems. In all these cases a new system is designed sometimes from scratch, based on the lessons learned from past developments and after a thorough analysis of the individual system components and their ability to work together.

For example, the development of a new processor with several billion gates goes through a rigorous process. This process starts with the development of detailed performance, power consumption, and reliability models. The next step is to experiment with the model. Simulators such as Simple Scalar (http://www.simplescalar.com/) and timing analysis tools have been widely used by the industry and research groups for years. Benchmarks (https://www.spec.org/benchmarks.html) used as input to the simulator allow us to predict the performance for different workloads.

Applying these ideas to computer clouds is far from trivial. While we can model in great detail the operation of an individual server, *the interactions among the set of servers is what gives the cloud infrastructure its flexibility and power* and require an analysis of the system as a whole. Moreover, a model useful for understanding the effect of new CRM policies is even more complex because the model should also describe the interactions of the infrastructure with an environment consisting of a large population of users, rather than describing the infrastructure in isolation. Unfortunately, detailed models of a cloud environment are yet to be developed.

It is extremely challenging to capture the dynamic interaction of individual servers in a model, then test several policies and mechanisms under different workloads. It is also not helpful that the organization of the infrastructure of existing systems, their policies, and the internal mechanisms for resource management are rather opaque. The CSPs are reluctant to disclose the inner working of their infrastructure, thus, it is not feasible to compare new policies and mechanisms with existing ones. This hinders not only the investigation of alternative CRM policies, but also standardization and efforts for supporting cloud interoperability.

A realistic alternative is to develop high-level (rather than detailed) models of the cloud infrastructure, conduct simulation experiments using these models, and draw qualitative conclusions from the simulation results. Such models must be carefully crafted and avoid details that unnecessarily complicate the simulation, or make it infeasible. The goal should be to *identify trends and determine the effect of different model parameters to gain insights based on a qualitative, rather than a quantitative analysis of the simulation results.*

An important step of model development is the identification of performance metrics likely to be affected by a new policy. Once these metrics are identified, the model should capture the processes affecting each one of them and quantify their effects.

The simulation models should exploit homogeneity whenever feasible. For example, assuming that all severs in a rack of a WSC are identical reduces the complexity of the simulation model and it is realistic, as it reflects the practice of current system architecture. These principles are applied in the analysis of market mechanisms based on coalition formation and combinatorial auctions for CRM discussed in this chapter.

The next three sections discuss simulation studies. The first simulation experiments compare hierarchical control with market-based policies for CRM. The second compares HB coalitions and JST coalitions, and the third covers experiments with an algorithm for combinatorial auctions.

5.7 HIERARCHICAL CONTROL VERSUS MARKET MECHANISMS

Hierarchical control in large-scale systems is ubiquitous. A distributed hierarchical management scheme seems a natural choice for a cloud infrastructure given the hierarchical topology of WSC networks. This motivates the choice of comparing the hierarchical control with the market mechanisms as reported in [163] and discussed in this section.

Hierarchical control means that decisions are made at different levels of the hierarchy of a cloud infrastructure similar to the one presented in Section 4.4. The decision process at each level of the hierarchy must be based on information about the state of the system components at the levels below it. The state information required by hierarchical control is collected periodically by a monitoring process and communicated to the decision agents.

Some of the desirable properties and the problem posed by the application of market mechanisms to CRM, discussed in Section 4.8, deserve to be further investigated. From the wide range of choices for the market mechanisms, a simple bidding scheme is chosen. In this scheme individual servers offer services and the decision process at the WSC level attempts to match service requests to services offered by the system. A qualitative analysis of hierarchical control and market mechanisms in a hierarchically organized computer cloud is presented next.

A simulation experiment. The simulation experiments are conducted on the Amazon cloud using *c3.8xlarge*[1] EC2 instances. It is challenging to simulate systems with 4–8 WSCs efficiently, the execution time for each one of the simulation experiments reported in this section is about 24 hours, and each simulation requires 5–6 days wall clock time.

It is important to understand how the scale and the load of the system, as well as several other parameters of the resource management system affect the ability of the cloud infrastructure to respond to service requests. An important measure of the effectiveness of a resource management system is the communication complexity expressed by the number of messages at each level of an interconnection infrastructure.

The communication latency increases and the bandwidth of the interconnection infrastructure decreases from the rack to the cell and then to the WSC level. We expect the communication complexity of a hierarchical resource management system to be dominated by monitoring and by the effort for locating a server capable to process a service request.

The simulation model assumes a time-slotted system. A service request is characterized by three parameters:

1. Service type.
2. Service duration—expressed as a number of time slots.
3. Service intensity—expressed as the number of vCPUs.

The system size, the system load, the service time, the total number of service types supported by the system, and the number of service types supported by a server affect the system performance. From the broad set of system performance metrics the following are the most relevant:

- The number of messages exchanged at the three levels of system hierarchy, rack, cell, and WSC for mapping the service requests. These numbers reflect the overhead of the request processing process.
- The ability of the system to balance the load, measured as the coefficient of variation (the variance versus the average) of the system load per allocation slot.
- The rejection ratio, the ratio of service requests rejected because no server able to match the service type, the service intensity, and the service duration demanded by the clients could be found, to the total number of requests.

---

[1] Compute-optimized instance with 32 vCPU and 60 GiB memory.

The system configuration is derived from the data in [27] and the parameters of the simulation model have been chosen as realistic as possible. The experiments were conducted with two system configurations, 4 and 8 WSCs. A WSC has the following configuration: 24 cells, 100 racks per cell, 40 servers in each rack, and 4 processors per server. Thus, a WSC has 88,000 servers and 352,000 processors. All servers have the same capacity, 10 vCPUs.

The simulation environment is flexible. A configuration file describes the system infrastructure, the network speed, the server load, and the parameters of the model. For example, the system configuration for the high initial load case is:

```
% System configuration
  static const int serverNum = 40;
 static const int cpuNum = 4;
 static const int rackNum = 100;
 static const int cellNum = 25;
 static const int WSCsNum = 4;
 static const int servers_capacity =100;
% Network speeds and load parameters
  static const int interRackSpeed = 1;
 static const int intraRackSpeed = 10;
 static const int MIN_LOAD = 80;
 static const int MAX_LOAD = 85;
% Model parameters
 static const int NUMBER_OF_TYPES = 100;
 static const int vCPU_MAX_REQUES = 800;
 static const int vCPU_MIN_REQUEST =10;
 static const int vCPU_PER_SERVER = 10;
 static const int MAX_SERVICE_TIME = 10;
 static const int MONITORING_PERIOD = 10;
 static const int SIMULATION_DURATION = 200;
 static const int TYPES_FOR_SERVER = 5;
 static const int TYPES_FOR_REQUEST = 5;
 static const int RACK_CAP =  serverNum * servers_capacity;
 static const int CLUS_CAP= rackNum * RACK_CAP;
 static const int WSC_CAP= clusterNum * CLUS_CAP;
 static const int SYSTEM_CAP= WSCsNum * WSC_CAP;
```

The amount of resources in a service request has a broad range, between 10 and 800 vCPUs, while a single server can provide 10 vCPUs. The spectrum of service types offered is quite large, initially 500 types and then reduced to 100.

The time is slotted and a batch of service requests with a random distribution of the service time, type, and intensity arrive in each slot. The individual service requests are randomly assigned to one of the WSCs. Practical considerations regarding simulation costs and time to get the results have limited the duration of simulation to 200 allocation slots.

Several simulation experiments with different system parameters are presented. In the first experiment the attributes of service requests are uniformly distributed and the ranges are: 1–100, 1–10, and 10–800 for service type, service time, and service intensity, respectively. A server supports 5 different service types randomly selected from a total of 500 possible service types. The monitoring interval is 10 allocation slots; for later experiments it will increase to 20 and then to 50 allocation slots. In a second experiment the effects of changing the parameters of the system model are investigated when:

1. Doubling the number of WSCs from 4 to 8; this gives an indication of the scalability of the model.
2. Increasing the average system load from about 20% to about 80% gives an indication about the robustness of the system and its ability to perform well under stress.
3. Reducing the number of requested service types from 500 to 100; we want to study the impact of the service diversity.
4. Reducing the number of types of services offered by each server from 5 to 2, though the more types of services, the more flexible the server configuration should be.
5. Changing the distribution of the service time from $(1 - 10)$ to $(1 - 20)$ time slots. The larger the range of the service time the broader the range of applications able to use the cloud infrastructure.
6. Increasing the monitoring interval for hierarchical control from 20 to 50 time slots; the monitoring interval is expected to have an effect on the quality of information used by load balancers.

Hierarchical control. In each time slot incoming service requests are randomly assigned to one of the WSCs. Each WSC periodically collects data from the cells, which in turn collect data from racks, which collect data from individual servers.

The communication complexity for this monitoring process increases linearly with the size of the system. The more frequent the monitoring at each level, the more accurate the information is, but the larger the volume of data and the interference with the "productive communication," communication initiated by running applications. The communication bandwidth at each level is limited and when the system load increases the communication latency is likely to increase significantly, as many applications typically exchange large volumes of data.

The simulation model assumes that load balancers at each level monitor the system they control. When a request is assigned to a WSC, the load balancer directs it to the cell with the lowest reported load and the process repeats itself at the cell level. The cell load balancer directs the request to the rack with the lowest reported load, which in turn directs it to server with the lowest reported load.

If the server rejects the request, the rack load balancer redirects the request to the server with the next lower load. If the rack cannot satisfy the request, it informs the cell load balancer, which in turn, redirects the request to the rack with the next lowest reported average load. The request is rejected if none of the cells of the WSC are able to find a server able to satisfy the type, duration, and intensity of the service request.

The simulation is conducted for two average initial system loads: low, around 20% and high, around 80% of the system's capacity. The total number of service requests for 4 WSCs and for low and high initial system load is around $(12 - 17) \times 10^6$ and $(42 - 57) \times 10^6$, respectively. In each case we show: (1) the number of WSCs; (2) the average initial and final system load for low and high load; (3) the initial and final coefficient of variation γ of the load; (4) the rejection ratio (RR); the number of messages for monitoring and control per service request at (5) WSC level; (6) cell level; and (7) rack level.

Simulation results for hierarchical control. The results of the first simulation experiment, Table 5.3, show that the rejection ratio, the coefficient of the variation of the final load, and the average number of messages required to map a service request to a server are more than three fold larger in the case of higher load; indeed, $7.1/2.2 = 3.22, 0.183/0.057 = 3.22$, and $984/276 = 3.2$, respectively. At higher load, more requests are rejected, load balancing is less effective, and the overhead for mapping a request is considerably higher. The increase in the number of messages means a

Table 5.3 Hierarchical Control—The Simulation Results for a System Configuration With 4 WSCs

WSCs	Initial/Final Load (%)	Initial/Final (γ)	RR (%)	# of Service Requests	WSC (Msg/Req)	Cell (Msg/Req)	Rack (Msg/Req)
4	22.50/19.78	0.007/0.057	2.2	14,335,992	0.98	3.18	271.92
	78.50/82.38	0.004/0.183	7.1	57,231,592	1.01	10.16	973.15
8	22.50/19.26	0.006/0.049	1.9	31,505,482	0.98	3.18	271.92
	78.50/81.98	0.005/0.213	8.7	94,921,663	1.01	11.36	1071.75

Shown are: the average initial and final system load for the low and high load; the initial and final coefficient of variation γ of the load; the rejection ratio (RR); and the average number of messages for monitoring and control per service request at WSC, cell, and rack level.

Table 5.4 Hierarchical Control: (Top Half) the Number of Service Types Is Reduced From 500 to 100; (Bottom Half) the Number of Service Types Offered by a Server Is Reduced From 5 to 2

WSCs	Initial/Final Load (%)	Initial/Final (γ)	RR (%)	# of Service Requests	WSC (Msg/Req)	Cell (Msg/Req)	Rack (Msg/Req)
4	22.50/21.15	0.003/0.051	1.9	16,932,473	1.00	3.53	337.34
	82.50/67.18	0.003/0.109	7.2	42,034,225	1.00	11.15	1097.00
8	22.50/22.13	0.008/0.055	5.4	38,949,889	1.00	4.22	470.35
	82.50/81.63	0.006/0.155	4.2	84,914,877	1.00	10.72	1038.96
4	22.50/21.15	0.003/0.051	1.7	17,341,885	0.99	3.22	276.34
	82.50/74.27	0.006/0.059	14.6	52,206,014	1.00	12.12	1255.40
8	22.50/16.27	0.006/0.035	1.3	37,750,971	0.99	3.18	268.27
	82.50/74.55	0.007/0.081	2.9	99,686,943	1.00	10.77	1036.64

All other parameters are identical to the ones for the experiment with results in Table 5.3.

substantial increase in the communication costs and also a longer waiting time before a request enters the service.

Doubling the size of the system does not affect the statistics for the same average system load. For example, when the initial average load is 22.50% the average number of messages exchanged per service request is the same at the three levels of the hierarchy for both system configurations. The rejection ratio varies little, 2.2% versus 1.9% and 7.1% versus 8.7% for 4 and 8 WSCs, respectively.

Table 5.4 (Top half) presents the results after reducing the total number of service request types from 500 to 100. A reduction of the rejection ratio and of the number of messages at high load for the larger configuration of 8 WSCs compared to the case in Table 5.3 is noticeable. Also, the rejection ratio decreases from 7.4% to 4.2% for configurations with 4 and 8 WSCs, respectively.

When the number of service types offered by a server is reduced from 5 to 2 and the system configuration changes from 4 to 8 WSCs the rejection rate decreases, see Table 5.4 (Bottom half). The reduction from 14.6 to 2.9 can be attributed to the fact that an incoming service request is randomly assigned to one of the WSCs; the larger the number of WSCs, the less likely is for the request to be rejected. The number of messages at the rack level is considerably larger for the smaller system configuration at high load, 1255 versus 973 in the first case presented in Table 5.3.

Table 5.5 Hierarchical Control: (Top Half) The Service Time Is Uniformly Distributed in 1–20 instead of 1–10 Allocation Slots; (Bottom Half) The Monitoring Interval Is Increased From 10 to 50 Reservation Slots

WSCs	Initial/Final load (%)	Initial/Final γ	RR (%)	# of Service Requests	WSC Msg/Req	Cell Msg/Req	Rack Msg/Req
4	22.50/22.41	0.005/0.047	0.20	12,352,852	1.00	3.13	261.11
	82.50/80.28	0.003/0.063	2.10	43,332,119	1.00	3.41	1108.12
8	22.50/22.77	0.005/0.083	1.30	25,723,112	1.00	3.11	236.30
	82.50/79.90	0.005/0.134	4.10	88,224,546	1.00	10.63	1029.56
4	22.50/21.07	0.003/0.033	1.00	12,335,103	0.99	3.21	270.07
	82.50/83.46	0.007/0.080	1.80	51,324,147	1.01	10.87	1040.63
8	22.50/19.16	0.005/0.030	1.30	29,246,155	1.00	3.37	304.88
	82.50/84.12	0.002/0.041	2.30	93,316,503	1.00	3.66	1005.87
All other parameters identical to the ones for the experiment with results in Table 5.3.							

Next, the monitoring interval is set to 20 allocation slots and the service time is uniformly distributed in the range 1–20 allocation slots. The results in Table 5.5 (Top half) show that the only noticeable effect is the reduction of the rejection rate.

In the following experiment, the monitoring interval is extended from 10 to 50 allocation slots. The service time is uniformly distributed in the range 1–10 allocation slots; even when the monitoring interval was 10 allocation slots, this interval is longer than the average service time thus, the information available to load balancers at different levels is obsolete.

The results in Table 5.5 (bottom half) show that increasing the monitoring interval to 50 slots has little effect for the 4 WSC configuration at low load, but it reduces substantially the rejection ratio and increases the number of messages at high load. For the 8 WSC configuration, increasing the monitoring interval reduces the rejection ratio at both low and high load, while the number of messages changes only slightly.

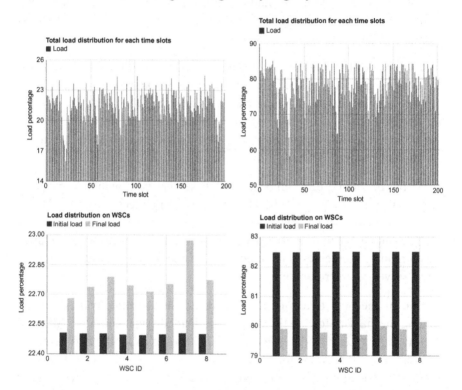

Fig. 5.9 Hierarchical control for a cloud with 8 WSCs. The monitoring interval is 20 allocation slots and the service time is uniformly distributed in the range 1–20 allocation slots. The initial average system load: (left) 20%; (right) 80% of system capacity. (Top) Time series of the average WSC load. (Bottom) Initial and final average WSC load.

Fig. 5.9 (top) shows the time series of the average system load for the low and the high initial load, respectively for the case in Table 5.3 when the monitoring interval is 20 time slots and the service time is uniformly distributed in the 1–20 slots range and there are 8 WSCs. The system workload has significant variations from slot to slot; for example, at high load the range of the average system load is from 58% to 85% of the system capacity. Fig. 5.9 (bottom) shows the initial and the final load distribution for the 8 WSCs; the imbalance among WSCs at the end of the simulation is in the range of $1 - 2\%$.

The results of the five simulation experiments are consistent, they typically show that at high load, the number of messages, and thus the overhead for request mapping increases three- to four-fold, at both cell and rack level and for both system configurations, 4 and 8 WSCs.

Simulation of a market model. In this resource management model, all servers of a WSC bid for service. A bid consists of the service type(s) offered and the available capacity of the bidder.

The overhead is considerably lower than that of the hierarchical control; there is no monitoring, and the information maintained by each WSC consists only of the set of unsatisfied bids at any given time. The servers are autonomous and act individually; there is no collaboration among them. Note that self-organization and self-management require agents to collaborate with each other.

At the beginning of an allocation slot, servers with available capacity above a threshold τ place bids. The bids are then collected by each WSC. A bid is *persistent,* if not successful in the current allocation slot it remains in effect until a match with a service request is found. This strategy to reduce the communication costs is justified because successful bidding is the only way a server can increase its workload.

One of the objectives of the investigation is the effectiveness of the bidding mechanism for lightly and heavily loaded system, around 20% and 80% average system load, respectively. The thresholds for the two cases are different, $\tau = 30\%$ for the former and $\tau = 15\%$ for the latter. The choice for the lightly loaded case is motivated by the desire to minimize the number of messages; a large value of τ, e.g., 40% would lower the rejection ratio but increase the number of messages. Increasing the threshold, e.g., using a value $\tau = 20\%$, would increase dramatically the rejection rate in the case of heavily loaded system; indeed, few servers would have 20% available capacity when the average system load is 80%.

Simulation results for the market model. The measurements reported for the hierarchic control are repeated under the same conditions as those for hierarchical control for a fair comparison; only bidding replaces monitoring and hierarchical control. The same performance indicators are used:

Table 5.6 Market Model: Simulation Results for a System Configuration With 4 WSCs

WSCs	Initial/Final Load (%)	Initial/Final (γ)	RR (%)	# of Service Requests	WSC (Msg/Req)	Cell (Msg/Req)	Rack (Msg/Req)
4	22.50/23.76	0.007/0.067	0.22	15,235,231	0.002	0.011	0.987
	82.50/80.32	0.004/0.115	5.44	63,774,913	0.003	0.042	4.155
8	22.50/22.47	0.006/0.033	0.18	30,840,890	0.002	0.011	0.987
	82.50/81.30	0.005/0.154	7.23	89,314,886	0.003	0.054	5.761

Shown are the initial and final system load for the low and high load, the initial and final coefficient of variation γ of the load, the rejection ratio (RR), and the average number of messages for monitoring and control per service request at WSC, cell, and rack level.

Table 5.7 Market Model: (Top) The Number of Service Types Is Reduced From 500 to 100; (Center) The Number of Service Types Offered by a Server Is Reduced From 5 to 2; (Bottom) The Service Time Is Uniformly Distributed in the Range of 1–20 Instead of 1–10 Allocation Slots

WSCs	Initial/Final Load (%)	Initial/Final (γ)	RR (%)	# of Service Requests	WSC (Msg/Req)	Cell (Msg/Req)	Rack (Msg/Req)
4	22.50/22.3	0.004/0.050	0.18	15,442,372	0.002	0.011	0.987
	82.50/79.88	0.004/0.098	6.01	56,704,224	0.002	0.059	5.968
8	22.50/23.0	0.007/0.049	0.3	31,091,427	0.002	0.011	0.987
	82.50/80.91	0.009/0.127	5.81	85,322,714	0.003	0.051	5.845
4	22.50/20.94	0.007/0.056	0.1	15,295,245	0.002	0.011	0.987
	82.50/77.83	0.008/0.133	10.1	49,711,936	0.003	0.063	6.734
8	22.50/22.33	0.007/0.063	0.02	31,089,191	0.002	0.011	0.987
	82.50/78.18	0.008/0.142	3.61	71,873,449	0.002	0.059	6.098
4	22.50/23.31	0.002/0.064	2.27	13,445,186	0.001	0.011	0.988
	82.50/84.05	0.007/0.101	3.75	57,047,343	0.002	0.042	6.329
8	22.50/18.93	0.007/0.038	2.94	28,677,012	0.001	0.011	0.988
	82.50/85.13	0.008/0.072	4.38	88,342,122	0.002	0.029	4.078

communication complexity, the efficiency of load balancing, and the rejection ratio. The results are shown in Tables 5.6 and 5.7.

The simulation results show a significant reduction of the communication complexity, more than two orders of magnitude in case of the market-oriented mechanism. For example, at low average load the average number of messages per reservation request at the rack level is 0.987, Tables 5.6 and 5.7, versus 271.92, Table 5.3 for 4 and 8 WSCs.

At high average load, the average number of messages for the market model and the hierarchical model, respectively, are: 4.155 versus 973.14 for the 4 WSC case and 5.761 versus 1071.75 for the 8 WSC case. A second observation is that when the average load is 20% of the system capacity, the communication complexity is constant, 0.987, for both configurations, 4 and 8 WSCs, regardless of the choices of simulation parameters. At high average load, the same value is confined to a small range, 4.078–6.734.

The organization is scalable, the results for 4 and for 8 WSCs differ only slightly. This is expected because of the distributed scheme where each WSC acts independently, it receives an equal fraction of the incoming service requests and matches them to the bids placed by the servers it controls.

The average rejection ratio at low average load decreases, see Tables 5.6 and 5.7. On the other hand, the rejection rate increases when the range of the service time increases from the 1–10 to 1–20, see Table 5.7 (bottom). This effect is most likely due to the fact that requests with a large service time arriving during later slots do not have time to complete during the 200 allocation slots covered by the simulation.

At high average system load, the average rejection ratio is only slightly better for market-based versus hierarchical control. Lastly, the market-based mechanism performs slightly better than hierarchical control in terms of slot-by-slot load balancing, the coefficient of variation of the system load per slot is $\gamma \leq 1.115$.

The number of different service types offered by the cloud and the number of services supported by individual servers, do not seem to affect the performance of the system see Table 5.7 (top) and (center).

Fig. 5.10 (top) shows time series of the average system load for the low and the high initial load, respectively. The actual system workload has relatively small variations from slot to slot; for example, at high load, the range of the average system load ranges from 77% to 82% of the system capacity. Fig. 5.10 (bottom) shows the initial and the final load distribution; the imbalance among the eight WSCs at the end of the simulation is in the 21–23% range at low load and in the 80–80.1% range at high load.

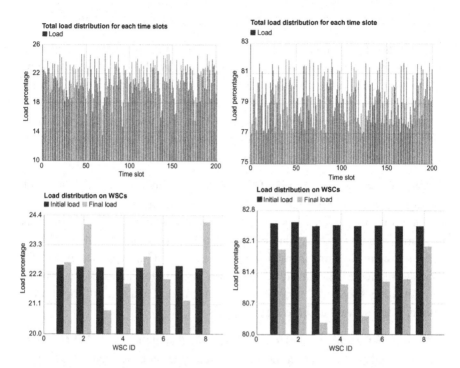

Fig. 5.10 Market model. A cloud with 8 WSCs, the monitoring interval is 20 allocation slots and the service time is uniformly distributed in the range 1–20 allocation slots. The initial average system load is: (left) 20%; (right) 80% of system capacity. (Top) time series of the average load. (Bottom) initial and final average load.

The results show that market-based policy performs well at high system load and this is extremely important. The average server utilization based on existing CRM policies reported in the literature is rather low. A policy that allows servers to operate effectively under heavy load is highly desirable.

The results of the simulation experiments discussed in this section confirm our intuition that monitoring required by a hierarchical resource management adds a significant overhead for resource management in a large-scale system and cannot provide accurate information about the state of system resources. We can only draw qualitative conclusions from the simulation experiments, the performance of the market mechanisms is significantly better for critical performance metrics than the results of hierarchical control and this effect is noticeable for experiments with different sets of parameter models.

5.8 HISTORY-BASED VERSUS JUST-IN-TIME COALITIONS

The results of a simulation experiment comparing the two strategies for coalition formation, HB and JST are reported in [164] and in [253] and reviewed in this section. The simulation is based on a simple model when a service request specifies the type of service, the service duration, and service intensity expressed as the number of vCPUs. For each service type, only racks offering that service form coalitions, provided that the autonomous servers in the rack have sufficient available capacity.

The system model. In the HB strategy, described in Section 5.3, a rack leader uses historic information about past successful coalitions in a window of w auctions to suggest the size of the coalitions that the servers in the rack join, provided that their available capacity allows participation in a coalition. Once the coalitions are formed, all racks of a WSC independently bid for services requested in that allocation slot. An auction takes place and the racks hosting successful coalitions are informed. Then this information is passed to the servers and the service starts.

In the JST strategy, service requests are dispatched to a WSC where they are analyzed to determine the service type and the desired coalition size for each. This information is then broadcast to the racks of the WSC where an attempt is made to dynamically create appropriate coalitions. Rack leaders initiate the coalition formation process, and finally, the information about newly formed coalitions is passed to the combinatorial auction system. The algorithm for JST coalition formation is similar to the one for the HB strategy. The only difference is that the coalition sizes are now the ones demanded by the service request rather than those determined by past activity.

The combinatorial auction protocol. The protocol is based on the clock algorithm discussed in Section 5.5. The auctioneer announces prices and the bidders indicate the quantities they wish to buy at the current price. Then the auctioneer adjusts the prices based on the current demand. In our simulation, after coalition formation, coalitions start bidding on the service request and the auctioneer analyzes these bids and prioritizes them based on the prices they offered.

Several criteria drive the decisions of the auctioneer when selecting the coalitions for the packages required by the work-flow. These decisions are based on the price discovered during the clock phase. The implementation of the auction is based on a hierarchical decision making process.

The decision factors in priority order are:

1. the *coalition size*—the larger the coalition size, the higher the priority;
2. the *requested service duration*—the longest duration has the highest priority;
3. the *rack load*—the lower the rack load, the higher the priority; and
4. the *cell load*—the lower the cell load, the higher the priority.

If two coalitions with the same size and same duration, but with different rack load levels bid for a request, priority is given to the coalition from the rack with lower load. This decision process aims to balance the load on racks and cells.

Simulation experiments. Several simplifications are necessary to simulate a cloud infrastructure with several WSCs:

1. Auctions are organized periodically and the time between two consecutive auctions is called an *allocation slot*.
2. A service request should specify the service duration as an integer number of slots.
3. The communication complexity is measured by the number of messages; this approximation avoids a detailed timing analysis of the communication delays, which would require modeling contention at different levels of the network hierarchy.
4. For practical reasons, the simulation is conducted for only 500 allocation slots. A longer history would lead to more accurate predictions of the size of successful coalitions for each service type, thus, we expect the results to improve in time for the HB strategy.

The choice of the system configuration is guided by data from the literature [27]. The simulated system consists of 4 WSC, each one with 25 cells; each cell has 100 racks and each rack has 40 servers. The server capacity, measured by the number of vCPU, is uniformly distributed in the range of 10–50 vCPU.

Sensible choices to describe the workload include: the number of coalitions in each package of services in a client's request, the number of different service types provided by the system, service intensity measured by the number of vCPU requested, and service duration. Each coalition request specifies the service type, the service duration, and the service intensity expressed as the number of vCPU. The last parameter is used to determine a sensible coalition size. Service requests are generated continually and all service requests, arriving after an auction has begun, wait to participate in the next auction.

The system offers 20 different service types. A request for service specifies the service type, intensity, and duration. The service intensity is uniformly distributed in the range 10–500 vCPUs and the service duration is uniformly distributed in the range 5–25 allocation slots. The number of coalitions in a package is uniformly distributed in the interval 5–25.

Simulation results. Figs. 5.11 and 5.12 display time series of the number of coalitions requested, coalitions successful during the auctions, as well as, the success ratio for two initial system loads, 20% and 80%, respectively, when all services are taken into account. It is rather difficult to control the average system load and we only report the initial system load. The duration of the simulation is 500 allocation slots and each bin shows the average over 10 of them. The mean and the variance of the three simulation results, the numbers of coalitions requested and coalitions formed, and the success ratios are summarized in the left columns of Table 5.8.

The average number of successful coalitions decreases when the load increases, about 16% for HB and about 7% for JST. This difference is not reflected in the success ratios of the two strategies; as we shall see next, it is most likely a sign that HB better reflects the internal state of the system than JST.

The coalition formation success ratio varies only slightly with the load. When the initial average system load increases from about 20% to 80% the success ratio decreases only slightly for HB, from 68% to 66% and increases slightly for JST, from 66% to 67%. *This is remarkable and shows that both market-based strategies are robust and indicate a much higher resource utilization than the average one reported for existing systems.*

Table 5.9 shows the communication complexity at the low and high average initial system load for the two strategies HB and JST. We differentiate between messages exchanged at the rack level and those exchanged at higher levels of the network hierarchy (cell and WSC), where contention for network access is more intense.

As expected, the total number of messages for the HB strategy decreases significantly with the load, from about 47×10^6 to 20×10^6; as the load increases, fewer servers are available for coalition formation. The situation is reversed for JST, and we notice a sharp increase from about 21×10^6 to 37×10^6. This is expected because the coalition formation process is

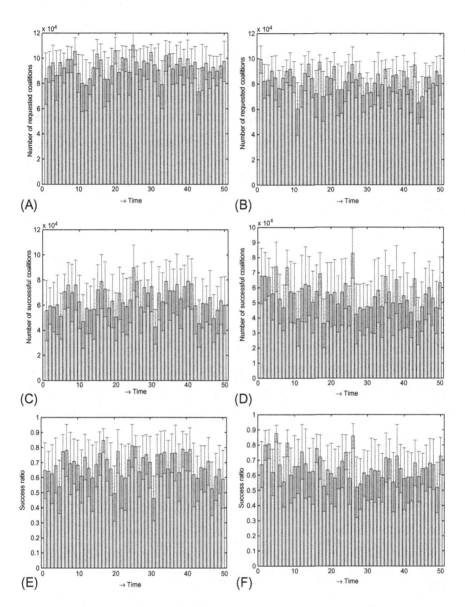

Fig. 5.11 Time series of the number of coalitions requested, successful, and the success ratio at 20% initial system load for all service types. Strategies for coalition formation: HB (A) requested, (C) successful, and (E) success ratio; JST (B) requested, (D) successful, and (F) success ratio.

driven by the external service requests. Note that in the case of JST, 70% of all messages exchanged at high load are at the cell and WSC level, where contention for communication bandwidth is considerably higher.

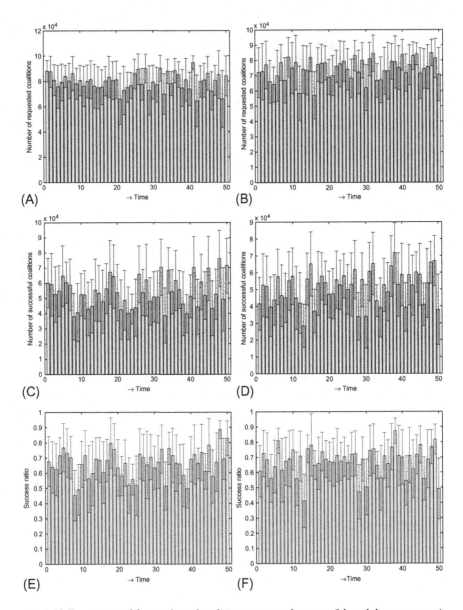

Fig. 5.12 Time series of the number of coalitions requested, successful, and the success ratio at 80% initial system load for all service types. Strategies for coalition formation: HB (A) requested, (C) successful, and (E) success ratio; JST (B) requested, (D) successful, and (F) success ratio.

In HB, the coalition formation process is driven by the internal state: only servers with available capacity participate in coalition formation and subsequently in the combinatorial auctions, while in the case of JST the process is driven by external factors. At low load, the number of rack-

Table 5.8 Statistical Results for the Two Coalition Formation Strategies, HB and JST, for Two Different Initial Loads, 20% and 80%

Method	Initial Load	Stats	Requested All	Successful All	SR All	Requested Two Types	Successful Two Types	SR Two Types
HB	20%	Mean/	93,648.96/	64,805.99/	68%	11,991.71/	7124.12/	60%
		Std	7691.05	10,134.88	0.09	1076.32	1101.33	0.09
	80%	Mean	79,882.37/	54,192.35/	66%	10,421.61/	5957.67/	57%
		Std	6540.43	9786.67	0.09	1037.72	1149.43	0.08
JST	20%	Mean/	83,194.86/	55,565.27/	66%	10,689.07/	6068.37/	57%
		Std	8445.98	9787.62	0.09	881.93	1035.98	0.09
	80%	Mean	74,572.12/	51,381.41/	67%	9672.03/	5690.32/	59%
		Std	6602.59	9699.45	0.09	924.87	1128.16	0.09

The mean and the variance of the number of coalitions requested and the number of successful coalitions chosen during the auctions, and the success ratio (SR). Results are shown for: (left) all types of service requests; (right) two randomly chosen types.

Table 5.9 Communication Complexity of HB and JST for All Service Types and Two Different System Initial Loads, 20% and 80%

Method	Load	Nr	Nt	SRr	SRt	SCFr	SCFt
HB	20%	18,823,492	46,824,480	201	500	290	722
	80%	6,299,012	19,970,590	79	250	116	368
JST	20%	8,129,402	20,798,714	98	250	146	374
	80%	14,241,563	37,286,059	191	500	277	725

Number of messages: Nr, at rack level; Nt, at all level; SRr, per service request at rack level; SRt, per service request at all levels; SCFr, per successful coalition formation at rack level; and SCFt, per successful coalition formation at all levels.

level messages per either service request, or successful coalition formation, is almost twice larger for HB than for JST, e.g., 201 versus 98 and 290 versus 146, respectively, see Table 5.9. At high load the situation is reversed 79 versus 191 and 116 versus 277. The same observation applies to the total number of messages per service request and per successful coalition formation. At low load the ratios for HB and JST are 500 versus 250 and 722 versus 374, respectively. At high load the ratios are 250 versus 500 and 368 versus 725.

Fig. 5.13 presents the life-time of coalitions for all service requests when the initial load is 20% and 80% of system capacity, for the HB and LST reservation systems, respectively. This life-time of a successful coalition reflects the duration of the corresponding service request.

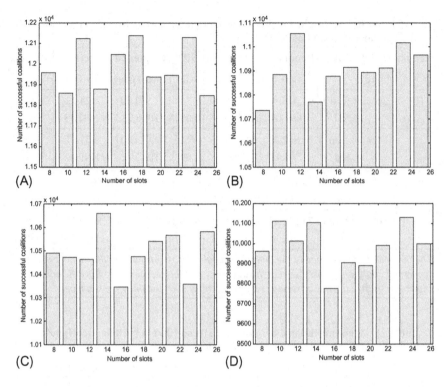

Fig. 5.13 Histograms of coalition lifetime. Average initial load 20% of system capacity: (A) HB; (B) JST. Average initial load 80% of system capacity: (C) HB; (D) JST.

Lastly, two particular types of service are randomly selected to study their behavior. The results, summarized on the right-hand side of Table 5.8, show that indeed the number of requests, as well as, the number of successful coalitions is about one-tenth of the total number of the corresponding entries for all service requests. Fig. 5.14 shows time series of the success ratios for the two randomly selected service types.

5.9 ANALYSIS AND EVALUATION OF THE PROXY PHASE

The results of simulation experiments to gain some insight into the proxy phase of the clock-proxy auction of the protocol are presented next. The system we evaluate requires the description of the environment in which the auction takes place, the reservation requests, and the services offered:

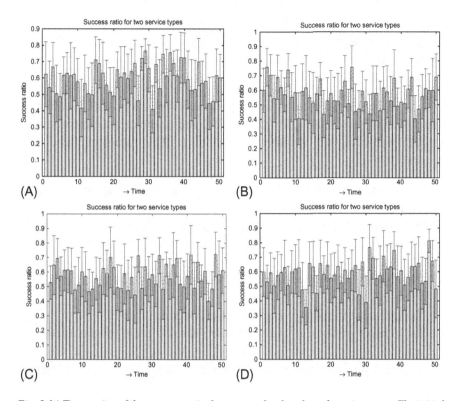

Fig. 5.14 Time series of the success ratio for two randomly selected service types. The initial load is : (top) 20%; (bottom) 80%. Two strategies for coalition formation: (A) and (C) HB; (B) and (D) JST.

1. The environment elements: n—the number of coalitions offering services in this round; m—the number of clients; and κ—the number of slots auctioned.
2. The package j requested by client i: α_i^n—the number of services in the package; the slots desired by the service S_k, ordered by the length of the run of consecutive slots; $r_{k,j}$—the intensity of service S_k in slot j; $p_{i,j}$—the price per unit of service for slot j if client i was a provisional winner of that slot during the clock phase.
3. The service S_k provided by coalition $\mathbb{C}_k$ includes: γ_k—the largest run of consecutive slots for each offered service S_k; the profile of the service S_k—the slots offered ordered by the length of consecutive slots, when it is available; $q_{k,j}$—the quantity of service S_k offered in slot j; and p_k—the price per unit of service offered by coalition $\mathbb{C}_k$.

For simplicity, it is assumed that a coalition offers one service only and the number of services is $\nu < n$. It is also assumed that all platforms have a maximum capacity of 100 vCPUs and that $q_{k,j}$, the quantity of service S_k offered for auction, and $r_{k,j}$, the quantity of S_k requested in slot j, are the same for all the slots of an offered/requested run. The number of slots auctioned is fixed, $\kappa = 50$.

The range and the distribution of parameters for the protocol evaluation are chosen to represent typical cases. The parameters of the simulation are random variables with a uniform distribution. The parameters and their ranges are:

1. The number of coalitions and clients requesting reservations, n and m, respectively; the interval is [200–250].
2. The number of services offered and requested ν; the interval is [10–20].
3. The number of clients bidding for each service in a given slot; the interval is [0–4].
4. The capacity offered for auction for a service in a given slot; the interval is [60–90] vCPUs.
5. The services offered by a coalition; the interval is [1–ν].
6. The number of consecutive slots a service is offered in; the interval is [1–κ].
7. The number of services in the package requested by a client; the interval is [1–3].
8. The number of consecutive slots of the services in the package requested by a client; the interval is [1–κ].

The slots are randomly chosen when the client is the provisional winner. The evaluation process consists of the following steps:

1. *Initialization.*
2. *Preliminary rounds.* Carry out γ preliminary rounds with $\gamma = \max_k \gamma_k$.
   - Auction κ_1 slots of service S_1, κ_2 slots of service S_2, and so on, in the first preliminary round.
   - Identify the first slot of each run and the reservation request that best matches the offer.
   - Identify the provisional winners if such matches exist and remove the corresponding runs from the set of available runs. A match exists if the run consists of the same number of slots or if one slot is longer than requested and if the capacity offered is at least the one required by the reservation request. For services without a match, remove the last slot, add both the shorter run and the last slot to the list of available runs.
   - Continue this process until only single slots are available.

3. *Final round.* In this round the following actions are carried out:
- Identify the packages for each client and if multiple packages exist determine the one which best matches the request.
- Compute the cost for the winning package for each client.

Fig. 5.15(A–F) shows several performance metrics including the customer satisfaction index, the service mismatch index, the auction success ratio, the spot opportunity index, the temporal fragmentation index, and the capacity allocation index. The simulation covers 50 time slots.

The 5% confidence intervals for the mean of all performance metrics are computed for 25 batches, each one of 200 realization of each random variable. The simulation times are 6.4 s for 2,000 runs and 11.7 s for 5,000 runs. The confidence intervals are rather tight; this indicates that the performance of the protocol is relatively stable for the range of parameters explored in this evaluation.

The auction success rate is high, typically above 80%. The initial low auction success rate is an artifact of the decision to randomly select the service startup time. The spot allocation opportunity index is correlated with the auction success rate and shows that a significant fraction of the capacity is available for spot allocation. This result is correlated with the one in Fig. 5.15(F) which shows that on average, some 50% of the server capacity is not allocated by the reservation system and it is available for the spot market.

A reservation system covering 50% of the server capacity is probably the most significant result; it shows that self-management based on auctions can drastically improve server utilization. We live in a world of limited resources and cloud over-provisioning is not sustainable either economically or environmentally.

The service mismatch index is fairly high, typically in the 50% range and it is above 60% in a few slots. The customer satisfaction is correlated with the service mismatch and typically is in the region of 50%. In a realistic scenario, when coalitions maintain statistics regarding the services offered and avoid offering services unlikely to be demanded by the cloud users, the service mismatch would not affect the performance of the algorithm. Temporal fragmentation, though rather low, is undesirable. The overbidding factor $64 \pm 2.93\%$ is another indication that the protocol needs to be finely tuned.

Self-organization cannot occur instantaneously in an adaptive system and this simple observation has important consequences. It is critical to give

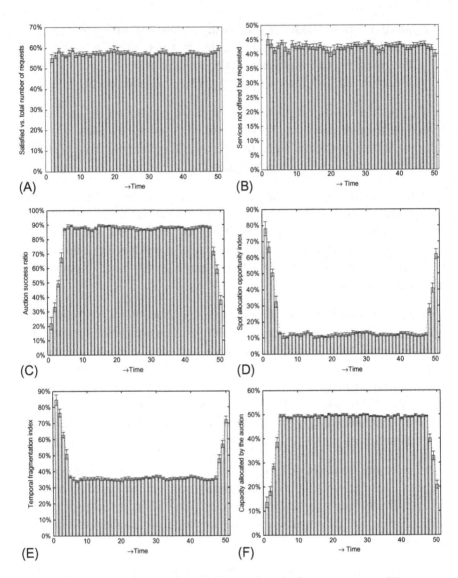

Fig. 5.15 Proxy phase of an auction with 50 time slots. Performance metrics: (A) customer satisfaction; (B) service mismatch; (C) auction success; (D) spot allocation opportunity; (E) temporal fragmentation; (F) capacity allocation.

autonomous cloud platforms, interconnected by a hierarchy of networks, the time to form coalitions in response to services demanded. Thus, self-management requires an effective reservation system and our results indicate that the reservation protocol is working well.

5.10 SOFTWARE ORGANIZATION FOR A RESERVATION SYSTEM

This section presents a software organization for a cloud reservation system for Big Data applications. The software implements the algorithms for the HB coalition formation and the combinatorial auctions introduced earlier in this chapter. The reservation system supports a primitive form of self-organization and self-management. Indeed, no monitoring is involved, the information about available resources flows from the bottom to the top, from the individual servers to the WSCs, where service requests are matched to a set of available coalitions.

The software organization reflects the WSC organization presented in Section 4.4 and illustrated in Fig. 4.4 and assumes that all servers in a rack have the same architecture and identical configuration, but the servers in different racks may have a different architecture and configuration. The racks are homogeneous, while a WSC is a heterogeneous collection of different racks.

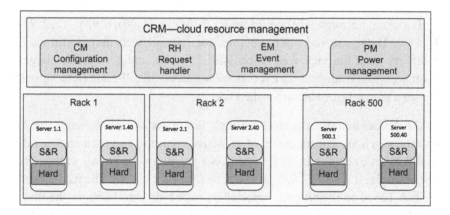

Fig. 5.16 The software organization for a reservation system using history-based coalition formation and combinatorial auctions. All servers in a rack run the S&R control system responsible for coalition formation. Global functions are provided by the CRM running on dedicated servers.

The software for the reservation system includes the *Server and Rack* (S&R) control system and the CRM system (see Fig. 5.16). The S&R control system is responsible for coalition formation and resource management at the rack level.

A rack leader manages the coalition formation process in each rack. The role of rack leader is passed from one server to the next to balance the load and to ensure some degree of fault-tolerance. The rack leader may or may not be included in any coalition. Selection of a rack leader can be done automatically to avoid a communication-intensive election process. For example, when the server IDs are $\{1, 2, \ldots, j, \ldots, S\}$ then in slot k the role of rack leader can be automatically assigned to the server with ID $j = k \mod S$.

The coalition formation process involves several steps:

1. Ranking of coalitions most likely to succeed based on historic performance data;
2. Assignment of available servers to coalitions according to their bids; and
3. Sharing information about successful coalitions after an auction.

To reduce communication complexity, all servers maintain a list of successful coalitions in previous auctions. This list is ordered according to the revenues brought in by the coalitions with the same number of servers. The coalition with the largest number of servers is placed before the others in case of a tie. The list could be extended to include the most likely combinations of successful coalitions.

For example, such a list could be $\mathcal{R} = \{6(75), 11(40), 8(43), \ldots, 2(97), 1(198)\}$. Data gathered after previous auctions showed that coalitions of 6 servers from the rack were successful 75 times and brought the largest revenue, while coalitions of 1 server were successful 198 times and brought the least amount of revenue for the rack.

At the beginning of a slot, the rack leader receives bids from the N_a servers which are not members of an active coalition and then chooses the coalition set to compete for service packages in the current allocation slot. For example, if $N_a = 27$ this set could be $\mathcal{C} = \{6, 11, 8, 2\}$. The leader ranks the bids based on the revenue reported by each bidder and assigns the first 6 servers to the first coalition, then the next 11 servers to the second coalition and so on. Finally, after the auction, the leader broadcasts the information about successful coalitions, e.g., $\{6, 8\}$ and verifies that the leader for the next allocation slot is ready to carry out its duties.

The CRM includes a large number of components including the Configuration Management System (CMS), the Request Handler System (RHS), the Event Management (EM) system, and the Power Management System (PMS). The CMS describes the organization of the entire infrastructure including the number of WSCs, the cells in each WSC, the racks in each cell, and the architecture and configuration of individual servers in each rack.

Racks with identical servers have an identical rack-description record. The CMS includes a network-configuration file with a detailed description of the interconnect fabric. The CMS also supports the Health Monitoring Center (HMC) tasked to provide data about the performance and state of all system components. Another component of the CMS is the System Administrator Access (SAA) system which supports privileged system access for system administrators.

The Request Handler System has multiple functions, some supporting an application-centric environment, and others implementing the market-oriented mechanisms for resource allocation. Its main components are:

1. Client Access Console (CAC),
2. Intelligent Concierge (IC),
3. Blueprint Interpreter (BPI),
4. Admission Control System (ACS),
5. Combinatorial Auction Management System (CAMS),
6. Spot Allocation System (SAS),
7. Task Management System (TMS),
8. Workflow Management System (WMS),
9. Error Recovery System (ERS), and
10. Accounting System (AS).

The Client Access Console supports a set of high-level services for cloud users. CAC allows users to create and manage an account, request services, list all active instances, monitor the execution of running instances, gather performance data for active instances, terminate an instance, report on storage utilization, and get accounting data. The Intelligent Concierge aims to improve the user experience. The Intelligent Concierge collects history data, builds user profiles, suggests blueprints for different activities, supports workflow definition, profiles applications, and suggests alternatives for application optimization.

The role of the Blueprint Interpreter is to parse a *blueprint,* a request for service expressed in a Service-oriented Description Language, and generate the internal format of a service request. The blueprint can specify a specific service, e.g., MapReduce, or it can describe the characteristics of the application such as CPU intensive, data intensive, memory intensive and let the system identify the type of instance best suited for the application. The blueprint can also specifies the workflow of the application and the package of services. The internal format includes the service description, the service duration, and the service intensity for each service in the package.

The Admission Control System uses the internal format produced by BPI to create: (i) SRA—a list of service requests to participate at the auction organized at the beginning of the next allocation slot and (ii) SRSA—a list of service requests for *spot allocation*. The Combinatorial Auction Management System implements the combinatorial auction algorithm. CAMS gathers the bids from different coalitions and attempts to match them with the service requests in SRA. After an auction, the SAS invites bids for spot allocation from servers in unsuccessful coalitions and matches them to service requests in the SRSA.

The Task Management System starts an instance and supervises its execution. The Error Recovery System interacts with the TMS and restarts the instance, if the error is due to hardware failure, or activates the error recovery procedure specified by the blueprint. The Accounting System records the resources used by all instances and generates accounting records for system users.

The Event Management is a distributed event processing system. All system software components use the publish-subscribe paradigm to interact with the EM. Event logs are maintained by the EM and used whenever compliance issues occur. Last, but not least, the task of Power Management System is to minimize power consumption. This means to keep servers operating in an optimal mode as discussed in [186], turn servers to a sleep mode whenever the system load is low and wake them up whenever the load increases.

5.11 AN INTEGRATED STRATEGY FOR CLOUD SOFTWARE DEVELOPMENT

Once a model of the system has been thoroughly analyzed, the next step is the development of system software. The software development is a complex process requiring multiple iterations; the insights gained after each iteration should lead to changes of system components and overall better system performance. Such insights can only be gained through the simulation of the system behavior, therefore, a first objective is to develop a simulation environment for investigating the behavior of a realistic system subject to realistic working conditions.

The simulation software should implement as accurately as possible the algorithms and protocols for all system components and should allow the simulation of different system configurations. Another challenge is to conduct simulation with a realistic workload. Initially, a synthetic workload can be used, but more realistic results can only be obtained using trace data gathered from runs on a small-scale system. Therefore, the second objective is to conduct experiments on a testbed system and collect trace data. At this stage, two difficult problems arise: first, ensuring that the testbed operates in a manner consistent with the system model; second, scaling up the simulation results.

The implementation should progress from the model development, to high-level description of the software and then translation of the high level system description to: (i) software for the testbed system and (ii) simulation software. This solution ensures compatibility between the software for system simulation, the software running on the testbed system, and the final product, the software for a realistic cloud infrastructure. Fig. 5.17 illustrates this process; it shows testbed experiments running realistic applications and generating trace date for the simulation of a realistic a cloud infrastructure with a realistic workload.

The simulated cloud infrastructure is generated using as input: (i) a configuration file describing the organization of a rack, the number of

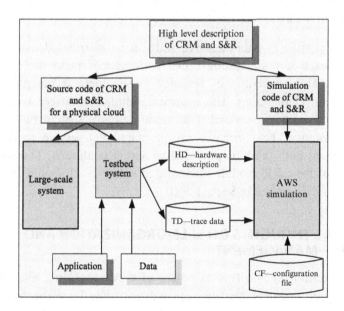

Fig. 5.17 The integration of system simulation, software development for the testbed system, and the development of code for the management of a large-scale physical cloud.

racks, and the number of cells; (ii) a hardware description file containing detailed data about the architecture and the configuration of each server. The interconnection network must also be described by the hardware configuration file; it typically consists of a hierarchy of Gigabit Ethernet (GE) networks and rack and cell switches, and border routers.

The scale of the simulated system is limited, as the simulation environment must keep track of the state of all servers and of the interconnection network. While it may be feasible to simulate a system with 50,000–100,000 servers, the simulation of a cloud with 10^8 servers seems unrealistic at this time. One of the most difficult tasks is to simulate communication among the servers within the rack, among the racks of a cell, and among the cells of a WSC.

The trace data generated on the testbed system is used as input to multiple simulated instances to create a realistic workload. The volume of trace data collected for realistic applications running over extended periods of time is likely to be of the order of terabytes, or possibly petabytes, thus, such simulations can only be carried on the most powerful instances available from AWS. If the architecture and the configuration of servers used to collect trace data is identical with that of simulated servers, then the simulated execution of an application simply advances the simulated time based on the events in the trace file.

The simulation is data-intensive and can be distributed over a set of instances, each one simulating a cell with tens of racks and thousands of servers. The simulation of resource management is communication-intensive and challenging. The instances simulating different cells must communicate with the simulated admission control system running on a separate instance. This instance accepts simulated service requests and matches them with the bids provided by server coalitions. The simulated operation of the S&R module operating at server level should implement the algorithm discussed in Section 5.10.

5.12 FINAL THOUGHTS ON SELF-ORGANIZATION AND SELF-MANAGEMENT

Self-organization and self-management offer an appealing alternative to existing cloud resource management policies; they have the potential to significantly alter the cloud computing landscape. So far, pragmatic means for the adoption of self-organization principles for large-scale computing and communication systems have eluded us. A main reason for this state of affairs is that self-management has to be coupled with some mechanisms for cooperation; these mechanisms should allow autonomous servers to act in concert towards global system goals. Cooperation means that individual systems have to partially surrender their autonomy. Striking a balance between autonomy and cooperation is a challenging task, it requires a fresh look at the mechanics of self-organization and the practical means to achieve it.

Practical implementation of cloud self-organization is challenging for several reasons, including the absence of a technically suitable definition of self-organization, a definition that could hint to practical design principles for self-organizing systems and quantitative evaluation of the results. Computer clouds exhibit the essential aspects of complexity and controlling complex systems is inherently difficult.

The investigation reported in this chapter started with a realistic model of the cloud infrastructure, the hierarchical organization reported in [27] which seems inherently tied to hierarchical control. First, the hierarchical control based on monitoring was compared with a market model in which the servers of a WSC place bids for service requests and found out that the latter is much more effective than the hierarchical control [163].

In the simple market model the servers act individually, rather than cooperating with each other, a fundamental aspect of self-organization. But cooperation is clearly needed because individual servers may not be able to supply the resources demanded by many data-intensive application. Thus, it was concluded that servers have to form coalitions to offer larger pools of resources. At the same time, it seemed obvious to us that complex applications with multiple phases would require packages of resources offered by different coalitions.

Algorithms for coalition formation based on combinatorial auctions are at the heart of the cloud ecosystem discussed in this chapter. Auctions have been successfully used for resource management in the past. Auctions do not require a model of the system, while traditional resource management strategies do. The auction-based protocol is scalable, and the computations can be done efficiently, though the computational algorithms involved are often fairly complex.

We end now where we started, attempting to answer the question if self-organization and self-management are feasible in large-scale, cyber-physical systems. An important step is to accept that the systems cannot be examined in isolation. The systems have to adapt to the environment and this can only be done by learning the patterns of events and interactions with the environment over a period of time. Fortunately, the rate of events generated by the environment is very high, thus, the history of events and the responses to these events could be compressed. While initially the system may perform suboptimally, after days, weeks, maybe months, the system should be able to accumulate enough knowledge and avoid to be surprised by changes of the environment.

To assess the quality of system responses, it is necessary to have a clear and easily implementable definition of utility. This is extremely challenging in most cases because the utility measures the impact of a system action on the global system state. Determining accurately the state of a large-scale system after each event is not feasible. The only solution is to periodically assess the system state and correlate the set of events and the system's actions leading to that state with previous observations. A large database of events, actions, and system state can then be used by a reinforced learning algorithm to guide the future system behavior. The auction system discussed in this chapter avoids these hard problems as individual servers bid for services.

BIBLIOGRAPHY

[1] R. Abbott. "Complex systems engineering: putting complex systems to work," *Complexity,* **13**(2):10–11, 2007.

[2] B. Abrahao, V. Almeida, J. Almeida, A. Zhang, D.Beyer, and F. Safai. "Self-adaptive SLA-driven capacity management for Internet services." *Proc. IEEE/IFIP Network Operations & Management Symposium (NOMS06)*, pp. 557–568, 2006.

[3] D. Abts, M. Marty, P. M. Wells, P. Klausler, and H. Liu. "Energy proportional datacenter networks." *Proc. Int. Symp. Comp. Arch. (ISCA10)*, pp. 238-247, 2010.

[4] L. A. Adamic, R. M. Lukose, A. R. Puniyami, and B. A. Huberman. "Search in power-law networks." *Phys. Rev. E,* **64**(4):046135, 2001.

[5] B. Addis, D. Ardagna, B. Panicucci, and L. Zhang. "Autonomic management of cloud service centers with availability guarantees." *Proc. IEEE 3rd Int. Conf. on Cloud Computing*, pp. 220–227, 2010.

[6] L. Adleman. " Molecular computations of solutions to combinatorial problems." *Science,* **266**:1021–1024, 1994.

[7] L. Adleman. "Computing with DNA." *Scientific American,* **279**(2):54–61, 1998.

[8] S. Airiau and W. Jamroga. "Coalitional games." *European Agent Systems Summer School, EASSS 2009,* http://www.di.unito.it/~argo/easss09.pdf, pp. 265–288, 2009.

[9] R. Albert, H. Jeong, and A.-L. Barabási. "The diameter of the world wide web." *Nature,* **401**:130–131, 1999.

[10] R. Albert, H. Jeong, and A.-L. Barabási. "Error and attack tolerance of complex networks." *Nature,* **406**:378–382, 2000.

[11] R. Albert and A-L. Barabási. "Statistical mechanics of complex networks." *Reviews of Modern Physics,* **72**(1):48–97, 2002.

[12] L. A. N. Amaral and J.M. Ottino. "Complex networks." *Eur. Phys. J. B,* **38**:147–162 (2004)

[13] "Amazon elastic compute cloud." http://aws.amazon.com/ec2/ (Accessed April 2016).

[14] Amazon Docker. http://aws.amazon.com/docker (Accessed May 2015).

[15] D. Ardagna, B. Panicucci, M. Trubian, and L. Zhang. "Energy-aware autonomic resource allocation in multi-tier virtualized environments." *IEEE Trans. on Services Computing,* **5**(1):2–19, 2012.

[16] S. Arif, S. Olariu, J. Wang, G. Yan, W. Yang and I. Khalil. "Datacenter at the airport: Reasoning about time-dependent parking lot occupancy." *IEEE Trans. on Parallel and Distributed Systems,* **23**(11):2067–2080, 2012

[17] W. R. Ashby. "Principles of self-organizing system." *Principles of Self-Organization: Transactions of the University of Illinois Symposium,* H. Von Foerster and G. W. Zopf, Jr. (Eds.), Pergamon Press, London, UK, pp. 255–278, 1962.

[18] L. Ausubel and P. R. Milgrom. "Ascending auctions with package bidding." *Frontiers of Theoretical Economics,* **1**(1):1–42, 2002.

[19] L. Ausubel and P. Cramton. "Auctioning many divisible goods." *Journal European Economic Assoc.,* **2**(2-3):480–493, 2004.

[20] L. Ausubel, P. Cramton, and P. Milgrom. "The clock-proxy auction: a practical combinatorial auction design." *Chapter 5*, in *Combinatorial Auctions*, P. Cramton, Y. Shoham, and R. Steinberg, Eds. MIT Press, 2006.

[21] P. Bak, C. Tang, and K. Weisenfeld. "Self-organized criticality." *Phys. Rev.* A, **38**:364–374, 1988

[22] P. Bak. *How Nature Works; The Science of Self-organized Criticality*. Springer Verlag, New York, 1996.

[23] D. J. Baker and A. Ephemides. "The architectural organization of a mobile radio network via a distributed algorithm." *IEEE Trans. Comm*, **11**:1694–1701, 1981.

[24] J. S. Bell. newblock *Speakable and Unspeakable in Quantum Mechanics*. Cambridge University Press, Cambridge, UK, 1987.

[25] A. Barrat and M. Weight. "On the properties of small-worlds network models." *European Physical Journal B*, **13**(3):547–560, 2000.

[26] L. A. Barosso and U. Hölzle. "The case for energy-proportional computing." *IEEE Computer*, **40**(2):33–37, 2010.

[27] L. A. Barossso, J. Clidaras, and U.Hözle. *The Datacenter as a Computer; an Introduction to the Design of Warehouse-Scale Machines*. (Second Edition). Morgan & Claypool, 2013.

[28] J. Baliga, R.W.A. Ayre, K. Hinton, and R. S. Tucker. "Green cloud computing: balancing energy in processing, storage, and transport." *Proc. IEEE*, **99**(1):149–167, 2011.

[29] A-L. Barabási and R. Albert. "Emergence of scaling in random networks," *Science*, **286**:509–512, 1999.

[30] A-L. Barabási, R. Albert, and H. Jeong. "Scale-free theory of random networks; the topology of World Wide Web." *Physica A*, **281**:69–77, 2000.

[31] G. Bell. "Massively parallel computers: why not parallel computers for the masses?" *Proc. 4-th Symp. on Frontiers of Massively Parallel Computing*, pp. 292–297, 1992.

[32] Y, Benenson, B. Gil, U Ben-Dor, R. Adar, and E Shapiro. "An autonomous molecular computer for logical control of gene expression." *Nature*, **429**(6990):423–429, 2004.

[33] C. H. Bennett. "Dissipation, information, computational complexity, and the definition of organization." in *Emerging Syntheses in Science, Pines D. (Ed.)*, Addison-Wesley, Redwood City CA, pp. 215–233, 1985.

[34] C. H. Bennett. "On the nature and origin of complexity in discrete, homogeneous, locally-interacting systems." *Foundations of Physics*, **16**(6):585–592, Springer, 1986

[35] C. H. Bennett. "Notes on Landauer's principle, reversible computation and Maxwell's Demon." *Studies in History and Philosophy of Modern Physics*, **34**:501-520, 2003.

[36] L. Von Bertalanffy. *General System Theory: Foundations, Development, Applications*. Penguin University Books, 1956.

[37] M. Blackburn and A. Hawkins. "Unused server survey results analysis." *www.thegreengrid.org/media/WhitePapers/Unused%20Server%20Study_WP_101910_v1.ashx?lang=en* (Accessed December 2013).

[38] A. Bogomolnaia and M. O. Jackson. "The stability of hedonic coalition structures." *Games and Economic Behavior*, **38**(2):201–230, 2002.

[39] E. Bonabeau, M. Dorigo, and G Theraulez. *Swarm Intelligence: From Natural to Artificial Systems*. Oxford University Press, Oxford, UK, 1999.

[40] K. E. Boulding. "General systems theory; the skeleton of science." *Management Science*, **2**:197–208, 1956.

[41] G. K. Brennen, C. M. Caves, P. S. Jessen, and I. H. Deutsch. "Quantum logic gates in optical lattices." *Phys. Rev. Lett.*, **82**(5):1060–1063, 1999.

[42] N. F. Britton. *Essential Mathematical Biology.* Springer Verlag, New York, NY, 2004.

[43] D. Bruneo. "A stochastic model to investigate data center performance and QoS in IAAS cloud computing systems." *IEEE Trans. on Parallel and Distributed Systems,* 25(3):560–569, 2014.

[44] T. E. Carroll and D. Grosu. "Formation of virtual organizations in grids: a game-theoretic approach." *Concurrency and Computation: Practice and Experience,* 22(14):1972–1989, 2010.

[45] G. J. Chaitin. "On the length of programs for computing binary sequences." *J. Assoc. Comp. Mach.* 13:547–569, 1966.

[46] S. Chaisiri, B. Lee, and D. Niyato. "Optimization of resource provisioning cost in cloud computing." *IEEE Trans. on Services Computing,* 5(2):164–177, 2012.

[47] V. Chang, G. Wills, and D. De Roure. "A review of cloud business models and sustainability." *Proc. IEEE Cloud Computing,* pp. 43–50, 2010.

[48] B. N. Chun and D. E. Culler "Market-based proportional resource sharing for clusters." *Technical Report,* U. C. Berkeley, 2000.

[49] P. Cilliers. "Boundaries, hierarchies and networks in complex systems." *Int. J. of Innovation Management,* 5(2):135–147, 2001.

[50] J. I. Cirac and P. Zoller. "Quantum computation with cold trapped ions." *Phys. Rev. Lett.,* 74(20):4091–4094, 1995.

[51] J. I. Cirac and P. Zoller. "A scalable quantum computer with ions in an array of microtraps." *Nature,* 404:579–581, 2000.

[52] E. H. Clarke. "Multipart Pricing of Public Goods." *Public Choice,* IX:13–33, 1971.

[53] M. Clerc and J. Kennedy. "The particle swarm - Explosion, stability, and convergence in a multidimensional complex space." *IEEE Transactions on Evolutionary Computation,* 7(1): 58–73, 2002.

[54] R. Cohen, K. Erez, D. ben-Avraham, and S. Havlin. "Resilience of the Internet to random breakdowns." *Phys. Rev. Lett.,* 85: 4626, 2000. Also arXiv:cond-mat/0007048.

[55] R. Cohen, K. Erez, D. ben-Avraham, and S. Havlin. "Breakdown of the Internet under intentional attack." *Phys. Rev. Lett.,* 86:3682, 2001. Also arXiv:cond-mat/0010251.

[56] R. Cohen and S. Havlin. "Scale-free networks are ultrasmall." *Phys. Rev. Lett.,* 90(5):058701, 2003.

[57] T. C. Collier and C. Taylor. "Self-organization in sensor networks," *Journal of Parallel and Distributed Computing,* 64(7):866–873, 2004.

[58] F. J. Corbato. "On building systems that will fail." *Turing Award Lecture 1991,* http://larch-www. lcs.mit.edu:8001/~corbato/turing91/

[59] D. G. Cory, A. F. Fahmy, and T. F. Havel. "Ensemble quantum computing by NMR spectroscopy." *Proc. National Academy of Science,* 94(5):1634–1639, 1997.

[60] T. M. Cover and J. A. Thomas. *Elements of Information Theory* (Second Edition), Wiley-Interscience, Hoboken, NJ, 2006.

[61] P. Cramton, Y. Shoham, and R. Steinberg, Eds., *Combinatorial Auctions,* MIT Press, Boston, MA, 2006.

[62] F. Crick and J.D. Watson "The complementary structure of deoxyribonucleic acid." newblock *Proc. of Royal Society of London Series A,* 223:80–96, 1954.

[63] J. P. Crutchfield, J. D. Farmer, N. Packard, and R. Shaw. "Chaos." *Scientific American,* 255(6): 46–57, 1986.

[64] J. P. Crutchfield. "The calculi of emergence: computation, dynamics, and induction." *Physica D: Nonlinear Phenomena,* 75(1–3):11–54, 1994.

[65] J. P. Crutchfield and J. P. Shalizi. "Thermodynamic depth of causal states: objective complexity via minimal representation," *Phys. Rev. E*, **59**:275–283, 1999.

[66] CUDA "CUDA 7.0 performance report." http://on-demand.gputechconf.com/gtc/2015/webinar/gtc-express-cuda7-performance-overview.pdf, May 2015 (Accessed April 2016).

[67] C. Darwin. *The Origin of Species by Means of Natural Selection or the Preservation of Favored Races in the Struggle for Life.* Penguin Classics,1985 (first published in 1859).

[68] R. Dawkins. *The Selfish Gene.* (2nd edition), Oxford University Press, Oxford, UK, 1989.

[69] IBM DB2. http://www-01.ibm.com/software/data/db2/.

[70] C. Delimitrou and C. Kozyrakis. "Quasar: Resource-efficient and QoS-aware cluster management." *Proc. ASPLOS14*, pp. 127–144, 2014.

[71] D. Deutsch. "Quantum theory, the Church-Turing principle and the universal quantum computer." *Proc. of the Royal Society London A*, **400**:97–117, 1985.

[72] D. P. DiVincenzo. "Quantum gates and circuits." *Phil. Trans. Royal Soc. London A*, **454**:261–276, 1998, Also, Proc.: Mathematical, Physical and Engineering Sciences, Vol. 454, No. 1969, Quantum Coherence and Decoherence (January 1998), pp. 261–276 Also, Preprint, arxiv.org/quanth-ph/9705009, May, 1997.

[73] D. P. DiVincenzo. "The physical implementation of quantum computation." *Fortschritte der Physik*, **48**(9-11):771–783, 2000.

[74] M. Dorigo. "Optimization, learning and natural algorithms." *PhD thesis*, Politecnico di Milano, 1992.

[75] M. Dorigo and C. Blum. "Ant colony optimization theory: A survey." *Theoretical Computer Science*, **344**:243–278, 2005.

[76] M. Dorigo. "Ant colony optimization." *Scholarpedia*, **2**(3)1461, 2007. Also http://www.scholarpedia.org/article/Ant_colony_optimization (Accessed December 2015).

[77] X. Dutreild, N. Rivierre, A. Moreau, J. Malenfant, and I. Truck. "From data center resource allocation to control theory and back." *Proc. IEEE 3rd Int. Conf. on Cloud Computing*, pp. 410–417, 2010.

[78] P. Erdös and A. Rényi. "On random graphs." *Publicationes Mathematicae*, **6**:290–297, 1959.

[79] L. Euler. "Solutio problematis ad geometriam situs pertinentis." *Commentarii Academiae Scientiarum Petropolitanae*, 8, pp. 128–140, 1741. See also http://eulerarchive.maa.org/pages/E053.html. (Accessed December 2015).

[80] R. Feynman. "Simulating physics with computers." *Int. J. Theoretical Physics*, **21**(6/7):467–488, 1982.

[81] R. Feynman. "Quantum mechanical computers." *Optics News*, **11**:11–46, 1985.

[82] R. Feynman. *Lecture Notes on Computation. Addison-Wesley*, Readings, MA,1996.

[83] R. Gallagher. "A perspective on multiaccess channels," *IEEE Trans. Inf. Theory*, IT **31**(2):124-142, 1985.

[84] A. Gandhi, M. Harchol-Balter, R. Raghunathan, and M.Kozuch. "AutoScale: dynamic, robust capacity management for multi-tier data centers." *ACM Trans. on Computer Systems*, **30**(4):1–26, 2012.

[85] A. G. Ganek and T. A. Corbi, "The dawning of the autonomic computing era." *IBM Systems Journal*, **42**(1):5-18, 2003.Also, https://www.cs.drexel.edu/~jsalvage/Winter2010/CS576/autonomic.pdf.

[86] J. O. Gutierrez-Garcia and K. M. Sim. "Self-organizing agents for service composition in cloud computing." *Proc. 2nd IEEE Int. Conf. on Cloud Computing Technology and Science*, pp. 59–66, 2010.

[87] M. Gardner. "The fantastic combination of John Conwey's new solitary game Life." *Scientific American*, **223**:120–123, 1970.

[88] C. Gershenson. "Design and control of self-organizing systems." *Ph. D. Dissertation*, Vrije Universiteit Brussels, Belgium, 2007.

[89] M. Gell-Mann. "Simplicity and complexity in the description of nature." *Engineering and Science*, Caltech, **LI**(3):3–9, 1988.

[90] M. Gell-Mann. *The Quark and the Jaguar: Adventures in the Simple and the Complex.* W.H. Freeman Publishers, San Francisco, 1994.

[91] M. Gerla and J.T. Tsai. "Multicluster, mobile, multimedia radio networks." *Wireless Networks*, pp. 255–265, 1995.

[92] J. Gleick. *Chaos. Making a New Science. Viking*, New York, NY, 1987.

[93] D. Gmach, J. Rolia, and L. Cerkasova. "Satisfying service-level objectives in a self-managed resource pool." *Proc. 3rd. Int. Conf. on Self-Adaptive and Self-Organizing Systems*, pp. 243–253, 2009.

[94] Google Docker. https://cloud.google.com/container-engine (Accessed May 2015).

[95] K. I. Goh, B. Kahang, and D. Kim. "Universal behavior of load distribution in scale-free networks." *Physical Review Letters*, **87**:278701, 2001.

[96] J. Goldstein. "Emergence as a construct: history and issues." *Emergence: Complexity and Organization*, **1**(1):49–72, 1999.

[97] S. J. Gould and N. Eldredge. "Punctuated equilibria: the tempo and mode of evolution reconsidered." *Paleobiology*, **3**(2):115–151, 1977.

[98] M. Grabisch, Y. Funaki. "A coalition formation value for games in partition function form." *European Journal of Operational Research*, Elsevier, pp.175–185, 2012.

[99] G. Greco, E. Malizia, L. Palopoli, and F. Scarello. "On the complexity of the core over coalition structures." *Proc 22 Int. Joint Conf. on Artificial Intelligence*, pp. 216–221, 2011.

[100] T. Groves. "Incentives in teams." *Econometrica*, **41**:617–631, 1973.

[101] M. Gu, C. Weedbrook, A. Perales, and M. A. Nielsen. "More reality is different." *Physics D; Nonlinear Phenomena*, **238**(9-10):835–839, 2009.

[102] V. Gupta and M. Harchol-Balter. "Self-adaptive admission control policies for resource-sharing systems." *Proc. 11th Int. Joint Conf. Measurement and Modeling Computer Systems (SIGMETRICS'09)*, pp. 311–322, 2009.

[103] J. O. Gutierrez-Garcia and K.- M. Sim. "Self-organizing agents for service composition in cloud computing." *Proc IEEE 2nd Int. Conf. on Cloud Computing Technology and Science*, pp. 59–66, 2010.

[104] J. D. Halley and D. A. Winkler. "Classification of emergence and its relation to self-organization," *Complexity*, **13**(5):10–15, 2008.

[105] G. Hardin. "The tragedy of the commons." *Science*, **162**:1243-1248, 1968.

[106] S. Havlin. "Lecture notes on complex systems." http://havlin.biu.ac.il/course1.php (Accessed October 2015).

[107] T. He, J. Stankovic, C. Lu, and T. Abdelzaher. "SPEED: A real-time routing protocol for sensor networks." *Proc. Int. Conf. on Distributed Computing Systems*, p.46, Providence, RI, 2003.

[108] L. He and T. R. Ioerger. "Forming resource-sharing coalitions: a distributed resource allocation mechanism for self-interested agents in computational grids." *Proc. ACM Symp. on Applied Computing*, pp. 84–91, 2005.

[109] W. Heinzelman, A. Chandrakasan, and H. Balakrishnan. "Energy efficient communication protocol for wireless microsensor networks." *Proc. Hawaii Int. Conf. System Sciences*, Hawaii, 2000.

[110] J. L. Hennessy and D. A. Patterson. *Computer Architecture - A quantitative Approach* (Fifth Edition). Morgan Kaufmann, Waltham, MA, 2012.

[111] M. Herrmann. "Lectures on natural computing." http://www.inf.ed.ac.uk/teaching/courses/nat/, 2010 (Accessed October 2015).

[112] F. Heylighen. "Publications on complex, evolving systems: a citation-based survey." *Complexity* 2 (5):31–36, 1997.

[113] F. Heylighen. "The science of self-organization and adaptivity." *Knowledge Management, Organizational Intelligence and Learning, and Complexity* in: The Encyclopedia of Life Support Systems, EOLSS, pp. 253–280, 1999.

[114] F. Heylighen and C. Gershenson. "The meaning of self-organization in computing", *IEEE Intelligent Systems,* May/June, 18(4):72–75, 2003.

[115] M. Hinchey, R. Sterritt, C. Rouff, J. Rash, W. Truszkowski. "Swarm-based space exploration." *ERCIM News* 64:26, 2006.

[116] B. Hindman, A. Konwinski, M. Zaharia, A. Ghodsi, A.D. Joseph, R. Katz, S. Shenker, and I. Stoica. "Mesos: A platform for fine-grained resource sharing in the data center." *Proc. 8th USENIX Symp. on Networked Systems Design and Implementation*, pp. 295–308 2011.

[117] J. H. Holland. *Adaptation In Natural and Artificial Systems.* University of Michigan Press, Ann Arbor, MI, 1975.

[118] J. H. Holland. *Hidden Order: How adaptation builds complexity.* Addison-Wesley, Reading, MA, 1996.

[119] J. H. Holland. *Emergence: from Chaos to Order.* Addison- Wesley, Reading, MA, 1998.

[120] J. Hopfield. "Neural networks and physical systems with emergent collective computational abilities." *Proc. National Academy of Science,* 79:2554–2558, 1982.

[121] A. W. Hübler. "Understanding complex systems," *Complexity,* 12(5):9–1, 2007.

[122] R. J. Hughes, G. I. Morgan, and C. G. Peterson. "Quantum key distribution over a 48 km long optical fibre network." *J. of Modern Optics,* 47:533–547, 2000.

[123] J. S Huxley and T. H. Huxley. *Evolution and Ethics.* The Pilot Press, London, UK, 1947.

[124] IBM Corporation. "Bringing big data to the enterprise." http://www-01.ibm.com/software/data/bigdata/what-is-big-data.html (Accessed April 2016).

[125] N. Israeli, and N. Goldenfeld. "Computational irreducibility and the predictability of complex physical systems." *Phys. Rev. Lett.* 92:074105, 2004.

[126] K. R. Jackson, L. Ramakrishnan, K. Muriki, S. Canon, S. Cholia, J. Shalf, H. Wasserman, N. J. Wright. "Performance analysis of high performance computing applications on the Amazon Web services cloud." *Proc. IEEE Second Int. Conf. on Cloud Computing Technology and Science,* pp. 159–168, 2010.

[127] D. Jaksch, H.-J. Briegel, J. I. Cirac, and P. Zoller. "Entanglement of atoms via cold controlled collisions." *Phys. Rev. Lett.,* 82(9):1975–1978, 1999.

[128] M. Joa-Ng. "Spread spectrum medium access protocol with collision avoidance using controlled time of arrival." *Telecommunication Systems,* 18(1–3):169–19, 2001.

[129] J. P. Kahan and A. Rapoport. *Theories of Coalition Formation.* Lawrence Erlbaum Associates, 1984.

[130] E. Kalyvianaki, T. Charalambous, and S. Hand. "Self-adaptive and self-configured CPU resource provisioning for virtualized servers using Kalman filters." *Proc. 6th Int. Conf. Autonomic Comp. (ICAC2009)*, pp. 117–126, 2009.

[131] L. Kari and G. Rozenberg. "The many facets of natural computing." *Comm. ACM*, **51**:(10):72–83.

[132] D. Katz and R. L. Kahn. *The Social Psychology of Organizations*. Wiley, New York, NY, 1966.

[133] J. Kennedy and R. Eberhart. "Particle swarm optimization." *Proc. IEEE Int. Conf. Neural Networks*, IEEE Press, pp.1942–1948, 1995.

[134] J. O . Kephart and D. M. Chase. "The vision of autonomic computing." *Computer*, **36**(1):41–50, 2003.

[135] J. O. Kephart, H. Chan, R. Das, D. Levine, G. Tesauro, F. Rawson, and C. Lefurgy. "Coordinating multiple autonomic managers to achieve specified power-performance tradeoffs." *Proc. 4th Int. Conf. Autonomic Computing (ICAC2007)*, pp. 100-109, 2007.

[136] J. O. Kephart and R. Das. "Achieving self-management via utility functions." *IEEE Internet Computing*, **11**(1):40-48, 2007.

[137] J. O. Kephart. "Autonomic computing, the first decade." *Int. Conf. on Autonomic Computing*, http://www3.cis.fiu.edu/conferences/icac2011/files/Keynote_Kephart.pdf, 2011 (Accessed July 2015).

[138] S. U. Khan and I. Ahmad. "A cooperative game theoretical technique for joint optimization of energy consumption and response time in computational grids." *IEEE Trans. on Parallel and Distributed Systems*, **20**(3):346–360, 2009.

[139] A. N. Kolmogorov. "Three approaches to the quantitative definition of information." *Problemy Peredachy Informatzii*, **1**:4-7, 1965.

[140] J. G. Koomey, S. Berard, M. Sanchez, and H. Wong. "Implications of historical trends in the energy efficiency of computing." *IEEE Annals of Computing*, **33**(3):46-54, 2011.

[141] B. Krishnamachari, S. B. Wicker, and R. Bejar. "Phase transition phenomena on wireless ad-hoc networks." *Proc. IEEE Globecom01*, pp. 2921–2925, 2001.

[142] P. R. Krugman. *The Self-organizing Economy*. Blackwell Publishers, New York, NY, 1996.

[143] Kubernets. https://cloud.google.com/container-engine/docs/tutorials (Accessed May 2015).

[144] D. Kusic, J. O. Kephart, N. Kandasamy, and G. Jiang. "Power and performance management of virtualized computing environments via lookahead control." *Proc. 5th Int. Conf. Autonomic Comp. (ICAC2008)*, pp. 3–12, 2008.

[145] T. D. Ladd, F. Jelezko, R. Laflamme, Y. Nakamura, C. Monroe, and J. L. O'Brien. "Quantum Computers." *Nature*, **464**:4552, 2010.

[146] R. Landauer. "Irreversibility and heat generation in the computing process." *IBM Journal of Research and Development*, **5**:183-191, 1961.

[147] D. S. Lee, K. I. Goh, B. Kahng, and D. Kim. "Evolution of scale-free random graphs: Potts model formulation." *Nuclear Physics B.*, **696**:351–380, 2004.

[148] K. Lerman and O. Shehory. "Coalition formation for large-scale electronic markets." *Proc. ICMAS 2000 - 4th Int. Conf on Multiagent Systems*, pp. 167–174, 2000.

[149] C. Li and K. Sycara. "Algorithm for combinatorial coalition formation and payoff division in an electronic marketplace." *Proc. AAMAS02 - First Joint Int. Conf. on Autonomous Agents and Multiagent Systems*, pp. 120–127, 2002.

[150] H. Li, C. Wu, Z. Li, and F. Lau. "Profit-maximizing virtual machine trading in a federation of selfish clouds." *Proc. IEEE INFOCOM*, pp. 25–29, 2013.

[151] H C. Lim, S. Babu, J. S. Chase, and S. S. Parekh. "Automated control in cloud computing: challenges and opportunities." *Proc. First Workshop on Automated Control for Datacenters and Clouds,*, ACM Press, pp. 13–18, 2009.

[152] A. Livnat, C. Papadimitriou, J. Dushoff, and M. W. Friedman. "A mixability theory for the role of sex in evolution." *Proc. Natl. Acad. Sci. USA,* **105**(50):19803–19808, 2008.

[153] J. Machta. "Complexity, parallel computation, and statistical physics," *Complexity,* **11**(5):46–64, 2006.

[154] B. B. Mandelbrot. *The Fractal Geometry of Nature.* Freeman Publishers, New York, NY,1983.

[155] D. Mange, A. Stauffer, L. Peparaolo, and G. Tempesti. "A macroscopic view of self-replication." *Proc. of the IEEE,* **92**(12):1929–1945, 2004.

[156] D. C. Marinescu and G. M. Marinescu. *Approaching Quantum Computing.* Prentice Hall, Upper Saddle River, NJ, 2005.

[157] D. C. Marinescu, X. Bai, L. Bölöni, H. J. Siegel, R. E. Daley, and I-J. Wang. "A macroeconomic model for resource allocation in large-scale distributed systems." *Journal of Parallel and Distributed Computing,* **68**:182–199, 2008.

[158] D. C. Marinescu, H. J. Siegel, and J. P. Morrison. "Options and commodity markets for computing resources," In *Market Oriented Grid and Utility Computing,* R. Buyya and K. Bubendorf, Eds., Wiley, New York, NY, ISBN: 9780470287682, pp. 89–120, 2009.

[159] D. C. Marinescu, C. Yu, and G. M. Marinescu. "Scale-free, self-organizing very large sensor networks." *Journal of Parallel and Distributed Computing,* **50**(5):612–622, 2010.

[160] D. C. Marinescu and G. M. Marinescu. *Classical and Quantum Information.* Academic Press, New York, NY, 2012.

[161] D. C. Marinescu. *Cloud Computing; Theory and Practice.* Morgan Kaufmann, Waltham, MA, 2013.

[162] D. C. Marinescu. "High probability trajectories in the phase space and system complexity." *Complex Systems,* **22**(3):233–246, 2013.

[163] D. C. Marinescu, A. Paya, J. P. Morrison, and P. Healy. "Distributed hierarchical control versus an economic model for cloud resource management." http://arXiv:.org/pdf/1503.01061.pdf, 2015.

[164] D. C. Marinescu, A. Paya, and J. P. Morrison. "Coalition formation and combinatorial auctions; applications to self-organization and self-management in utility computing." http://arXiv:.org/pdf/1406.7487.pdf, 2015.

[165] D. C. Marinescu. "Cloud energy consumption." *Encyclopedia of Cloud Computing, Chapter 25,* Wiley, New York, NY,2016.

[166] von der Marlsburg, C. "Network Self-organization." In *An Introduction to Neural and Electronic Networks.* S. Zonetzer, J. L. Davis, and C.Lau (Eds.), pp. 421–432, Academic Press, San Diego, CA, 1995.

[167] L. Mashayekhy, M.M.Nejad, and D.Grosu. "Cloud federations in the sky: formation game and mechanisms." *IEEE Trans. on Cloud Computing,* **3**(1):14–27, 2015.

[168] M. W. Mayer. "Architecting principles for system of systems." *Systems Engineering,* **1**(4):267–274, 1998.

[169] D. W. McShea. " Metazoan complexity and evolution: Is there a trend?" *Evolution* **50**:477–492, 1996.

[170] S. Milgram. "Behavioral study of obedience." *Journal of Abnormal and Social Psychology,* **67**(4):371–378, 1963.

[171] M. Minsky. *Computation: Finite and Infinite Machines.* Prentice Hall, New York, 1967.

[172] I. Müller, R. Kowalczyk, and P. Braun. "Towards agent-based coalition formation for service composition." *Proc. IEEE/WIC/ACM Int. Conf. on Intelligent Agent Technology,* pp. 73-80, 2006.

[173] J. K. Navlakha. " A survey of system complexity metrics." *The Computer Journal,* **30**(3):233–239, 1987.

[174] M. E. J. Newman. "The structure of scientific collaboration networks." *Proc. Nat. Academy of Science,* **98**(2):404–409, 2001.

[175] M. A. Nielsen and I. L. Chuang. *Quantum Computing and Quantum Information.* Cambridge University Press, Cambridge, UK, 2000.

[176] D.Niyato, A.Vasilakos, and Z.Kun. "Resource and revenue sharing with coalition formation of cloud providers: Game theoretic approach." *Proc. IEEE/ACM Intl. Symp. on Cluster, Cloud and Grid Comp.,* pp. 215–224, 2011.

[177] G. Nicolis and I. Prigogine. *Exploring Complexity.* Freeman Publishers, New York, NY, 1989.

[178] P-A. Noël, C. D. Brummitt, and R. M. D'Souza. "Controlling self-organizing dynamics on networks using models that self-organize." *Phys. Rev. Lett.* **111**, 078701, 2013.

[179] M. Ogihara and A. Ray. "Simulating Boolean circuits on a DNA computer." *Algorithmica,* **25**:239–250, 1999.

[180] M. J. Osborne and A. Rubinstein. *A Course in Game Theory.* MIT Press, Boston, MA, 1994.

[181] A. Padovitz, A. Zaslavsky, S. W. Loke. "Awareness and agility for autonomic distributed systems: platform-independent publish-subscribe event-based communication for mobile agents." *Proc. 14th Int. Workshop on Database and Expert Systems Applications (DEXA?03),* pp. 669–673, 2003.

[182] C.H. Papadimitriou, K. Steiglitz. *Combinatorial Optimization - Algorithms and Complexity.* Dover Publications, New York, NY, 1982.

[183] C. H. Papadimitriou. "Computational insights and the theory of evolution." http://web.stanford.edu/class/ee380/Abstracts/120425-slides.pdf (Accessed December 2015).

[184] Gh. Paun. "Computing with membranes." *Journal of Computer and System Sciences,* **61**(1):108–143, 2000.

[185] G. Paun. *Membrane Computing: An Introduction.* Springer Verlag, Heidelberg, 2002.

[186] A. Paya and D. C. Marinescu. "Energy-aware load balancing and application scaling for the cloud ecosystem." *IEEE Trans. on Cloud Computing,* Vol. PP, Issue 99, DOI: 10.1109/TCC.2015.2396059, 2015.

[187] S. Penmatsa and A. T. Chronopoulos. "Price-based user-optimal job allocation scheme for grid systems." *Proc. Parallel & Distributed Processing Symp.,* pp. 8–16, April 2006.

[188] V. Phua, A. Datta, R. Cardell-Oliver. "A TDMA-based MAC protocol for industrial wireless sensor network applications using link state dependent scheduling." *Proc Globecom,* pp. 1–6, 2006.

[189] I. Prigogine and I. Stengers. *Order out of Chaos.* Bantam Books, New York, 1984.

[190] L. Qian and E. Winfree. "Scaling up digital circuit computations with DNA strand displacement cascades." *Science,* **332**(6034):1196–1201, 2011.

[191] T. Rahwan, S. D. Ramchurn, N. R. Jennings, and A. Giovannucci. "An anytime algorithm for optimal coalition structure generation." *Journal of Artificial Intelligence Research,* **34**:521–567, 2009.

[192] S. D. Ramchurn, M. Polukarov, A. Farinelli, C. Truong, and N. R. Jenkings. "Coalition formation with spatial and temporal constraints." *Proc. 9th Int. Conf. on Autonomous Agents and Multiagent Systems (AAMAS 2010),* pp. 1181–1188, 2010.

[193] R. Rivest, A. Shamir, and L Adleman. "A method for obtaining digital signatures and public-key cryptosystems." *Communications of the ACM*, **21**(2):120–126, 1978.

[194] J. H. Saltzer and M. F. Kaashoek. *Principles of Computer System Design*. Morgan Kaufmann, Burlington, MA, 2009.

[195] N. Samaan. "A novel economic sharing model in a federation of selfish cloud providers." *IEEE Trans. on Parallel and Distributed Systems*, **25**(1):12–21, 2014.

[196] C. A. A. Sanches and N. Y. Soma. "A polynomial-time DNA computing solution for the Bin-Packing Problem." *Applied Mathematics and Computation*, **215**:2055–2062, 2009.

[197] M. Schwarzkopf, A. Konwinski, M. Abd-El-Malek, and J. Wilkes. "Omega: flexible, scalable schedulers for large compute clusters." Proc. EuroSys13, pp. 351–364, 2013.

[198] T. W. Sandholm, K. S. Larson, M. Andersson, O. Shehory, and F. Tohm. "Coalition structure generation with worst case guarantees." *Artificial Intelligence*, **111**(1-2):209–238, 1999.

[199] P. Schuster. "Nonlinear dynamics from Physics to Biology. Self-organization: An old paradigm revisited." *Complexity*, **12**(4):9–11, 2007.

[200] S. Sen and P. S. Dutta. "Searching for optimal coalition structures." *Proc. ICMAS 2000 - 4th Int. Conf on Multiagent Systems*, pp. 287–295, 2000.

[201] L. S. Shapley. "A value for n-person games." *In Contributions to the Theory of Games, volume II, H.W. Kuhn and A.W. Tucker, Eds. Annals of Mathematical Studies, Princeton University Press*, **28**:307–317.1953.

[202] L. S. Shapley and M. Shubik. "A method for evaluating the distribution of power in a committee system." *American Political Science Review*, **48** (3):787–792, 1954.

[203] O. Shehory and S. Kraus. "Methods for task allocation via agent coalition formation." *Artificial Intelligence*, **101**(1-2):165âĂŞ-200, 1998.

[204] J. Shneidman, C. Ng, D. C. Parkes, A. AuYoung, A. C. Snoeren, A. Vahdat, A., and B. Chun. "Why markets could (but don't currently) solve resource allocation problems in systems." *Proc. 10th Conf. on Hot Topics in Operating Systems*, 2005.

[205] P. W. Shor. "Algorithms for Quantum Computation: Discrete Log and Factoring." *Proc., 35 Annual Symp. on Foundations of Computer Science*, IEEE Press, Piscataway, NJ, pp. 124–134, 1994.

[206] P. W. Shor. "Scheme for Reducing Decoherence in Quantum Computer Memory." *Phys. Rev. A*, **52**(4):2493–2496, 1995.

[207] P. W. Shor. "Fault-Tolerant Quantum Computation." *37th Annual Symp. on Foundations of Computer Science*, IEEE Press, Piscataway, NJ, 56–65, 1996.

[208] P. W. Shor. "Polynomial-Time Algorithms for Prime Factorization and Discrete Logarithms on a Quantum Computer." *SIAM J. of Computing*, **26**:1484–1509, 1997.

[209] H. Simon and A. Ando. "Aggregation of variables in dynamic systems." *Econometrica*, **29**:111–138, 1961.

[210] H. Simon. "The architecture of complexity." *Proc. American Phil. Soc.* **106**(6):467–482, 1962.

[211] M. Sims, C. V. Goldman, and V. Lesser. "Self-organization through bottom-up coalition formation." *Proc. Int. Conf. on Autonomous Agents and Multi Agent Systems*, pp. 867–874, 2003.

[212] R. G. Smith. "The contract net protocol; high-level communication and control in a distributed problem solver." *IEEE Trans. on Computers*, Vol. C **29**(12):1104–1114, 1980.

[213] J. Smuts. *Holism and Evolution*. MacMillan, New York, NY, 1926.

[214] B. Snyder. "Server virtualization has stalled, despite the hype." http://www.infoworld.com/print/146901 (Accessed December 2013).

[215] K. Sohrabi, J. Gao, V. Ailawadhi, and G. Pottie." "Protocols for self-organisation of a wireless sensor network." *IEEE Personal Communications,* 7(5):16–27, 2000.

[216] I. Sommerville, D. Cliff, R. Calinescu, J, Keen, T. Kelly, M. Kwiatowska, J. McDermid, and R. Paige. "Large-scale IT complex systems." *Communications of the ACM,* **55**(7):71–77, 2012.

[217] P. D. Straffin. "Game Theory and Strategy." *New Mathematical Library,* vol 36, The Mathematical Association of America, Washington, 1993.

[218] M. Stokely, J. Winget, E. Keyes, C. Grimes, and B. Yolken. "Using a market economy to provision compute resources across planet-wide clusters." *Proc. Int. Parallel and Distributed Processing Symp. (IPDPS 2009),* pp. 1–8, 2009.

[219] R. Subrata, A. Y. Zomaya, and B. Landfeldt. "Game-theoretic approach for load balancing in computational grids." *IEEE Trans. on Parallel and Distributed Systems,* **19**(1):66–76, 2008.

[220] G. Tesauro, N. K. Jong, R. Das, and M. N. Bennani. "A hybrid reinforcement learning approach to autonomic resource allocation." *Proc. Int Conf. on Autonomic Computing, ICAC-06,* pp. 65–73, 2006.

[221] R. Thom. *Structural Stability and Morphogenesis: An Outline of a General Theory of Models.* Reading, MA: Addison-Wesley, ISBN 0-201-09419-3, 1989.

[222] "Top 500 supercomputers." http://top500.org/featured/top-systems/ (Accessed January 2016).

[223] Z. Toroczkai and K. E. Bassler. "Jamming is limited in scale-free systems." *Nature,* **428**:716, 2004.

[224] A.M. Turing. "The chemical basis of morphogenesis." *Philosophical Transactions of the Royal Society of London Series B,* **237**:37–72, 1952.

[225] B. Tsybakov and N. Vvedenskaya. "Random multiple access stack algorithms." *Prob. Inform. Trans.* **16**:230–241, 1980.

[226] A. Verma, L. Pedrosa, M. R. Korupolu, D. Oppenheimer, E. Tune, and J Wilkes. "Large-scale cluster management at Google with Borg." *Proc. EuroSys15,* pp. 124–139, 2015.

[227] W. Vickrey. "Counterspeculations, auctions, and competitive sealed tenders." *The Journal of Finance,* **16**(1):8–37, 1961.

[228] VMware. "VMware vSphere Storage Appliance." https://www.vmware.com/files/pdf/techpaper/ VM-vSphere-Storage-Appliance-Deep-Dive-WP.pdf (Accessed August 2015).

[229] H. Von Foerster. "On self-organizing systems and their environments." *In Self-organizing systems,* M.C. Yovits and S. Cameron (eds.), Pergamon Press, London, UK, pp. 31–50, 1960.

[230] S. V. Vrbsky, M. Lei, K. Smith, and J. Byrd. "Data replication and power consumption in data grids." *Proc IEEE Int. Conf. on Cloud Computing Technology and Science,* pp. 288–295, 2010.

[231] J. von Neumann. "Proof of the quasi-ergodic hypothesis." *Proc. Natl. Acad. Sci. USA,* **18**(1): 70–82, 1932.

[232] J. von Neumann. "Physical applications of the ergodic hypothesis." *Proc. Natl. Acad. Sci. USA,* **18**(3):263–266, 1932.

[233] J. von Neumann. "First draft of a report on the EDVAC." https://web.archive.org/web/ 20130314123032/http://qss.stanford.edu/~godfrey/vonNeumann/vnedvac.pdf, 1945 (Accessed November 2015).

[234] J. von Neumann. *Mathematical Foundations of Quantum Mechanics.* Princeton University Press, Princeton, NJ, 1953.

[235] J. von Neumann. "Probabilistic logic and synthesis of reliable organisms from unreliable components." In *Automata Studies,* C. E. Shannon and J. McCarthy, Editors. Princeton University Press, Princeton, NJ, 1956.

[236] J. von Neumann. "Fourth University of Illinois Lecture." *Theory of self-reproduced automata,* A. W. Burks, Editor. 66, University of Illinois Press, Urbana, IL, 1966.

[237] J. von Neumann and O. Morgenstern. *Theory of Games and Economic Behavior.* Wiley, New York, NY, 1967 (original edition 1944).

[238] S de Vries and R. Vohra. "Combinatorial auctions; a survey." *INFORMS Journal of Computing,* **15**(3):284–309, 2003.

[239] "Crossbow," http://www.xbow.com.

[240] H-J. Zhang, Q-H. Li, and Y-L. Ruan. "Resource co-allocation via agent-based coalition formation in computational grids." *Proc Second Int. Conf. on Machine Learning and Cybernetics,*, pp. 1936–1940, 2003.

[241] E.C. Zeeman. "Catastrophe theory." *Scientific American,* **234**(4):65–70, 75–83, 1976.

[242] G. K. Zipf. *Human Behavior and the Principle of Least Effort: An Introduction to Human Ecology.* Addison-Wesley, Reading, MA,1949.

[243] M. M. Waldrop. "Complexity: The Emerging Science at the Edge of Order and Chaos." *Simon & Schuster,* New York, NY, 1992.

[244] D. J. Watts and S. H. Strogatz. "Collective-dynamics of small-world networks," *Nature,* **393**:440–442, 1998.

[245] G. Wei, A. Vasilakos, Y. Zheng, and N. Xiong. "A game-theoretic method of fair resource allocation for cloud computing services." *The Journal of Supercomputing,* **54**(2):252–269, 2010.

[246] W. Waver. "Science and complexity." *American Scientist,* **36**:536–547, 1948.

[247] D. Whitley. "A genetic algorithm tutorial." *Statistics and Computing,* **4**:65–85, 1994.

[248] N. Wiener. *Cybernetics: Or Control and Communication in the Animal and the Machine.* M.I.T. Press, Boston, MA, 1961.

[249] S. Wolfram. *Cellular Automata and Complexity: Collected Papers.* Addison-Wesley, Reading MA, 1994.

[250] S. Wolfram. *A New Kind of Science.* Wolfram Media, Champaign, IL, 2002.

[251] D. H. Wolpert and W. Macready. "Using self-dissimilarity to quantify complexity," *Complexity,* **12**(3):77–85, 2007.

[252] W. Ye, J. Heidemann, and D. Estrin. "An energy efficient MAC protocol for wireless sensor networks ." *Proc. IEEE Infocom 2002.* New York, June 2002.

[253] D. C. Marinescu, A. Paya, and J. P. Morrison. "A cloud reservation system for Big Data applications." *IEEE Trans. on Parallel and Distributed Systems,* Vol. PP, Issue 99, DOI: 10.1109/TPDS.2016.2594783, 2016.

INDEX

Note: Page numbers followed by *f* indicate figures and *t* indicate tables.

Printed in the United States
By Bookmasters